BY THESE HANDS

BY THESE HANDS

A
DOCUMENTARY
HISTORY OF
AFRICAN AMERICAN
HUMANISM

❏

Edited by

Anthony B. Pinn

NEW YORK UNIVERSITY PRESS
New York and London

NEW YORK UNIVERSITY PRESS
New York and London

Library of Congress Cataloging-in-Publication Data
By these hands : a documentary history of African American humanism / edited by
Anthony B. Pinn.
p. cm.
Includes bibliographical references and index.
ISBN 0-8147-6671-4 (acid-free paper)—ISBN 0-8147-6672-2 (pbk. : acid-free paper)
1. Humanism—United States—History—Sources. 2. African American philosophy.
3. African Americans—Religion. I. Pinn, Anthony B.

B821 .B9 2001
144'.089'96073—dc21   2001030437

New York University Press books are printed on acid-free paper,
and their binding materials are chosen for strength and durability.

Manufactured in the United States of America

10 9 8 7 6 5 4 3 2 1

Dedicated to
William R. Jones
and the
Ancestors

Human rebellion ends in metaphysical revolution. It progresses from appearances to acts, from the dandy to the revolutionary. When the throne of God is overturned, the rebel realizes that it is now his own responsibility to create the justice, order, and unity that he sought in vain within his own condition, and in this way to justify the fall of God.

—Albert Camus, *The Rebel*

There are those amongst you who will cry out for my indictment, brand me with meaningless words as: "Atheist! Infidel! Blasphemer! and Godless!" Meaningless words because they are nothing except criminal sounds, uttered to describe any truth-seeker who dares to point up the folly and fallacy in the present God-Concepts people allegedly serve.

—Robert H. deCoy, *The Nigger Bible*

CONTENTS

CONTENTS

PREFACE

Shortly after the publication of my first book—*Why, Lord? Suffering and Evil in Black Theology*—I knew many of my points needed additional support. There was no assumption on the part of many that African Americans in noteworthy numbers shared humanist thought and values. In this volume, I attempt to provide a documentary history of African American humanism. And although I alone am responsible for these pages, many individuals helped with the completion of this project. I would like to take this opportunity to thank them. I must also thank my editor, Stephen Magro, whose encouragement and support have been invaluable, as well as my copy editor, Betty Seaver. I would also like to thank Calvin Roetzel and the members of the Macalester College Religious Studies Department for support and encouragement. Other members of the Macalester community helped in numerous ways with the collection of documents: thank you to Patrick Guarasci and Jumaane Saunders.

My wife, Cheryl Johnson, has been supportive and kind beyond measure, and I am grateful. As always, my mother, my brother, and my sisters provided encouragement in many ways.

INTRODUCTION

Humanism in the U.S. Context

❑

Many argue that the United States of America is founded upon overtly religious ideals and desires. From the pilgrims onward, the common nation-story has revolved around religious freedom and the creation of a "new promised land." There may be some truth to this, but it is also the case that less than 30 percent of the colonists who populated this land in its early European years were actively involved in organized religion. The land fostered individualism and frontier life, making it difficult to provide sufficient missionaries to spread the gospel. Furthermore, the treatment of Native Americans, African Americans, women, and powerless Europeans points to a lack of attention to the basic principles of the Christian faith. It is safe to say that spiritual concerns, when present, took a back seat to economic concerns created by an unforgiving terrain. It is also possible that Christianity did not appeal to many of the colonists and their descendants because they found humanism better able to address their existential needs and concerns.

There were continual fears of a loss of concern for religion in the United States that centered on suspicion concerning the antireligious undertones of the French Revolution's impact upon U.S. thought. However, most of those living in the United States were not familiar with the issues that preoccupied elite New Englanders and others who would have been influenced by European thought. Yet humanist and free-thought ideas were present in the United States and manifested themselves in central figures and institutions. North America developed a humanist tradition because it (1) moved away from doctrinal and rigid control of knowledge by promoting free inquiry; (2) promoted intellectual vitality; (3) promoted human potential and progress—intrinsic ethical and intellectual worth, not moral depravity and mental impotence; (4) and enjoyment of earthly life.

Those who did not demolish Christianity, such as Thomas Paine, forced those who believed its doctrine to rethink it and defend it in ways that recognized its weaknesses and inconsistencies.[1] Furthermore, although Enlightenment ideas related to humanism and the like were under siege during the Great Awakening revivals, this questioning of God and the centrality of humanity was never completely wiped out. It took a variety of forms but was never eradicated.

In the United States the promise and pitfalls of a new democracy generated a concern for an understanding of human life. The blood and sweat that fed U.S. soil generated the fundamental questions of life's meaning and purpose: the Civil War, Reconstruction, and so on required the creation of a worldview that made sense of human promise and misery. The result was the emergence of humanist-inspired thought and organizations, drawing when useful from European thinkers.[2] It was also, in the final analysis, a response to modernity—one that embraced human potential for progress guided by reason and science.

Even within this brief historical survey, spotty though it is, there is sufficient reason to believe that humanism has had a long history within the United States. The basic humanist principles have helped guide this country's development with respect to values and aspirations. Nonetheless, I am unwilling to state, as some do, that the fundamental, daily aims of U.S. citizens are humanistic in nature. It is sufficient, I believe, to simply note and briefly document the presence of humanistic principles as an important thread within the fabric of U.S. thought. The theoretical importance of humanism has been long recognized. What has been more difficult is its practical application—the ethical and moral standards that concretely and overtly inform activity. That is, the questions continue: What do humanists do? What informs and anchors their activities? With these questions in mind, the pressing task is to give some attention to the ethics and morals that guide humanists. Although a full discussion is beyond the scope of this introductory essay, I would like to highlight quickly some general components of humanist ethics. However, it might be helpful to begin with a few remarks concerning the nature of humanism.

Corliss Lamont, who has written classic treatments such as *The Philosophy of Humanism,* argues that humanism as a system is defined by eight basic propositions. They can be summarized as follows. Humanism rejects notions of the supernatural, and recognizes nature as the basis of all life. Attached to this is an understanding of humanity as an intimate component of nature that developed through a process of evolution, not creation, and with death human personality ceases to exist. Connected to this linking of body and mind is an understanding of reason or thinking as the result of humanity's interaction with the natural environment. Hence, ideas cannot be separated from experience. Through reason and the advances of science, humanists believe humankind is capable of solving its problems; in this sense humans are, in the words of the poet William Ernest Henley, masters of their own fate.[3]

Furthermore, Lamont asserts that humanism entails an appreciation of culture and works to advance the arts. This includes respect for nature that necessitates efforts to safeguard it. Connected to this is concern for humanity around the globe, demonstrated through efforts to ensure peace and health. Finally, these principles, according to Lamont, are enacted through an ethic that "grounds all human values in this-worldly happiness, freedom and progress—economic, cultural, and ethical—of all mankind, irrespective of nation, race or religion."[4] The connotations of this position entail a balance between individualism and a concern for community. That is to say, humanists, according to the above principles, are responsible for living in the world in ways that promote not only individual happiness but the health and welfare of the larger community. Ultimate happiness is achieved, hence, only through service to others. It should be noted that these principles, although somewhat unified and, in varying degrees, embraced by most humanists, are not connected to one homogenous system rightfully known as humanism. Lamont and others quickly remark that there are various forms of humanism; for Lamont, these include agnostic humanism, atheistic humanism, religious humanism. One could easily add to this list freethinkers (who reject religious revelation and the authority of the church), rationalists (for whom reason and verifiability through experience are supreme), members of Ethical Culture societies (who are dedicated to the "right"), advocates of "dialectical materialism" (premised upon the work of Karl Marx), scientific humanism, democratic humanism, skepticism, and deism. Even with these additions, the list may not be complete. Yet, what tends to run through all of these, is an appreciation for naturalistic thought—a grounding of all thought and action in nature rather than the supernatural—and a commitment to human activity as the only source of hope for the world.

These principles outlined by Lamont, including the vague sketch of a humanistic ethic, predate the publication of his text. In fact, in 1933, a group of humanists—clergy, academics, and others—felt the need to clarify exactly what humanists think and do. This took the form of the *Humanist Manifesto I*.[5]

Drawing from principles noted in the founding documents of the

United States, humanists such as philosopher John Dewey, clergyman John H. Dietrich, and thirty-two others presented the basic humanist perspective. In the words of the signatories,

> The time has come for widespread recognition of the radical changes in religious beliefs throughout the modern world. The time is past for mere revision of traditional attitudes. Science and economic change have disrupted the old beliefs. Religions the world over are under the necessity of coming to terms with new conditions created by a vastly increased knowledge and experience. In every field of human activity, the vital movement is now in the direction of a candid and explicit humanism.[6]

As those who have studied *Manifesto I* often indicate, it stands upon three secure pillars: reason, science, and democracy. Attached to these three pillars are the following ideas: (1) Humans are part of nature and nature reflects an evolutionary process, not a moment of divine creation; (2) a rejection of a mind/body split based upon a sense of reason and experience as co-dependent; (3) supernatural rationales and explanations for human life are rejected, and religion is understood as being a human construct; (4) human potentiality and creativity must be exalted, and both personal fulfillment and social well-being promoted.

Manifesto I quickly became dated as a result of "New World" concerns and problems such as World War II and the civil rights movement, which made necessary its replacement. What resulted was the *Humanist Manifesto II* (1973), which opens with the following words:

> It is forty years since *Humanist Manifesto I* (1933) appeared. Events since then make that earlier statement seem far too optimistic. . . . As we approach the twenty-first century, however, an affirmative and hopeful vision is needed. Faith, commensurate with advancing knowledge, is also necessary. In the choice between despair and hope, humanists respond in this

5

Humanist Manifesto II with a positive declaration for times of uncertainty.[7]

Humanist Manifesto II expanded the issues addressed in the 1933 document, and also presented a system of ethics. The system of ethics was grounded in human experience and is situational in that it had to change as the needs and problems of the world changed: "ethics stems from human need and interest."[8] In part, this situational ethics was a response to Christian notions of ethics that anchored what humans "ought to do" in unalterable divine revelations and mandates, which were not always understood with respect to worldwide needs. In opposition to this, *Humanist Manifesto II* describes an ethical system of conduct that calls attention to "united actions—positive principles relevant to the present human condition. [It is] designed for a secular society on a planetary scale."[9] Ethical conduct requires a respect and appreciation for the insights of groups other than one's own. All of this is balanced by "compassion, empathy" and tolerance. There is a sense in which this optimism, according to *Manifesto II,* must be tempered and contained. It must recognize the horrific deeds done by humans toward other humans and the larger reality of nature. Understanding this, humanism asserts that liberation or transformation is a possibility but is in no way guaranteed. Nonetheless, human creativity and ingenuity are important and powerful resources.

Adhering to the above principles, humanists seek to enhance freedom and dignity—individual fulfillment and communal health on all levels of existence—within a open, peaceful, and global society.[10] Although controlled, there is an optimism behind this project clearly expressed in the final section of *Humanist Manifesto II:*

> What more daring a goal for humankind than for each person to become, in ideal as well as practice, a citizen of a world community.
>
> It is a classical vision; we can now give it new vitality. Humanism thus interpreted is a moral force that has time on

its side. We believe that humankind has the potential intelligence, good will, and cooperative skill to implement this commitment in the decades ahead.[11]

Yet, what is important for humanists is the manner in which this optimism is controlled by a growing awareness of the world and human nature.

Subsequent work on humanistic ethics has been done by Paul Kurtz, the president of Prometheus Books and the founder of the Council for Secular Humanism, Inc. Related to such topics as ethics, Kurtz has produced numerous texts, including *Forbidden Fruit* and *Moral Problems in Contemporary Society*.[12] In the former, Kurtz raises the following question: "If all moral systems are products of human culture and if we remove the self-deceptive faith systems that sanctify them, is it still possible to lead an authentic ethical life in which a responsible morality can be developed?"[13] His response is an emphatic yes. His basic assertion affirms the individual's ability to maintain an ethically and morally sound life without a theistic orientation. Humanism does not, of necessity, collapse into a state of nihilism. In fact, the radical sense of accountability and responsibility humanism requires of humanity can foster a strong sense of creativity and ingenuity leading to self-and social transformation.

Although Kurtz's work places strong emphasis on agnostic, atheistic, and skeptical forms of humanism—with their strong critique of traditional forms of theism—Kurtz, as did Lamont and the signers of both manifestos, acknowledges that there are basic elements of a humanistic system of ethics that are embraced by all humanist camps. The various categories of humanism mentioned throughout this essay are distinctive due to the emphasis given to particular humanist principles as opposed to more intrinsic differences. Within each of these camps is a recognition that human purpose and meaning are developed and articulated only in respect to the needs, interests, and experiences of living species.[14] That is to say,

7

Life has no meaning per se; it does, however, present us with innumerable opportunities, which we can either squander and retreat from in fear or seize with exuberance. The meaning of life is not to be found in a secret formula discovered by ancient prophets or priests, who withdraw from it in quiet contemplation and release.

It can be discovered by anyone and everyone who can untap an inborn zest for living. It is found within living itself, as it reaches out to create new conditions of experience.[15]

How does one act upon the above conviction? First, humanists assert that humans have an obligation to value time and to bring fullness to each moment because we have only this one physical existence. Furthermore, humans must work toward individual development, and the construction of a larger society in which all have healthy life options and positive avenues for fulfillment based upon full human rights and civil liberties. Humanists recognize that this is a normative claim, a normative value. The process also entails a recognition of humanity as being a part of nature without special status and without the possibility of appeal to a "higher power" capable of breaking into and altering human history. (It is no wonder that so many humanists are actively involved with organizations such as the American Civil Liberties Union, the ACLU.)

This system of ethics recognizes the risk involved in living, and acknowledges that our success with respect to the above striving will be accompanied by moments of failure. Yet, this does not result in despair and apathy because humanistic ethics means a repostulation of what it is to achieve and be successful. What becomes important is not the "end" of struggle—guaranteed outcomes—but that success is located in positive action itself. Kurtz relates this reevaluation of success to the Greek myth of Sisyphus, who continually rolled a rock uphill only to reach the top and have it fall to the bottom again, and again. In Kurtz's words:

The myth of Sisyphus has exaggerated the dilemma, because there can be significant enjoyment and enrichment in working to reach our goals. . . . There are great and exciting expectations and desires that stimulate us to action, and there are great thrills in experiencing and striving for them.[16]

Within Kurtz's various writings, readers will find the basic principles outlined earlier in the work of figures such as John Dewey, John Dietrich, and Corliss Lamont in individual documents and collective treaties such as the manifestos. In addition to their common humanist principles, the four also have something else in common: they are all white men. Yet, this should not suggest that humanism is the exclusive position of white Americans, a stereotypical depiction. What is of interest for this volume is that two of the signers of the second manifesto are African Americans: A. Philip Randolph and James Farmer. Although only these two signed this document, they are not the lone humanists within the African American community.

This volume attempts to shed light on the presence of a greater "cloud of witnesses." When more attention is given to issues of race as connected to other forms of oppression, one sees more clearly the manner in which humanism has lived and functioned within African American communities, as well as the rationale for the involvement of African Americans such as Randolph and Farmer.

Readers will notice throughout this volume that African American humanism has an origin different from the Renaissance and the Enlightenment. Ideas from these may be present in African American humanist thought, yet it is an indirect reference because African American humanism draws its strength directly from the experiences of African Americans in the Americas. With this said, readers should understand, however, that African American humanism shares the values and ethical principles of the larger U.S. humanist community but with a stronger emphasis on certain issues because of African American needs and concerns. That is, African American humanism contains all the variety of the various humanist camps mentioned above, but with a common thread premised upon the significance of race (and race tied to other forms of oppression) in the United States. African American humanists in these pages are atheistic, agnostic, skeptical, and so on in perspective, yet, they share elements of a basic ethics defined by the following elements: (1) understanding of humanity as fully (and solely) accountable and responsible for the human condition and the correction of its plight; (2) suspicion toward or rejection of supernatural explanation and claims, combined with an understanding of humanity as an evolving part of the natural environment as opposed to its having been created; (3) tied to this is an appreciation for African American cultural production and a perception of traditional forms of Black religiosity as having cultural importance as opposed to any type of "cosmic" authority; (4) a commitment to individual and societal transformation; and (5) a controlled optimism that recognizes both human potential and human destructive activities.

In earlier work, I have attempted to demonstrate the manner in which humanism functions as a religious system within African American communities.[17] In part, this was my effort to understand both the theistic and "nontheistic" manifestations of religiosity within African American life. Such is not my concern, however, in this volume; I'm not interested in debating here the religious or philosophical nature of African American humanism or humanism in more general terms. Rather, I am open to both possibilities. My concern is to demonstrate the manner in which humanism—however constructed as religion or philosophy—has served as a grounding for liberative action within African American history. Despite the physical dominance of Black churches on the streets of Black communities, not all African Americans are swayed by Christianity or other theistic forms of orientation. Despite the prevalence of Christian rhetoric and the assumed dominance of theistic assumptions, not all are "warmed by those fires." But this has not meant inactivity, hermetic existence for the "nonbelievers." They have been active, but guided by a different set of directives. Those of this disposition are generally understood as humanists who rely solely on humanity for societal and personal transformation.[18]

It is possible to speak of humanists without rejection of a God concept. However, keep in mind earlier statements concerning the various humanist camps. This anthology is limited, for the most part, to humanists who doubt or deny the existence of God as a component of their humanistic stance. Those interested in humanism that maintains a notion of God might find some of my earlier work of interest. See, for example, *Why, Lord? Suffering and Evil in Black Theology.* I place such restrictions on the term *humanism* in order to avoid broad definitions—concern with humanity—that would embrace all "freedom fighters." This is important because my goal here is to highlight a distinctive impetus for Black liberation efforts, one that is distinctive from the Black church tradition and the theistic orientation it exemplifies.[19]

For too long, many have thought of Christian churches or the Nation of Islam—some theistic and institutional form of thought— as the motivation or rationale for African American progressive activities. This volume demonstrates that humanism has not resulted in nihilism or radical individualism; rather, it has served as the basis for action. This ground of motivation has been embraced by a variety of prominent figures in African American thought and letters. I seek here to present humanism as a system of belief that is embraced on a variety of levels.

Much of the praxis marking the character and tone of the African American movement toward social transformation is attributable to the humanist leanings of major African American figures, as well as the liberation workers who have remained nameless. Historically, humanism has provided many African Americans with direction that sparked their sense of being in the world, and their efforts to shape the world. Therefore, to understand what motivates African Americans to construct their "world" in certain ways—to understand responses to African American experience—attention must be given to a full range of philosophical or religious motivations. Unfortunately, many scholars of African American life have restricted their discussion of these motivational forces or ideologies to the influence of the Christian church or traditions such as the Nation of Islam. Hence, whereas the Christian perspective (and Black church tradition) of Martin Luther King, Jr., for example, is understood as a major factor in his civil rights work, and the Islamic beliefs of Malcolm X are recognized as providing the framework for his critique of U.S. society, few have been willing to note the manner in which the humanism of James Forman, for example, played a role in his SNCC involvements.

This volume seeks to correct for this by documenting the presence and impact of humanism on African American life and thought. Only Norm Allen's *Anthology of African American Humanism* has attempted this. Although an invaluable tool, his volume does not provide the scope and thematic structure achieved herein. For example, it does not provide the same attention to the "religion versus philosophy" debate concerning humanism, nor does it provide the same full range of humanist expression in politics, the arts, and so on. *By These Hands* also offers important contextual essays that give weight to the text missing from Allen's treatment. In short, this volume provides important information concerning a component of African American expression that has been long ignored, yet one that helps explain the motivation for the African American struggle for equality. What is presented here, in short, is the personal commitment to some form of humanism that undergirds the ethics and actions of important African American leaders, in a variety of life areas.

The focus of this text is not an apology for humanism as a religious system, but it is important to acknowledge this debate. It should be noted that although I personally understand humanism as a religious system, the humanists in this volume are allowed to speak for themselves; I do not attempt to "force" them into a "religious" mode.

Rather, the opinions offered in the various documents point to the complex process of defining humanism.

This anthology counters arguments and demonstrates the complexity of African American communities through the documentation of African American humanism. In terms of structure, the volume is divided into two parts, the nineteenth century and the twentieth century. Each begins with a short description that places humanism within the historical context of the period, which is then followed by two short essays outlining the general development of African American humanism within cultural production and within politics. Next, personal narratives document the humanistic orientation guiding the thought and activity of central figures in African American liberation struggles. Documents within the two divisions are chronologically ordered. This arrangement, I believe, allows for presentation of a more "natural" and historical development of African American humanism's concerns and issues.

Little attention is given to biographical information. Rather, the emphasis is on demonstrating the connection between their praxis and humanism. However, although primacy is accorded their "conversion" to humanism, some contextual information is provided in a summary statement before each personal narrative. In part, I am suggesting and offering a new way of understanding the African American commitment that motivates action through an archaeology project involving autobiography. The personal narratives precede general statements concerning humanism.

Those for whom these figures are familiar will begin to recognize the ways in which humanism has helped shape extremely important liberation movements in the United States—labor movements, progressive politics, the Black aesthetic movement or the Black Arts Movement, the Harlem Renaissance, Black social science as an academic and transforming enterprise, the Black power movement, the civil rights movement, the full citizenship efforts through communism and socialism, and liberation theology. There should be no question as to the vitality and role of humanism as an underpinning for African American liberation work done by human hands alone.

Through this volume, I hope to accomplish several tasks: (1) to counter revisionist approaches to the connection between the church and social activism, and the religiosity of African Americans; (2) to add another layer to the sensibilities of African Americans; (3) to heighten awareness of the presence of humanism in Black communities; (4) to provide additional information on the development of African American identity and praxis; and (5) to refine further the philosophical/religious influences on Black thought and praxis.

This project entails a deep respect and appreciation for the various African American "freedom fighters," to borrow a phrase, who have made this volume possible. In working toward the completion of the above tasks, I believe the true diversity of thought within African American communities is given important recognition. And, the depth of African American creativity and ingenuity is celebrated. Of course, only readers can judge the success of my efforts.

NOTES

1. See for example: Thomas Paine, *Common Sense: Rights of Man* (New York: Gryphon Editions, 1992).

2. On humanism within the context of Europe, see, for example, Albert Rabil, Jr., *Renaissance Humanism: Foundations, Forms, and Legacy,* vol. 3, *Humanism and the Disciplines* (Philadelphia: University of Pennsylvania Press, 1988); Henry F. May, *The Enlightenment in America* (New York: Oxford University Press, 1976).

3. Corliss Lamont, *The Philosophy of Humanism* (New York: Philosophical Library, 1949); William Ernest Henley, "Invictus."

4. Lamont *The Philosophy of Humanism,* 19–21.

5. *Humanist Manifestos I and II* (Buffalo: Prometheus Books, 1973).

6. Ibid., 7.

7. Ibid., 13.

8. Ibid., 17.

9. Ibid., 15.

10. Ibid., 17–21.

11. Ibid., 23.

12. Paul Kurtz, *Forbidden Fruit: The Ethics of Humanism* (Buffalo: Prometheus Books, 1988); Paul Kurtz, ed., *Moral Problems in Contemporary Society* (Englewood Cliffs, N.J.: Prentice-Hall, 1969).

13. Kurtz, *Forbidden Fruit,* 17.

14. Ibid., 239.

15. Ibid., 240.

16. Ibid., 244–246. I am indebted to Sharon Welch for first introducing me to the idea of an ethic of risk. Her lectures at Harvard Divinity School during my student days and her *Feminist Ethic of Risk* (Minneapolis: Fortress Press, 1990) have been invaluable resources.

17. See, for example, Anthony B. Pinn, *Varieties of African American Religious Experience* (Minneapolis: Fortress Press, 1998), chap. 4. Some of the material on humanism presented here is also present in my article titled "Of Works and Faith? Reflection on the New Religious Right and Humanist Ethics," *Religious Humanism* (forthcoming).

18. In addition to the above, readers can gather additional concise, presentations concerning the nature of humanism in *Free Inquiry* 16, no. 4 (fall 1996).

19. Additional short autobiographical pieces are routinely published in the *AAH Examiner,* the newsletter of African Americans for Humanism. It is published in Buffalo and is available by contacting Mr. Norm Allen, Jr., P.O. Box 664, Buffalo, NY, 14226-0664. Sources for the biographical information for figures contained in this volume are Larry G. Murphy, J. Gordon Melton, and Gary L. Ward, ed., *Encyclopedia of African American Religions* (New York: Garland Publishing, 1993); Henry Louis Gates, Jr., and Nellie Y. McKay, gen. ed., *The Norton Anthology: African American Literature* (New York: W. W. Norton, 1997); Michael W. Williams, ed., *The African American Encyclopedia* (New York: Marshall Cavendish, 1993);

Jack Salzman, David Lionel Smith, Cornel West, ed., *Encyclopedia of African-American Culture and History* (New York: Macmillan Library Reference, 1996); and Charles D. Lowery and John F. Marszalek, eds., *Encyclopedia of African-American Civil Rights: From Emancipation to the Present* (New York: Greenwood Press, 1992).

PART I

NINETEENTH-CENTURY HUMANISM

Nineteenth-Century African American History

SCHOLARS LERONE BENNETT and Ivan Van Sertima assert that the movement of Africans into the Americas occurred prior to the presence of Europeans. This aside, an African presence in the "New World" dates from *at least* the beginning of the fifteenth century. Concerning this, historical record indicates that Africans traveled with European explorers and were among the first to encounter the Caribbean. Despite the time frame used to track the presence of Africans in the Americas, one thing is certain: the first Africans to encounter the Americas did not come as slaves. Their presence in the Americas and Caribbean first revolved around work as explorers and indentured laborers. However, this would change.

As early as 1508, word circulated concerning the importance of the "New World" for the economic welfare of Europe. The tremendous potential for wealth through gold and agriculture combined with a decrease in the native populations fostered a search for a new labor force. Initially, christianized Africans were brought to locations such as Cuba from Spain. However, this supply did not meet the labor demand. Earlier concerns about the use of "raw" Africans could not withstand the need for free labor. Over the course of a few decades, the number of slaves would greatly increase. Their presence was not limited to the Caribbean and South America. Some slaves who had been seasoned, or trained for their lot in life in the Caribbean, would eventually be brought to the North American colonies by the British. Although Africans arriving in Jamestown, Virginia, in 1619, came as indentured servants, service for life would become statutory by 1640; and according to some sources there was statutorily acknowledged slavery in Virginia by 1661.

The harsh circumstances of Africans brought to the colonies through this new and peculiar institution is well documented. For some, there was some access to opportunity, but for most, life was brutal. Stories of beatings, rape, disrupted families, and the general efforts to dehumanize enslaved Africans fill volumes. The issue, for planters and overseers, was not the welfare of the Africans but economic profit. As one ex-slave recounts,

> Some white folks might want to put me back in slavery if I tells how we was used in slavery time, but you asks me for the truth. The overseer was 'straddle his big horse at three o'clock in the mornin', roustin' the hands off to the field. . . . The rows was a mile long and no matter how much grass was in them, if you leave one sprig on your row they beats you nearly to death. . . . All the hands took dinner to the field in buckets and the overseer give them fifteen minutes to git dinner. He'd start cuffin' some of them over the head when it was time to stop eatin' and go back to work. He'd go to the house and eat his dinner and then he'd come back and look in all the buckets and if a piece of anything that was there when he left was et, he'd say you was losin' time and had to be whipped. He'd drive four stakes in the ground and tie a nigger down and beat him till he's raw. Then he'd take a brick and grind it up in a powder and mix it with lard and put it all over him and roll him in a sheet. It'd be two days or more 'fore that nigger could work 'gain.[1]

Revolts by slaves because of maltreatment were not uncommon. In addition to the well-known cases of Denmark Vesey, Nat Turner, and Gabriel Prosser, who understood the destruction of slavery and slave owners as a religious and moral obligation, were the more common forms of subversion such as the breaking of tools and work slowdowns.

Enslaved Africans knew that the system could not stand forever, and they would fight to gain their freedom. Such lessons were easily gathered from the successful revolution of Haitian slaves, led by Toussaint L'Ouverture. Even some who benefited from the system recognized that it was premised upon injustice and could not last. The nature of this system could result in the ruination of the country, the country that had gained its independence only in 1776.

In fact, such was almost the price paid for this free labor. The Civil War threatened to destroy the union, and to avoid this, Abraham Lincoln freed the slaves as part of a process of preserving the union. According to John Hope Franklin:

> From the very beginning of the war there had been speculation as to whether or when the slaves would be emancipated. Most Northern Democrats were opposed and said unequivocally that slavery was the best status for Blacks. The abolitionists supported the Republicans in 1860 principally because their platform was antislavery; and they demanded that the party fulfill its pledge by setting the slaves free.
>
> Lincoln had to move cautiously, however, for constitutional, political, and military reasons. His views on emancipation were well known. As early as 1849 he had introduced a bill in Congress for the gradual emancipation of slaves in the District of Columbia.[2]

Although the motivation was political and not the result of moral and ethical considerations, the Emancipation Proclamation issued by Lincoln on January 1, 1863, asserted the freedom of African Americans in all states.

The Emancipation Proclamation signaled new life options and possibilities for African Americans. This circumstance was reenforced during the Reconstruction period after the war ended (1865); troops were positioned in the Southern states to assist African Americans gain a certain measure of equality and to help Southern states—in a more general sense—reconstruct themselves. Against the wishes of the "Old" South, Reconstruction promised to provide African Americans with access to political authority, economic opportunity, and social progress. With the collapse of Reconstruction in 1877, African Americans lost those advantages and new forms of discrimination were enacted to "remind" African Americans of their place in southern society. The political, economic, and social backlash was enforced, if necessary, through mob violence and intimidation.

African Americans, although no longer slave labor, and poor whites were restricted for the most part to less than desirable forms of employment, including share cropping. Efforts toward economic advancement were undertaken at great risk because they could result in death. Even the North, considered the home of true freedom for many African Americans, was not free of racism and repression. As Jim Crow regulations and other forms of repression gained strength, and as agricultural crops failed, many African Americans would eventually leave rural areas of the South and move into both southern and northern cities, part of what became known as the "Great Migration." More is said regarding this phenomenon in the second section of this volume.

History, from the first presence of Africans in the Americas, is marked by the efforts of African Americans to forge identity and gather resources that would allow for healthy life options. It is certain that Black churches and their leadership played a role in these efforts, of which there are countless examples. However, not all who survived the hardships of U.S. treatment of African Americans, not all who fought for the progress of African Americans, based their activities upon traditional religious roots. There are many who fought for freedom based upon the demands of a humanist perspective. It is to this group of humanists that attention is given in the following pages.

NOTES

1. Ira Berlin, Marc Favreau, and Steven F. Miller, ed., *Remembering Slavery: African Americans Talk about Their Personal Experiences of Slavery and Emancipation* (New York: New Press in association with the Library of Congress, 1998), 75–76.

2. John Hope Franklin, *From Slavery to Freedom: A History of Negro Americans,* 5th ed. (New York: Alfred A. Knopf, 1980), 212.

SUGGESTED READING

Lerone Bennett, Jr., *Before the Mayflower: A History of the Negro in America, 1619–1964,* rev. ed. (Baltimore: Penguin Books, 1964).

Ira Berlin, Marc Favreau, and Steven F. Miller, ed., *Remembering Slavery: African Americans Talk about Their Personal Experiences of Slavery and Emancipation* (New York: New Press in association with the Library of Congress, 1998).

John Hope Franklin, *From Slavery to Freedom: A History of Negro Americans,* 5th ed. (New York: Alfred A. Knopf, 1980).

Paula Giddings, *When and Where I Enter: The Impact of Black Women on Race and Sex in America* (New York: Bantam Books, 1984).

James Oliver Horton and Lois E. Horton, *In Hope of Liberty: Culture, Community and Protest among Northern Free Blacks, 1700–1860* (New York: Oxford University Press, 1997).

Winthrop D. Jordan, *White over Black: American Attitudes toward the Negro, 1550–1812* (Chapel Hill: Published for the Institute of Early American History and Culture at Williamsburg, Va., by the University of North Carolina Press, 1968).

Albert J. Raboteau, *Slave Religion: The "Invisible Institution" in the Antebellum South* (New York: Oxford University Press, 1978).

Ronald Segal, *The Black Diaspora: Five Centuries of the Black Experience outside Africa* (New York: Farrar, Straus and Giroux, 1995).

Ivan Van Sertima, *They Came before Columbus* (New York: Random House, 1976).

Gayraud Wilmore, *Black Religion and Black Radicalism: An Interpretation of the Religious History of Afro-American People,* 2d ed., rev. and enlarged (Maryknoll, N.Y.: Orbis Books, 1983).

A

History, Culture, and Politics

I

RELIGIOUS HUMANISM

Its Problems and Prospects in Black Religion and Culture

William R. Jones

❏

In 1973, William R. Jones, of Florida State University, published a book that brought into question several of the basic assertions of theology as done by African Americans: Is God a White Racist? A Preamble to Black Theology *(Garden City, N.Y.: Anchor Press/Doubleday, 1973). In it Jones argues that African American theology makes claims concerning God's work on behalf of oppressed African Americans that must be proven. That is to say, God's efforts to help African Americans end racism must have historical evidence. Without such evidence, it is just as likely that God is a white racist who is actually concerned with the genocide of Black people. In Jones's words:*

> *It has often been said that asking the right question is as important as supplying the correct answer. Whether correct or incorrect, this generalization describes the purpose in the following pages. To paraphrase Kant's admonition, my objective is to force the black theologians and their readers to pause a moment and, neglecting all that they have said and done, to reconsider their conclusions in the light of another question:*

Is God a white racist? My concern throughout is to illuminate the issues this pregnant question introduces. (xiii)

Jones argues that theology done by African Americans (Black liberation theology) is by nature an extended treatment of the theodicy question: What can be said about the justice of God in light of human suffering? In place of the traditional theistic responses to this question offered by Black liberation theologians, Jones suggests humanocentric theism. This position gives humans more responsibility, an "exalted" position for their work toward liberation; humans have functional ultimacy with respect to issues of oppression and liberation. Although Jones offers this position, he acknowledges that his personal position is one of humanism. It is in later articles, such as the following piece, that Jones gives more attention to his understanding of humanism and the historical development of this perspective in African American communities. This article is not limited to a survey of humanism in nineteenth-century African American thought, but it does provide a useful secondary analysis of humanism within this period and its continuity with later humanistic discussions. In this way, it offers a useful segue to the second section of this volume.

For more information on the work of William Jones, see his "Reconciliation and Liberation in Black Theology: Some Implications for Religious Education," *Religious Education (September–October 1972), 382–389;* "Theism and Religious Humanism: The Chasm Narrows," *Christian Century 92 (May 21, 1975): 520–525;* "The Legitimacy and Necessity of Black Philosophy: Some Preliminary Considerations," *Philosophical Forum: A Quarterly 9, nos. 2–3 (winter–spring 1977–78): 149–161;* "The Case for Black Humanism," *in William Jones and Calvin Bruce, ed.,* Black Theology II: Essays on the Formation and Outreach of Contemporary Black Theology *(Lewisburg, Pa.: Bucknell University Press, 1978); and* "Purpose and Method in Liberation Theology: Implications for an Interim Assessment," *in Deane William Ferm, ed.,* Liberation Theology: North American Style *(New York: International Religious Foundation, 1987).*

❑

As my contribution to this volume, I would have preferred to narrow my concern to a description of the controlling categories and inner logic of religious humanism,[1] thus providing the reader with a neatly packaged model to compare and contrast with competing perspectives in black theology and religion.[2] However, because of the actual circumstance and rank of religious humanism in black religion, I have found it necessary to adopt an approach that is decidedly more apologetic.

A quick survey of research patterns in black religion reveals the reason. Religious humanism is a neglected aspect of black culture. In discussions of black religion, humanism of all varieties is virtually ignored, and when it is unexpectedly remembered, it suffers the unfortunate fate of being misinterpreted and misunderstood. Its' situation parallels the predicament of the hero in Ralph Ellison's, *The Invisible Man,* who though flesh and blood, living and breathing, is treated as if he did not exist.

Researchers in black religion characteristically narrow their focus to the history of the black church and its monolithic theological perspective of Christian theism. Because the black church is the major institutional expression of black religion, one can readily acknowledge that its thought and practice should receive preeminent attention. Having said this, however, it must also be allowed that the concern to uncover the rich past of the majority position should not obscure the full content and scope of black religion. Nor should the effort to honor the black church and its particular theological tradition obliterate the total spectrum of competing species of black religion, especially the nontheistic perspective. Unfortunately, this has occurred.

I am confident that future research will confirm that there are two religious traditions in black culture: a mainstream tradition of Christian and non-Christian theism and a minority tradition of humanism or nontheism. There is unobscure evidence of a tradition of religious humanism in the black past that is opposed to Christian theism and the biblical perspective. Unable to fit the fact of black oppression and slavery into normative Christian categories and lacking confidence in God's love and concern for blacks, these ebony humanists, like Prometheus and Job's wife, refused to honor or worship the divine.

Evidence internal to black Christian theism, its major antagonist, confirms the presence of this "heretical" viewpoint. The testimony of Daniel Alexander Payne, a bishop of the African Methodist Episcopal Church, is worth noting in this regard.

> The slaves are sensible of the oppression exercised by their masters; and they see these masters on the Lord's day worshipping in his holy Sanctuary. They hear their masters praying in their families, and they know that oppression and slavery are inconsistent with the Christian religion; therefore they scoff at religion itself—mock their masters, and distrust both the goodness and justice of God. Yes, I have known them even to question his existence. I speak not of what others have told me, but of what I *have both seen and heard from the slaves themselves.* I have heard the mistress ring the bell for family prayer, and I have seen the servants immediately begin to sneer and laugh; and have heard them declare they would not go into prayers; adding if I go she will not only just read, "Servants obey your masters," but she will not read "break every yoke, and let the oppressed go free." I have seen colored men at the church door, *scoffing at the ministers,* while they were preaching, and saying you had better go home, and set your slaves free. A few nights ago . . . a runaway slave came to the house where I live for safety and succor. I asked him if he were a Christian; "no sir" said he, "white men treat us so bad in Mississippi that we can't be Christians."[3]

In the very limited cases where the presence of this nontheistic tradition is acknowledged, it is not labeled "religious," nor is it recognized as a legitimate part of the family of black religion. This is not primarily the consequence of its status as a numerical minority in black culture; rather, humanism itself is suspect as something alien to the black psyche. Both its opponent and champion can agree that religious humanism has not established itself as an indispensable perspective in black religion, the description of which is required for an accurate and adequate understanding of Afro-American religion. Outside of this volume, one is hard pressed to uncover a panoramic analysis of black religion which self-consciously includes the humanist perspective as one of the competing options in black religion. Religious humanism, in sum, has little standing as an accredited representative of the black religious experience. Hence, the necessity and purpose of this essay: to inaugurate the discussion that will hopefully establish religious humanism as an authentic expression of black religion and culture.

Black Religious Humanism: The Invisible Religion

Though there can be little question about the actual presence of nontheism in the black past, it is exceedingly difficult to determine the actual extent of this radical religious perspective. In addition to the testimony of Bishop Payne, researchers, such as Sterling Brown[4] and John Lovell,[5] call our attention to a musical/literary genre, the slave seculars, that also confirms a nontheistic tradition in black religion. The seculars, often called devil songs, ran counter to the spirituals, the musical embodiment of the black church and its theistic thoughtforms. Rejecting the biblical promises and the God-centered theology that the spirituals have etched in our collective memory, the seculars ridiculed the God their fellow slaves worshipped and bombasted the eschatological and soteriological "good news" of the spirituals.

In Lovell's monumental work on the spirituals, it is important to be reminded of the connection he establishes between the spirituals and the seculars. Though he is concerned to make the spirituals, as it were, the womb for fundamental features of black literature and culture, he does not trace the origin of the seculars back to the spirituals. Rather the devil songs and the spirituals are depicted as two different traditions existing side by side.

Other materials suggest a two-way movement between the spirituals and other varieties of slave music that exaggerates the difficulty in plotting the exact boundaries and religious consistency of each. In the first published collection of slave songs we find several revealing statements about the rich variety of musical types and their continuing intercourse.

> We must look among their non-religious songs for the purest specimens of Negro minstrelsy. It is remarkable that they have themselves transferred the best of these to the uses of their churches—I suppose on Mr. Wesley's principle that 'it is not right the Devil should have all the good tunes.' Their leaders and preachers have not found this charge difficult to effect; or at least they have taken so little pains about it that one often detects the profane *cropping out,* and revealing the origin of their most solemn 'hymns,' in spite of the best intentions of the poet and artist.[6]

The collectors of this first volume of spirituals also inform us that the spirituals, the theistic incarnation of the slave experience, comprise only part of the black experience that was fashioned into song.

> Fiddle-sings,' 'devil-songs,' 'corn-songs,' 'jig-tunes,' and what not are common . . . We have succeeded in obtaining only a very few songs of this character. Our intercourse with the colored people has been chiefly through the work of the Freedmen's Commission, which deals with the serious and earnest side of the negro character.[7]

This last confession points to the most formidable obstacle to substantiate the actual extent of religious humanism in black culture: the biased pattern of selectivity used to compile and transmit the black religious heritage. We must not forget the fact that the individuals who first recorded the spirituals were white, and most of them were ministers. It is important to recognize the influence of these factors in determining both the genre and the number of songs recorded.

As Bernard Katz perceptively concludes:

> The vast majority of the songs that were rescued from oblivion were the songs of the Sabbath—of church worship. The songs of the rest of the week would have to creep out of hiding during a time when fewer men of the cloth were around. . . . Thus it is very possible that a great body of songs of secular social comment, too difficult to disguise for white ears, stayed underground . . . and would surface later in the blues and other forms.[8]

These materials highlight the risk involved in extrapolating from the number of extant seculars to the actual range and importance of the theological perspective they represent. Moreover, if one does extrapolate from the popularity of the blues, the acknowledged descendant of the seculars, then the cultural and theological matrix of religious humanism may be a more extensive and significant entity than is suggested by the paucity of seculars in the collection of black songs.[9]

For all of its deficiencies, the account of the Reverend Charles C. Jones is also significant for unearthing the history of black religious humanism. That Jones, in this account, is describing the different belief patterns the Christian missionary will encounter laboring among the slaves strongly suggests that we are dealing with a radical criticism of traditional theism that is not numerically insignificant.

> He discovers deism, skepticism, universalism . . . the various perversions of the Gospel, and all the strong objections which he may perhaps have considered peculiar only to the cultivated minds, the ripe scholarship and profound intelligence of *critics* and *philosophers*.[10]

Wilmore perceptively identifies another point that bears upon the history of humanism in black religion. He notes that figures like Edward W. Blyden enjoyed greater theological affinity with the radical left wing of New England Protestanism—the Channings, Theodore Parkers, and Emersons—who were more "dependable as friends of the Black man than the revival and camp-meeting preachers or the pious clerics of the main line denominations."[11]

Several points in Wilmore's analysis are revealing. He has identified members of Unitarianism, the radical theological movement of that era and which today is basically non-Christian and enthusiastically humanistic in its theological affirmations. What Wilmore accents as the basis for the theological congeniality is also revealing—their actions were more pointedly focused towards the liberation of blacks. What his analysis here suggests is that the radical theological left was a more dependable friend of black Americans than the orthodox theological tradition. Does it crucify the imagination to infer that slaves, convinced of the biblical and common sense maxim—"By their fruits shall you know them—" would not automatically reject a radical theological position that manifested itself concretely in the practice of liberation?

The Invisibility of the Black Humanism: Casual Factors

All that has been discussed thus far has attempted to make us aware of a competing, albeit minority, tradition in black religion. Having said all of this, however, the virtual invisibility of religious humanism in black religion becomes all the more perplexing, and the reasons both for its status as a numerical and a disvalued minority in black culture must be identified. In this connection a comprehensive treatment would analyze those factors which relate to the status of religious humanism as an authentic (a) religious and (b) Afro-American perspective, and those which accent the impact of (c) the context of blacks as an oppressed group in America and (d) the particular value and cultural orientation of Afro-Americans. Because of restraints of space and time only a select few of these factors can be discussed here.

To acknowledge the presence of black religious humanism as a minority tradition in black religion is to affirm that it has been constantly over-shadowed by the larger entrenched theism that continues in the black church. Accordingly, to explain the virtual invisibility of black religious humanism, we must focus on several features of institutionalized black theism and decipher their impact. First, we must accent the fact that religious humanism exists as a philosophical/theological *perspective* and not as an on-going *institution* like its rival, the black church. To state the obvious, an intellectual movement that lacks an institutional base has a limited life span.

Add to this the fact that humanism has been viewed as a hostile adversary, intent on exterminating religion in general and black Christian theism in particular, and it becomes clear why the black church would not be anxious to nurture a potential serpent in its own household.

If we highlight the connection between socio-economic-political context and one's theological/ethical outlook, we can identify another factor that accounts for religious humanism's status as a *numerical* minority. This, however, does not explain its position as a disvalued minority in black religion.

There are several different ways of connecting the cultural context and the minority status of religious humanism. Perhaps the most important and most controversial is the question: Is the historic oppression of blacks in America more conducive to the development of certain forms of theism than humanism? Put in other terms, is there a specific complex of socio-economic and political conditions that are correlated statistically with the respective world view of humanism and theism?

I must say at the outset that there are inadequate research data to

33

answer these questions confidently. However, I would hazard the opinion that humanism emerges most frequently in a situation that is antithetical to that which defines oppression and especially slavery. That is to say, a context of oppression is most generally connected with conceptual framework of theism. Accordingly, the actual historic situation of blacks in America is more likely to spawn certain types of theism than humanism.

Several factors lead me to advance this tentative hypothesis. The actual evolution of humanism seems to be associated with a firmly developed urbanized economy in contrast to an agricultural or pastoral one. Humanism, moreover, characteristically draws its adherents from the middle and upper socio-economic strata rather than those near the bottom of the economic ladder.

Because humanism affirms radical freedom/autonomy as the essence of human reality, humanism is most prominent in those cultures where individuals exercise in fact considerable control over their environment and history. The humanist understanding of wo/man comes into being, it appears, as the consequence of this type of experience and the material situation it presupposes.

The evolution of humanism in Greek culture, under the aegis of the Sophists, seems to confirm this tentative hypothesis. Gayraud Wilmore's invaluable treatment of the black church and its contribution to the radical wing of black thought and practice also supports this tentative conclusion about the socio-economic context for the evolution of black humanism. Wilmore identifies a "dechristianizing period" when the religious impulse self-consciously locates itself outside the circle of black Christian faith. Is it accidental that he identifies this secular nontheistic tradition with the intellectual, upper level groups of blacks? Is it accidental that a similar socio-economic context seems to be the base for those black writers associated with *The Messenger* and its radical critique of the black church?

At this juncture, it is important to make explicit the precise connection between humanism and socio-economic context that is being advanced. I am not arguing for either a strict relation of necessary or sufficient condition. Rather I am illuminating an empirical generalization[12] about the actual development of humanism that can serve as a hypothesis for examining the relation between cultural context and faith content. What I see is a clear-cut movement towards the humanistic pole of the religious spectrum[13] as individuals and groups move away from or release themselves from the scourges of oppression. Perhaps, a more focused analysis of the contrast between the spirituals and the blues will clarify the point.

According to most interpreters, the blues and the spirituals reflect distinct theological perspectives and socio-economic contexts. James Cone's analysis of their contrasting outlook and existential situation provides a helpful specimen for our discussion.

The blues, also labeled "secular spirituals," gravitated to the nontheistic theological pole. Whereas the spirituals gird the black slaves to endure oppression with the belief that the God of Israel would eventually set them free, the theology of the blues rejects a God-centered perspective as the answer to the enigma of black suffering, choosing instead to address black oppression as if God, Jesus Christ, and the black church were all irrelevant.

Most interpreters also conclude that the blues surface in a less circumscribed socio-economic context.

> The spirituals are *slave* songs, and they deal with historical realities that are pre-Civil War. . . . The blues . . . are essentially post Civil War in consciousness. They reflect experiences that issued from Emancipation, the Reconstruction Period, and segregation laws. "The blues was conceived," writes Leroi Jones, "by Freed-men and ex-slaves. . . ." Historically and theologically, the blues express conditions associated with the "burden of freedom."[14]

Having noted this contrast, the general question I raise here is whether this nontheistic faith content is a reflexion of a less oppressive socio-economic environment? In like manner, the growing unchurched population among blacks triggers the same inquiry.

In discussing the connection between socio-economic context and conceptual content, mention must also be made of the impact of the value structure of black culture. Is it a reflection of its situation of oppression that black culture has not been a fertile environment for the cultivation of those intellectual and cultural products, such as philosophy and secularism, that have been historically associated with the development of a self-confident humanist perspective? Though religion has been blessed in black culture, philosophy has been denied a status comparable to its position in the larger culture. Though there are a heady number of black theologians, the number of black philosophers is, by contrast, minuscule.

Methodological and Semantic Obstacles

Other factors affecting the visibility of religious humanism as an authentic expression of black religion relate to specific methodological and semantic practices. The interpretive grids of most current researchers are ineffective instruments for illuminating the totality of the phenomenon of black religion, especially the nontheistic component. Hence, to materialize religious humanism from its spectral status, it is necessary to challenge the semantic apparatus and methodological presuppositions that control current research in black religion.

As a corrective I would advance several interpretive principles. With these principles we can accelerate the resurrection of this disvalued tradition for analysis and critical appraisal; without them black religious humanism will remain invisible, unloved, unappreciated.

Afro-American religion must be approached as a multi-faceted phenomenon that comprises the full spectrum of theistic and nontheistic options.

What this principle excludes is a reductionist approach that seeks to shrink black religion to a monolithic pattern. In that sense, the principle demands that we examine black religion as a pluralistic phenomenon. This means in methodological terms that the researcher should approach the data of black religion with the view in mind of identifying discrete philosophical and theological types as background for determining which major points of the religious spectrum are actually represented in black religion.

Semantically speaking, the principle dictates that we abandon the common, but question-begging, usage that collapses religion into theism, a particular—though admittedly the most prominent—subclass of religion.

I must make the obvious point. If religion and theism are equated, nontheism, by definition, is excluded as a religious perspective. Add to this the common tendency, especially in the context of monotheism, to equate non-theism and atheism, and the possibility of a research apparatus that illuminates religious humanism is exceedingly remote. Nontheistic positions will either be ignored or mistakingly assimilated into the general theistic camp. The consequence is the same in either case: black religion becomes a single tradition of theism for research purposes.

Much more is at stake than a recommendation for an accurate terminology. It should be clear to all that the case for black humanism both as an authentic religious perspective and a valid expression of the black religious tradition stands or falls on this seemingly innocuous issue about the meaning of theism and religion. In deciding about the parameters of black religion, one is in fact answering the fundamental question of the essence of religion itself, in particular the logical and phenomenological connection between it and theism.

If the advocate of black religious humanism does not challenge the equation of theism and religion, s/he also provides grounds for the claim that religious humanism is not authentically black. This line of argumentation is unavoidable once the following descriptions of black consciousness are advanced within a semantic framework where religion and theism are synonymous.

> We black people are a religious people. From the earliest time we have acknowledged a Supreme Being. With the fullness of our physical bodies and emotions we have unabashedly worshipped Him with shouts of joy and tears of pain and anguish. We neither believe that God is dead, white, nor a captive to some rationalistic and dogmatic formulation of the Christian faith which relates Him exclusively to the canons of the Old and New Testaments, and accommodate Him to the reigning spirits of a socio-technical age.[15]
>
> The question of existence in reference to God is not the real issue for blacks. This does not preclude the fact that many blacks are nonbelievers. This is often true . . . of many older black intellectuals who are humanistically oriented and are greatly influenced by the position of Auguste Comte. . . . But the return to religion, often as blind faith in middle life, together with the spiritual strivings of their children, leads me to believe that religion is native to most blacks. Religion in some form or other appears to be an Africanism.[16]

Several points here merit special comment. Unless religion and theism are equated, these statements are meaningless. Moreover, it should also be noted that here theism is not simply advanced as the majority viewpoint but rather as the normative perspective and the yardstick by which one identifies the authentic black consciousness. Indeed, by defining black religion exclusively in theistic terms and thus failing to make an allowance for nonthesitic perspectives, these statements come close to making the acceptance of theism a defining characteristic of being black.

It is true of course that researchers in this area espouse a pluralistic interpretation of black religion. Indeed the major research trend in black religion has been to attack monolithic and stereotyped interpretations of the black religious experience and its institutional expressions. Received traditions of the black church as an Uncle Tom institution, with a sugar tit strategy, have been countered by new interpretations of the black church as a formidable agency of protest and liberation at all levels of the slave's activity. Research such as John Lovell's treatment of the slave spirituals as protest songs with a this-worldly outlook, parallel this development. However, one searches in vain for the same approach to the humanist dimension of the Afro-American heritage. There is still monumental resistance to attack a remaining shibboleth: black religion as exclusively theistic.

Because of what is at stake, it is important at this juncture to articulate the inner logic of a pluralistic approach as a means of testing the actual, in contrast to the espoused, theory of researchers. Pluralism, in this context, involves, first, the recognition of at least two discrete perspectives in black religion; neither can be reduced to the other; and each is regarded as co-valuable in the sense that if either is omitted, the phenomenon under discussion will be incomplete or inadequate.

It is important to identify another feature of an authentic pluralistic interpretation: The numerical distinction between the majority and minority viewpoints cannot be the basis for establishing a qualitative difference between them. Concretely, the fact that theistic worshippers are numerically superior cannot by itself substantiate their status as the normative or authentic black perspective. If this principle is not allowed, black theists sabotage their own efforts to challenge those interpretations of traditional Christianity that are alleged to be a grotesque understanding of the gospel.

Again, the problem goes beyond the mere recognition of a nontheistic tradition in the black past; rather the basic issue is that of interpreting this point of view as both religious and a valid expression of the black religious experience.

Cecil Cone's recent volume, *The Identity Crisis in Black Theology,* illustrates the approach that is challenged here. His thesis is that black theology is in an identity crisis because it has failed to identify the essence of black religion and to make this the exclusive point of departure and source material for theological construction and analysis.

Cecil Cone defines black religion accordingly: "The divine and the divine alone occupies the position of ultimacy in black religion. Indeed, an encounter with the divine is what constitutes the core or essence of that religion. Such an encounter is known as the black religious experience."[17] This God-encounter, the resulting conversion experience, and the variety of responses to the latter define black religion for Cecil Cone.

Let it be clear at the outset that the black humanist does not question the accuracy of Cone's account as a description of black *theism.* Indeed, the issue would be resolved for the humanist if theism were inserted in each case where Cecil Cone speaks inaccurately of religion. What the humanist resists is the arrogant assumption that the black religious experience is somehow exhausted by the theistic experience.

We cannot escape the fact that black religion is reduced to a form of theism in Cone's definition. The rigidity of this semantic apparatus forces him to treat those materials which seem to fall outside the theistic tradition in a most dubious fashion.

Citing the slave seculars and the passage from Bishop Daniel A. Payne discussed above, Cone clearly acknowledges the existence of blacks who were unafraid to question God's intrinsic goodness and, like Prometheus, were willing to rebel on moral grounds. But how does Cone respond to this theological tradition that rejects the almighty sovereign God and the black church?

From one vantage point his response is simply to note the presence of this minority theological view without relating it to his definition of black religion or discussing it further. According to another interpretation, Cone assimilates the God-defying perspective into the theistic religious experience! The radical question about God's justice and/or existence becomes the *pre*-conversionist mentality of the black *theist* facing the absurdity of the slave condition. In this interpretation the slave experience, with its excruciating doubt and despair about

God's rule over the world, creates the dark night of the soul. This, however, is erased by the slave's Job-like encounter with the divine. The transformation is complete. The pressure of Cone's equation of religion and theism has magically transmuted the humanist into a converted theist!

The Cultural Matrix of Afro-American Religious Humanism

To resurrect black religious humanism requires a second interpretive principle that current researchers in black religion do not sufficiently honor: *The actual origin as well as the current position of black religious humanism must be seen as a response to perceived inadequacies of black Christian theism, its theological rival.*

Implicit in this principle is the hypothesis that black humanism emerges as part of a debate that is internal to black life and thought. It is not a spinoff of the enlightment, the scientific revolution or, as Deotis Roberts has suggested, a borrowing from Comte.

Rather, as Benjamin Mays, an eminent representative of black Christian theism, has correctly perceived, black incredulity about the divine, as well as agnosticism and atheism "do not develop as the results of the findings of modern science, nor from the observations that nature is cruel and indifferent; but primarily because in the social situation, [the black American] finds himself hampered and restricted . . . Heretical ideas of God develop because in the social situation the 'breaks' seem to be against the Negro and the black thinkers are unable to harmonize this fact with the God pictured by Christianity."[18]

Whether we encounter black humanism during the slave period or more recent eras of oppression, it appears as a critic of black Christian theism, questioning the latter's capacity to make sense of the history of black oppression and to accommodate the prerequisites of a viable theology of liberation. Substantiating this conclusion about the indigenous origin of black humanism is the telling statement of the heroine in Nella Larsen's *Quicksand.*

> The white man's God.—And his great love for all people regardless of race! What idiotic nonsense she had allowed herself to believe. How could she, how could anyone, have been so deluded? How could ten million black folk credit it when daily before their eyes was enacted its contradiction? [19]
>
> And this, Helga decided, was what ailed the whole Negro race in America, this fatuous belief in the white man's God, this childlike trust in full compensation for all woes and privations in 'Kingdom' come . . . How the white man's God must laugh at the great joke He had played on them, bound them at slavery, then to poverty and insult, and made them bear it unresistingly, uncomplainingly almost, by sweet promises of mansions in the sky, by and by.[20]

Any assessment of the relation between black humanism and traditional Western humanism must incorporate this understanding of the genesis of Afro-American nontheism. Though black humanists and those humanists who trace their lineage to the enlightenment or the scientific revolution are akin in attacking the superstructure of theism, their criticisms develop from radically different socio-economic contexts. Accordingly, the question of God is posed in quite different ways.

Scientific humanism poses the problem of the divine in terms of the coherence between the natural world and the supernatural realm. This query leads often to the denial of the divine reality, i.e., a form of atheism. Black humanists, contrastly, ask the question: *An Deus sit?* because of the crimes of human history, and this emerges frequently in the form: Is God a white racist?, a question that is absent from scientific humanism.

The radical theological questions that black humanism raises grow out of the context of black oppression. They cannot be reduced to the protests of a brainwashed black who has been seduced by white Western secularism. They are not imported, as it were, from the outside. Thus, it would appear that those who attempt to connect black humanism with non-black sources, e.g., Comte, are still handcuffed by the equation of theism and religion. Having equated the two, and having affirmed that blacks are a spiritual people, i.e., faithful theists, nontheism by definition would have to come from outside the black community.

A Liberation Theology: The Black Humanist Perspective

To understand black humanism of the past and to clarify its present agenda and interaction with the black church, it is necessary to identify yet another interpretive principle that is suggested by Helga's vehement protest. Black Humanism must be interpreted as a specific strategy for liberation that issues in a particular theology/philosophy of liberation. For the black humanist, this dictates a specific theological method which becomes part of the critical apparatus for assessing black Christian theism.

Before we outline this theological method, the intended interaction of black humanism with the black church must be made clear. The agenda of black religious humanism does not call for the destruction of the black church. Neither does it involve an absolute disapproval of the practice of the black church, past or present. As with its interpretive approach to black religion, black humanism endorses a pluralistic program for the mechanics of liberation. Though black humanism regards the black church as a "sleeping giant" in terms of its potential as a liberating force, it also recognizes that the history of the black church is checkered relative to liberation and further that the black church has never successfully corralled the majority of blacks to be its congregation. For these reasons "black humanism thinks it unwise for the fate of black liberation to depend upon whether the black church awakens from its slumber or continues to snore, however piously and rhythmically. . . . The emergence of black humanism as a formidable opponent may successfully prod the black church, as other secular movements have done, 'to be about its father's (and mother's) work.' "[21]

In this sense black humanism should not be looked upon as a replacement for the black church but rather as its necessary complement. Black humanism seeks its constituency from the rapidly growing group of unchurched blacks, many of whom find the theology of the black church unpalatable and an untrustworthy account of their religious history. This large unchurched group, the black humanist concludes, cannot be ignored if black liberation is to succeed.

Though the black humanist seeks a cooperative and complementary relationship with the black church in the struggle for liberation, s/he nonetheless cannot avoid challenging it and its theistic theology at several significant points. This must be done to legitimate black religious humanism. But more importantly, black humanism is forced into a critical or gad fly posture because of its primary concern to advance the cause of black liberation. All of this becomes clear, if we analyze Helga's protest, cited above, as a miniature theology of liberation from a black humanist perspective.

In ridiculing the doctrine of God and eschatology, Helga is voicing a common protest of black humanists as well as more recent theologians and philosophers of liberation. The oppressed are oppressed, in fundamental part, because of the beliefs they hold. They adopt or are indoctrinated to accept a belief system that stifles their motivation to attack the institutions and groups that oppress them.

This understanding of oppression is not restricted to humanism; leading black theists have advanced the identical conclusion. The basic argument of Benjamin Mays' *The Negro's God,* claims that blacks conform or rebel against their oppressive situation by virtue of the concept of God they endorse. Certain beliefs about ultimate reality help blacks to survive, "to endure hardship, suffer pain and withstand maladjustment, but . . . do not necessarily motivate them to strive to eliminate the source of the ills they suffer."[22]

Mays' autobiographical account is instructive here, particularly in light of the fact that he denounces, in the same work, the stereotyped view of the black religion as an opiate and otherworldly.

> Long before I knew what it was all about, and since I learned to know, I heard the Pastor of the church of my youth plead with the members of his congregation not to try to avenge the wrongs they suffered, but to take their burdens to the Lord in prayer. Especially did he do this when the racial situation was tense or when Negroes went to him for advice concerning some wrong inflicted upon them by their oppressors. During these troublesome days, the drowning of Pharaoh and his host in the Red Sea, the deliverance of Daniel from the Lion's Den, and the protection given the Hebrew children in the Fiery Furnace were all pictured in dramatic fashion to show that God in due time would take things in hand. Almost invariably after assuring them that God would fix things up, he ended his sermon by assuring them that God would reward them in Heaven for their patience and long-suffering on the earth. Members of the congregation screamed, shouted, and thanked God. The pent up emotions denied normal expression in every day life found an outlet. They felt relieved and uplifted. They had been baptized with the "Holy Ghost." They had their faith in God renewed and they could stand it until the second Sunday in the next month when the experience of the previous second Sunday was duplicated. Being socially proscribed, economically impotent, and politically browbeaten, they sang, prayed, and shouted their troubles away. This idea of God had telling effects upon the Negroes in my home community. It kept them submissive, humble, and obe-

dient. It enabled them to keep on keeping on. And it is still effective in 1937.[23]

In addition to examining the concept of God . . . , the black humanist would also painstakingly inspect the understanding of human suffering, especially as this relates to the oppressed's beliefs about ultimate reality. That is, the theological method of black humanism elevates the theodicy question to first rank, and this is the consequence of the nature of oppression and the inner logic of a liberation theology.

A phenomenological analysis will reveal that oppression is reducible to a form of negative suffering, a suffering that is regarded as detrimental or irrelevant to one's highest good. Moreover, given that the purpose of a theology of liberation is the annihiliation of oppression, the theologian of liberation must provide a sturdy rationale that establishes the negativity of the suffering that is the core of oppression. For instance, it must be shown that the suffering that is oppression is not sanctioned by God's will nor the unfolding of some fundamental laws of nature. In short, the suffering at question must be desanctified, or else the oppressed will not define their suffering as oppressive, nor will they be motivated to attack it.

Liberation Theology and Theological Method

With this understanding as background, the primary purpose and initial step of the liberation theologian is unobscure: to free the mind of the oppressed from the enslaving ideas and submissive attitudes that sabotage any movement towards authentic freedom. This means several things for theological method. First, an exorcist or castration method is dictated. The ideas and concepts that undergird oppression must be clearly identified and systematically replaced with more humanizing and liberating beliefs. In this connection a clear differentiation must be made between those theological constructs that enhance *survival* in contrast to those which promote *liberation.*

In addition the examination must be total and comprehensive. At the outset each and every theological category in Christian faith and the black church must be provisionally regarded as suspect, as an unwitting prop for oppression or a fatal residue of the slave master's world view. This means that God must also be ruthlessly crossexamined to determine her/his responsibility, if any, for the crimes of human history. In sum, black humanism concludes that a liberation theology must self-consciously adopt a *de novo* approach to Christian faith and its theological tributaries.

In advancing this theological method, the black humanist is well aware that he is challenging the fundamental premise of black theism and Christian faith; the intrinsic benevolence and justice of God. Since this challenge often serves as the grounds for questioning black humanism's status as an authentic expression of black consciousness, it is important to understand the rationale for this root and branch method.

The primary point to be made is that this approach follows from the concern of the black humanist to correct black oppression by formulating a viable theology of liberation. We have already seen that the primary goal of a liberation theology, to eliminate oppression, requires a theological method which isolates and excommunicates those enslaving beliefs, such as quietism, which smother the oppressed's motivation to replace the unjust social institutions. Until these manipulative and inauthentic elements of the tradition have been successfully identified and quarantined, the liberation theologian cannot recommend conformity to the tradition. Otherwise, s/he runs the risk of unwittingly endorsing ideas and concepts that support oppression, thus contradicting the explicit purpose of the liberation theology.

The black humanist also advocates a total root and branch analysis because the character of Christian faith as a vehicle for liberation is unsettled and, further, the boundary between authentic black theism and the counterfeit position of Whitianity is obscure.

As a representative of black humanism I have often raised suspicions about Christian faith as a potent means for liberation. Though I am persuaded of its excellence as a survival religion, its quality as a religion of liberation is, for me, still unresolved. This issue was posed most pointedly for me as a result of a fortuitous comparison of the Jewish and Christian liturgical calendars. I was struck by the way in which the Jewish calendar revolved around the celebration of events of ESP (economic-social-political) liberation: passover, purim, hanuk-kah, etc. In contrast, an examination of the general Christian calendar failed to reveal a single celebration of ESP liberation.

This absence is not accidental. Though Christianity began as the religion of an oppressed community, it appears that its liturgical calendar reflects an entirely different political and economic context.

I also inspected the calendar of the black church. It had not modi-fied the Christian calendar in a manner that reflected its own context as an oppressed people; nor had it significantly included its own black saints in a way that other ethnic communities had done.

I did not conclude from this discovery that Christianity is not a liberation religion or that the black church is still captive to Whitian-ity. Rather, it suggested to me the necessity of a certain theological method. Each and every aspect of the tradition must be examined to determine its liberation quotient, and on this basis, accepted or rejected.

The necessity of a *de novo* approach can also be substantiated through a logical analysis of the concept of intrinsic benevolence itself as well as its actual function in black theism for some worshippers.

> To believe that the universe is in the hands of God is to believe that there is a purpose in the world and that God will guaran-tee the successful working out of affairs in the universe. In this sense the idea is compensatory. One can rest secure and feel satisfied because he knows that nothing can go wrong in the world since God governs it.[24]

Black humanism insists that the root and branch approach must be applied to the theology of the black church as well as the more general Christian tradition. In this regard, the black humanist is actually raising the question: How black is black Christian theism? Is it an authentic expression of the black religious consciousness or is it Whitianity in black mask? Because the *de novo* approach advanced here has not been adequately executed, black humanism is uncertain where Whitianity ends and authentic black theism and Christian faith begin. Is the affirmation of God's intrinsic goodness and justice for instance an appropriation of the slave master's religion that creates a theology of survival rather than a theology of liberation?

John Mbiti's research on the African concept of the time strongly suggests to the black humanist that the particular eschatological emphasis of much of black religion, past and present, is an area where the religion of the slave master may have usurped the more liberating worldview of our African foremothers and forefathers. At least this radical shift in outlook supports the necessity of a total examination of the black tradition to determine the liberation quotient of each of its parts.

> For the Akamba, Time is . . . simply a composition of events that have occurred, those which are taking place now and those which will *immediately* occur. What has not taken place, or what is unlikely to occur in the immediate future, has not temporal meaning—it belongs to the reality of "no-Time . . ." From this basic attitude to Time, other important points emerge. The most significant factor is that Time is considered as a two-dimensional phenomenon; with a long "past," and a dynamic "present." The "future" as we know it in the linear conception of Time is virtually non-existent. . . . The future is virtually absent because events which lie in the future have not been realized and cannot, therefore, constitute time which otherwise must be experienced. . . . It is therefore, what has taken place or will occur shortly that matters much more than what is yet to be.[25]

There is also the growing acknowledgement that black theistic belief was formulated as a self-conscious theology of liberation.[26] That is, its specific theological emphasis was not constructed with the requirements of a self-consistent theology of liberation in mind. From this admission the black humanist again concludes that it is necessary to examine every jot and tittle of the thought and practice of the black church to assess its liberation quotient.

In all of this, the black humanist concludes that s/he is executing the actual operational methodology of current black theologians, though in a more consistent manner. It is easy to show that black theistic theologians do not simply read off their theologies from the testimonies of our foreparents. Black theology has not been simply the recording of a "latent, unwritten Black theology."[27] Instead a clear process of selection and rejection informs their approach to the tradition. Certain features of black religion, e.g., a pie-in-the-sky eschatology, have been black balled because of their quietist entailments. Indeed, the following theological method advanced by the leading black theologian, James Cone, is the precise point of view the black humanist wants to endorse.

> We cannot solve ethical questions of the twentieth century by looking at what Jesus did in the first. Our choices are not the same as his. Being Christian does not mean following "in his footsteps. . . ." His steps are not ours; and thus we are placed in an existential situation in which we are forced to decide without knowing what Jesus would do. . . . Each situation has its own problematic circumstances which force the believer to think through each act of obedience without an absolute ethical guide from Jesus. To look for such a guide is to deny the freedom of the Christian man.[28]

Having granted us this latitude of authority relative to Jesus, how can the black church theologian withdraw the same authority to those assessing the black church? Surely, there is a clear inconsistency in denying absolute merit to Jesus but assigning it to the past of black theism.

The Coming Debate

Black religious humanism speaks for a minority, too long voiceless and too long powerless, in black religion. It is a demand to interpret the black experience without the fetters of a theological apparatus that may be an inappropriate or inaccurate account of our actual history. Though now a still small voice in black religion, it is emerging as a major religious force that black Christian theism will undoubtedly encounter as a rival and most assuredly as a prominent ingredient in the cultural matrix where the black church operates.

The black humanist is persuaded that the controlling principle of humanism, the affirmation of the radical freedom/autonomy of humanity, points to a verity that theism in general and black theism in particular must eventually acknowledge as a given. As black Christian theologians wrestle with the theodicy question in its revised form of quietism and ethnic suffering, as they attempt to construct a theology of social, political, and economic liberation, as they seek to accommodate the enlarged theological particularity that informs black theology and as they search for interpretive models to describe the *totality* of the biblical conception of the human creature, the necessity and significance of this understanding of human reality will be evident.

The future impact of black humanism can best be described by paraphrasing Frederick Herzog's fateful prediction: "Black humanism forces us to raise questions about the very foundations of black religion. By the time we have understood what it is all about, we will have realized that the whole structure of Black Christian theology will have to be rethought."[29]

NOTES

1. In this essay I have not attempted to describe the theological Weltanschaaung of religious humanism, having outlined this elsewhere (Theism and Religious Humanism: The Chasm Narrows," *The Christian Century,* 92:18, May 21, 1975). My focus here is narrowed to an analysis of religious humanism as expressed in the Afro-American experience.

2. The following pairs will be used synonymously: black humanism and black religious humanism; black theism and black Christian theism; humanism and non-theism; Afro-American and black; humanism and religious humanism.

3. "Document: Bishop Daniel Alexander Payne's Protestation of American Slavery," *Journal of Negro History,* 52 (1967): p. 63. Emphasis in the original.

4. Sterling Brown, "Negro Folk Expression: Spirituals, Seculars, Ballads and Work Songs" in August Meier and Elliott Rudwick (eds.), *The Making of Black America* (New York: Atheneum, 1969).

5. John Lovell, "The Social Implications of the Negro Spiritual," in Bernard Katz (ed.) *The Social Implications of Early Negro Music in the United States* (New York: Arno Press, 1969).

6. Preface, *Slave Songs of the United States:* Francis Allen, Charles Pickard Ware and Lucy McKim Garrison, in B. Katz, *The Social Implications of Early Negro Music in the United States,* p. xxxii.

7. *Ibid.,* p. xxxiii.

8. B. Katz, "Introduction," *The Social Implications of Early Negro Music in the United Sates,* p. xii.

9. The problem of ascertaining the actual latitude of black religious humanism parallels the determination of the true dimensions of insurrectionary activity among the slaves. Recent research leads one to conclude that the number of slave revolts was considerably more numerous than the actual records indicate.

10. Charles C. Jones, *The Religious Instruction of Negroes in the United States* (Savannah: T. Purse Co., 1842), p. 127.

11. Gayraud S. Wilmore, *Black Religion and Black Radicalism* (New York: Doubleday & Co., 1972), p. 161.

12. Cf. the similar claim of Benjamin Mays. "The other-worldly idea of God . . . finds fertile soil among the people who fare worst in this world; and it grows dimmer and dimmer as the social and economic conditions improve." *The Negro's God as Reflected in His Literature* (New York: Antheneum, 1969), p. 28.

13. This is not to affirm an abandonment of theism per se but a movement towards those forms of theism which are closest to the anthropological position of humanism.

14. James Cone, *The Spiritual & the Blues* (New York: Seabury Press, 1972), p. 112.

15. "Message to the Churches from Oakland," the National Committee of Black Churchmen, 1969.

16. J. Deotis Roberts, *Liberation and Reconciliation: A Black Theology* (Philadelphia: The Westminster Press, 1971), pp. 82–3.

17. Cecil Cone, *The Identity Crisis in Black Theology* (Nashville: African Methodist Episcopal Church, 1975), pp. 143–44.

18. Mays, *op. cit.,* pp. 281–19. Mays correctly identifies the cultural matrix of black religious humanism, but future research, no doubt, will challenge his claim about the historical location of black humanism. "Prior to 1914, God is neither doubted nor is His existence denied. Doubt, lack of faith, and denial are definitely post-War developments. In other words, from 1760 to 1914 God's existence is not denied." *Op. cit.,* pp. 252. The presence of the slave seculars and Payne's account of the God-defying slaves both suggest that the last word has not yet been said about the presence of humanism in ante-bellum black thought.

19. Nella Larsen, *Quicksand* (New York: Alfred A. Knopf, 1928), pp. 292. Though I contend that the fact of black suffering forces the question: Is God a White Racist? I do not conclude that the mere fact of black suffering—no matter how severe—permits us to answer the question. In this sense, Helga's self-confident assertion of a logical contradiction is inaccurate.

20. *Ibid.,* p. 297. This accent on the seeming disharmony between traditional categories of black Christian theism and the existential situation of black oppression is a characteristic feature of the black humanist theology. It is still true today that the black humanist fails to perceive the inner

consistency between the claim that God is the God of the oppressed and the continued oppression of blacks and other minorities. The more "The God of the Oppressed" theme is pressed, the more inexplicable becomes the point of departure for a black theology of liberation: the designation of the black situation as oppressive. From the humanist perspective, the crucial issue for black Christian theology is not that of original *sin,* but the original *oppression* that triggers the necessity of black liberation. To be extricated from this dilemma, the black Christian theologian will have to move towards a more radical eschatological doctrine or adopt a view of human reality that will relieve God of the responsibility for the crimes of human history. The former will push the black Christian theologian periously close to a "pie-in-the-sky eschatology," a point of view that has been denounced. The latter cannot be accomplished without endorsing the radical view of human freedom/autonomy that is the acknowledged core of the humanist anthropology.

21. William R. Jones, "Toward a Humanist Framework for Black Theology," included in *Black Theology II,* ed. William R. Jones and Calvin E. Bruce, Bucknell Press, 1977.

22. Mays, *op. cit.,* pp. 23–24.

23. *Ibid.,* p. 26.

24. *Ibid.,* p. 149.

25. John Mbiti, *New Testament Eschatology in an African Background* (London: Oxford University Press, 1971), p. 24. Emphasis supplied.

26. "Black folk theology, despite its record of highly liberating activity, cannot be labeled exclusively a theology of liberation. Black masses unanimously intuit such a goal, but do not self-consciously characterize their beliefs as a body primarily designed for liberation. It is more likely a theology of existence or survival." Henry Mitchell, *Black Belief* (New York: Harper & Row, Publishers, 1975), p. 120.

27. Roberts, *op. cit.,* p. 16.

28. James Cone, *Black Theology and Black Power* (New York: Seabury Press, 1969), pp. 139–40.

29. Frederick Herzog, *Liberation Theology* (New York: Seabury Press, 1972), p. vii–viii.

2

NINETEENTH-CENTURY BLACK FEMINIST WRITING AND ORGANIZING AS A HUMANIST ACT

Duchess Harris

❏

Harris, of Macalester College's African American Studies Program and Political Science Department, argues for an understanding of Black feminist responses to lynching and the politics of representation as humanist acts. That is to say, according to Harris, one of the basic premises of humanism is a strong regard for the human body and the safeguarding of humanity's welfare. In keeping with this basic principle, figures such as Ida Barnett Wells and others fought against unjust acts perpetrated against African Americans. By means of this analysis, Harris provides readers with an interesting political context and vantage point from which to examine the nineteenth-century documents presented here.

For additional information related to these nineteenth-century activities and figures, readers should see Sharon Harley and Rosalyn Terborg-Penn, ed., The Afro-American Woman: Struggles and Images *(Port Washington: Kennikat Press, 1978); Judith Weisenfeld and Richard Newman, eds.,* This Far by Faith: Readings in African-American Women's Religious Biography *(New York: Routledge, 1996); Evelyn Brooks Higginbotham,* Righteous Discontent: The Women's Movement in the Black Baptist Church, 1880–1920 *(Cambridge: Harvard University Press, 1993).*

❑

"Here in this place, we flesh; flesh that weeps, laughs; flesh that dances on bare feet in grass. Love it, love it hard. Yonder they do not love your flesh."

—Toni Morrison, *Beloved*

In the context of a nation that does not love our flesh but rather utilizes our bodies as a commodity and demonizes our spirit, Black Americans are continually challenged, externally and internally, to defend our humanity. One of the central themes of African American humanism is to love one's flesh; to become human, in the sense that, your body and spirit are one; to locate a powerful self, to develop and maintain an empowered Black community. This article will focus on the intersection of feminism and humanism during slavery and Reconstruction. I will focus on former enslaved woman Harriet Jacobs and antilynching advocate Ida B. Wells to illuminate the racialization of gendered politics.

Feminism has a different relationship to the African American community than it does to the dominant culture. When one thinks of feminism in Anglo-America, we often associate it with suffrage. In the Black community however, feminism has always been a humanist endeavor associated with racial uplift, with an emphasis on creating patriarchal family structures within a formerly enslaved community.

Harriet Jacobs, who wrote under the name Linda Brent, suffered during the period of slavery for loving her own flesh and for trying to protect her own virtue in the absence of a Black patriarch. When one reads *Incidents in the Life of a Slave Girl,* it is not difficult to see that the pursuit toward a more humane life is gendered. *Incidents* evolves

56

from the autobiographical tradition of heroic male slaves and from a line of American white women's writings that attack oppression and sexual exploitation, and yet her work is limited by the conventions of both narrative traditions. Restricted by the conventions and rhetoric of the slave narrative, a genre that presupposes a range of options more readily available to men than to women, Harriet Jacobs, in her own narrative, borrows heavily from the rhetoric of the sentimental novel. Like the prototypical bildungsroman plot, the plot of the slave narrative does not adequately accommodate differences in male and female development because it often neglects the sexualized nature of female enslavement.

Jacobs's experience in slavery differed from that of a male hero like Frederick Douglass in two important ways. First, her escape to the North could not have been successful without the support of the women's community. William Andrews, in *To Tell a Free Story*, makes the insightful observation that Jacobs's accounts of her community in the North and South provide an important commentary on what Carol Smith-Rosenberg has called the "female world of love and ritual" in nineteenth-century America.[1] Smith-Rosenberg's sources introduce the reader to the female support networks that conducted the socializing rituals that white middle-class women underwent in the nineteenth century. Andrews observes, "*Incidents* unveils for us not just a private, but clandestine set of women's support networks, often interracial in their composition, which presided over perilous Black female rites of passage in which the stakes were, quite literally, life and death."[2] His assessment is important because it demonstrates that parallel homosocial networks in Jacobs's autobiography are maintained clandestinely outside male awareness because they subvert the patriarchal system.

The second way in which Jacobs's American reality is different from Frederick Douglass's is that Douglass is able to escape slavery by physically fighting against it when he beats up his master, Mr. Covey. As a woman, Jacobs does not have the physical prowess to overcome her master and therefore employs verbal warfare and defensive verbal postures as tools of liberation. Whenever Jacobs is under sexual attack, Jo Anne Braxton notes that Brent uses "sass" as a weapon of self-defense.[3]

In her autobiography, Jacobs tells of her movements from silence into voice. She describes her encounters with Dr. Flint, who is trying to force her to be his concubine; she defies—with what Braxton identifies as "sass"—his demand that she become his exclusively by becoming pregnant by another white man:

> As for Dr. Flint, I had a feeling of satisfaction and triumph in the thought of telling him. From the time he told me of his intended arrangement, I was silent. At last, he came and told me that the cottage was completed, and ordered me to go to it. I told him I would never enter it. He said, I have heard enough of such talk as that. You shall go, if you are carried by force; and you shall remain there. I replied, "I will never go there. In a few months I shall be a mother."[4]

Just as Harriet Jacobs "sasses" Dr. Flint, she "sasses" white society by centralizing the voice of a Black woman who has been oppressed by racism, sexism, and class exploitation. "Sass" proves to be a successful tool with which Jacobs challenges the sociopolitical conditions of society. She suggests a tension in the Black woman's relation to various dominant discourses: history, literature, and social thought. *Incidents* is an artifact created by Brent's impulse to control and dominate in language those who controlled and dominated her. Language, becomes infinitely more powerful and more resonant than a lash or chain could ever be.

Jacobs is effective in contributing to the field of humanism because her story gives voice to a group of people who have been virtually silent in academia. A basic aesthetic pattern for defining the slave narrative lies in voice. This voice is projected in the foreground figure of the slave author who is in the process of transforming her experiences from object to subject. In the words of bell hooks, Harriet Jacobs is "talking back, thinking feminist, and thinking Black."[5]

Nestled within the framework of *Incidents in the Life of a Slave Girl*, is the notion that, as a Black woman, Jacobs had "nothing to fall back on; not maleness, not whiteness, not ladyhood, not anything."[6] Free or enslaved, Jacobs stands beyond the bounds of Victorian womanhood and yet takes her place within the American canon.

The theme that Black women stood beyond the confines of Victorian womanhood is echoed in the work of Beverly Guy-Sheftall. Guy-Sheftall notes that when the "cult of domesticity" received attention from women's studies scholars in the 1970s, Black women were virtually absent from the scholarly discourse surrounding the cult of true womanhood.[7]

Hazel Carby is one of the few Black women Americanists who has received recognition. In *Reconstructing Womanhood: The Emergence of the Afro-American Women Novelist,* she supports my claim that Jacobs's place in the American canon is as significant as Douglass's. In the chapter " 'In the Quiet Undisputed Dignity of My Womanhood': Black Feminist Thought after Emancipation," she argues that although many Americanists would like to characterize African-American culture at the turn of the century as the age of Booker T. Washington and W. E. B. Du Bois, the period was in fact one of intense activity and productivity for Black women.[8]

In 1891, Emma Dunham Kelly published the novel *Megda,* and 1892 was the year of publication not only of *Iola Leroy* but also of Anna Julia Cooper's *A Voice from the South* and Ida B. Wells's *Southern Horrors: Lynch Law in All Its Phases.* In 1893, at the Congress of Representative Women, Frances Harper, Fannie Barrier Williams, Anna Julia Cooper, Fanny Jackson Coppin, Sarah J. Early, and Hallie Q. Brown delivered addresses on various aspects of the progress of African-American women. In that same year Victoria Earle published *Aunt Lindy,* and in 1894 Gertrude Mossell published *The Work of Afro-American Women.*

The club movement among African-American women grew rapidly, and in 1895, the first Congress of Colored Women of the United States was convened in Boston. The National Federation of Afro-American Women was an outgrowth of the conference, then in 1896 the National Federation and the National League of Colored Women united in Washington, D.C., to form the National Association of Colored Women (NACW). Thus, for the first time, African-American women became nationally organized to confront the various modes of their oppression. The scholarly neglect of the history of Black women is nowhere more apparent than in the works that focus on white women in the nineteenth and early twentieth centuries.

Henry Louis Gates, Jr., has made an enormous contribution to unearthing the works of these previously erased women with publication of the Schomburg Library of Nineteenth-Century Black Women Writers. The short stories of Angelina Weld Grimké complement readings of Jacobs's autobiography and Ida B. Wells's speeches. After emancipation, the intersection of Black feminism and humanism meet at the linchpin of lynching. One could argue that Black feminist organizing during Reconstruction concerned itself with upholding the "quiet undisputed dignity of Black womanhood" by bringing humanity to Black manhood. The Black women's club movement focused on improving the race by lifting Black men as Black women climbed. Black women activists thought that the problem of the nineteenth century was the emasculinazation of the head of the household. In fact, for many Black women this spilled over into the twentieth century. Women like Dorothy Height thought that Du Bois's notion about the color line needed a male emphasis. Throughout the 1960s and 1970s the National Council of Negro Women (NCNW)—an offspring of the club movement—subordinated concerns for women as a group to those for the Black community, which meant Black men, during the peak of the civil rights movement. The Black women during this time period had the ills of the previous century to reflect on.

Angelina Weld Grimké's writings in the nineteenth century poetically articulate Black women's fears during her time, and even today. Her entire corpus—fiction, nonfiction, and drama—focuses almost exclusively on lynching and racial injustice. These works take on Black cultural grief rather than personal grief as their thematic focus, and they express great outrage over the lynchings of Blacks in the South, over the failure of northern whites to band together and demand an end to the crimes, and over racial injustice in general.[9] Lynching is a particularly affecting theme in Grimké's play *Rachel* (1920). The play depicts the effects of lynching on the desire to live and the attraction toward genocide for members of the Black community. The theme appears in her fiction as well, in such stories as "The Closing Door."

> An orderly mob, in an orderly manner, on a Sunday morning—
> I am quoting the newspapers—broke into the jail, took him
> out, slung him up to the limb of the tree, riddled his body
> with bullets, saturated it with coal oil, lighted a fire underneath
> him, gouged out his eyes with red hot irons, burnt him
> to a crisp and then sold souvenirs of him, ears, fingers, toes.
> His teeth brought five dollars each.[10]

Even though the lynching in "The Closing Door" is fictional, Grimké's depiction of it gives credence to the work of Ida B. Wells.

Ida B. Wells's nineteenth-century antilynching campaign demonstrates Black women's response to America's continued dismissal of Black humanity. In Toni Morrison's *Beloved,* the freedom of loving one's flesh in the segregated space of Baby Suggs's clearing is threatened once one steps into integrated space. Outside the clearing, humanistic action works to ensure that one does not find one's humanity dangling like "Strange fruit . . . from the poplar trees."[11]

On March 9, 1892, three Black men, Thomas Moss, Calvin McDowell, and Henry Steward, co-owners of The People's Grocery, were taken outside the Memphis city limits to be hung and shot. Wells, a close friend of Moss's, was in Natchez at the time of the lynchings. She quickly replied to the lynchings in the next issue of *Free Speech*:

> The city of Memphis has demonstrated that neither character nor standing avails the Negro if he dares to protect himself against the white man or become his rival. There is nothing we can do about the lynching now, as we are out-numbered and without arms. . . . There is therefore only one thing left that we can do; save our money and leave a town which will never protect our lives and property, nor give us a fair trial in the courts, but takes us out and murders us in cold blood when accused by white persons.[12]

This editorial marks the beginning of Wells's antilynching campaign, which would span the next several decades, exposing and examining thousands of lynchings of Black Americans. Slavery had not only served to imagine Black people as commodifiable, it also perpetuated the colonialist assumption of a spiritless body. The division of body and spirit was a key factor in the justification of slavery; because Black people had no moral spirit, they were dismissable as nonhuman. Wells notes, "During the slave regime, the Southern white man owned the Negro body and soul. It was to his interest to dwarf the soul and preserve the body."[13] It was commercially profitable to maintain the body of a slave. Emancipation brought the loss of direct economic profitability of a Black body, and in turn the "freedom" to lynch. At the same time, emancipation altered the image of Black men from innocent, malleable children to animalistic sexual deviants. This shift in imagery was due to the shift from economic profitability to economic threat.

In 1892, 241 persons were lynched in the United States. Of this number, 160 were Black, 5 were women, and 2 were children. The reasons given for the lynchings:

Rape	46	Attempted rape	11
Murder	58	Suspected robbery	4
Rioting	3	Larceny	1
Race prejudice	6	Self-defense	1
No cause given	4	Insulting women	2
Incendiarism	6	Desperadoes	6
Robbery	6	Attempted murder	2
No offense stated, boy and girl,	2[14]		

By May of 1892, Wells's campaign had turned from a statement of atrocities and call to flight, to an all-out challenge of white supremacist practices of subordination. Wells began to detail the violence of individual lynchings in her paper, *Free Speech*. The overwhelming percentage of Black men charged with the rape of, or communication with, white women led to Wells's concentration on the credibility of charges placed against the lynched.

Wells stated that she, too, had previously believed that Black men were raping white women throughout the South. After the lynching of Moss and Wells's tabulation of lynch statistics, the falseness of popular conceptions of Black men raping white women as the central cause of lynching became evident. On May 21, 1892, Wells wrote in *Free Speech:*

> Eight Negroes lynched since last issue of the "Free Speech" . . . three for killing a white man, and five on the same old racket— the new alarm about raping white women. The same program of hanging, then shooting bullets into the lifeless bodies was carried out to the letter. Nobody in this section of the country believes the old threadbare lie that Negro men rape white women. If Southern men are not careful, they will over-reach themselves and public sentiment will have a reaction; a conclusion will then be reached which will be very damaging to the moral reputation of their women.[15]

Throughout her writings, Wells explains the multiple ways in which constructing the necessity of protecting the virtue of southern white women was used to establish cause for lynching. Black men speaking with white women, consensual affairs, the need to explain a dark-skinned baby emerging from a white body, and cases of mistaken identity, all could result in the death of a Black man.

Wells contended that Black men's feared sexual prowess and southern white men's chivalry were not the central causes of lynching. She points out that no charges of rape were heard of during slavery, and that white men were prepared to leave their wives and daughters at home in the care of Black men when they went to war. "Lynching really was . . . [a]n excuse to get rid of Negroes who were acquiring wealth and property and thus keep the race terrorized and 'keep a nigger down.' "[16] Blacks had started to gain an economic foothold in the South, including facets other than labor positions. Businesses like The People's Grocery threatened the profit margins of white-owned businesses. This, coupled with fear of miscegenation of black men and white women, resulted in white men's fear of emasculation. To ensure their own manhood, white men castrated black men.

Her contempt for the lack of a strong public response, led to Wells's greatest humanist critique and challenge to action:

> Men who stand high in the esteem of the public . . . for normal and physical courage, for devotion to the principles of equal and exact justice to all . . . stand as cowards who fear to open their mouths to this great outrage. They do not see that by their tacit encouragement, their silent acquiescence, the black shadow of lawlessness in the form of lynch law is spreading its wings over the whole country.[17]

Wells's language challenges the humanity of those who relegate themselves to inaction. She points out that those who may believe themselves to be humanitarians, and moral human beings, looked the other way while the annual number of lynchings remained at more than 125 from 1885 to 1899. Her antilynching campaign was one woman's attempt to ensure that black flesh could become prosperous and survive in the United States, and she fought with statistics and documentation that demonstrated that Black people were lynched because they were imagined to be spiritless bodies. In essence, the campaign was "in the defense of her race."

One way that dominant culture tried to discredit the activism of Ida B. Wells and the humanism of the Black community as a whole was through the dissemination of the Aunt Jemima image. The company that made Aunt Jemima famous was founded in the early 1890s by a white man named Chris Rutt, who hired Nancy Green, a Black woman, to dress in costume and flip pancakes at the 1893 World's Fair (also known as the Columbian Exposition). There are many ironies implicit in the fact that the Columbian Exposition was used to launch Aunt Jemima products. As Patrcia A. Turner notes, Nancy Green was flipping pancakes while Wells was distributing the protest pamphlet *The Reason Why: The Colored American Is Not in the World's Columbian Exposition.*[18] Wells and her supporters wanted the public to know how inadequate they believed the fair's attention to Black Americans was.

The Wells pamphlet was further undermined by another pamphlet created around the same time by Purd Wright, *When Robert E. Lee Stopped at Aunt Jemima's Cabin.*[19] Aunt Jemima's fictionalized biography is told by an aging Confederate general who returns to the Old South after twenty years looking to revisit the best meal he ever had. According to Kenneth Goings, the story is that Aunt Jemima had worked her whole life on the Higbee plantation in Louisiana. In 1864, the general and his orderly became separated from the other troops and almost starved to death. On their third day of hunger they came across a cabin where the "mammy" fed them pancakes such as they had never eaten before. Years later, the general wanted to return to the cabin to see if she was still there. She was, and he persuaded her to sell him the recipe, which allowed him to introduce the product to northern consumers at a sizeable profit. Goings's critique of this biography is apropos: it is only in the fiction-dominated minds of White America that Aunt Jemima would not have joined the migration north but instead would have remained on the plantation like a "happy" former slave waiting to make pancakes for Robert E. Lee.[20] I would like to add to this critique the observation that the authenticity of this biography was not challenged in the way that Harriet Jacobs's autobiography was sixty years later.

Referring to the real-life objectification of Aunt Jemima, Turner states:

> In her homespun calico garb with a turban around her head, Aunt Jemima comforted the public; in her businesslike attire with a fashionable hat on her head, Ida B. Wells vexed the public. Aunt Jemima's was the kind of face people wanted to remember; Ida B. Wells was the kind they wanted to forget. And that is exactly what happened.[21]

I agree with Turner that the writings and activism to achieve humanism by Jacobs, Grimké, and Wells have been overshadowed by gross caricatures of Black American life.

This article has been an attempt to highlight the work of Black feminists in the nineteenth century who understood humanism as a process, an existential process by which one finds and lives humanity while also fighting for the humanity of others.[22]

NOTES

1. Carol Smith-Rosenberg, "The Female World of Love and Ritual: Relations between Women in Nineteenth Century America," *Signs* 1 (1975): 1–29.

2. Williams Andrews, *To Tell a Free Story: The First Century of Afro-American Autobiography, 1769–1865* (Urbana: University of Illinois Press, 1986), 58.

3. JoAnne Braxton, *Black Women Writing Autobiography: A Tradition within a Tradition* (Philadelphia: Temple University Press, 1989), 34.

4. Linda Brent, *Incidents in the Life of a Slave Girl* (Orlando: Harcourt Brace Jovanovich, 1973), 116.

5. bell hooks, *Talking Back: Thinking Feminist, Thinking Black* (Boston: South End Press, 1989), 74.

6. Paula Giddings, *When and Where I Enter: The Impact of Black Women on Race and Sex in America* (New York: William Morrow, 1984).

7. Beverly Guy-Sheftall, "Daughters of Sorrow: Historical Overview of Black Women, 1880–1920," in *Black Women in United States History*, ed. Darlene Clark Hine (Brooklyn: Carlson, 1990), 16.

8. Hazel Carby, *Reconstructing Womanhood: The Emergence of the Afro-American Woman Novelist* (New York: Oxford University Press, 1987), 116.

9. Alfreda Duster, ed., *Crusade for Justice: The Autobiography of Ida B. Wells* (Chicago: University of Chicago Press, 1970), 48–52.

10. Angelina Weld Grimké, "The Closing Door," in *Selected Works of Angelina Weld Grimké*, ed. Carolivia Herron (New York: Oxford University Press, 1991), 272.

11. "Strange Fruit," as sung by Billie Holliday, 1939. See David Margolick, *Strange Fruit: Billie Holliday, Cafe Society, and an Early Cry for Civil Rights* (Philadelphia: Running Press, 2000).

12. Ida B. Wells-Barnett, *A Red Record: Tabulated Statistics and Alleged Causes of Lynching in the United States, 1892–1893–1894* (Chicago: Donohue and Henneberry, 1895); reprinted in *Selected Works of Ida B. Wells-Barnett*, ed. Henry Louis Gates, Jr., comp. Trudier Harris (New York: Oxford University Press, 1991), 219.

13. Ida B. Wells-Barnett, *The Reason Why: The Colored American Is Not in the World's Columbian Exposition* (Chicago: Self-published, 1893); reprinted in *Selected Works of Ida B. Wells-Barnett*, ed. Gates, comp. Harris, 78.

14. hooks, *Talking Back*, 145–146.

15. Duster, *Crusade for Justice*, 64.

16. Ida B. Wells-Barnett, *Southern Horrors: Lynch Law in All Its Phases* (New York: New York Age Print, 1892); reprinted in *Selected Works of Ida B. Wells-Barnett*, ed. Gates, comp. Harris, 30.

17. Ibid.

18. Patricia A. Turner, *Ceramic Uncles and Celluloid Mammies: Black Images and Their Influence on Culture* (New York: Anchor Books, 1994), 50.

19. Purd Wright, *When Robert E. Lee Stopped at Aunt Jemima's Cabin*, pamphlet, in personal holdings of Kenneth Goings, Florida Atlantic University.

20. Kenneth Goings, *Mammy and Uncle Mose: Black Collectibles and American Stereotyping* (Bloomington : Indiana University Press, 1994), 31.

21. Turner, *Ceramic Uncles and Celluloid Mammies,* 50.

22. Unitarian Universalist Commission on Appraisal to the General Assembly, *Empowerment: One Denomination's Quest for Racial Justice, 1967–1982* (Boston: Unitarian Universalist Association, 1984), 24.

B

Personal Accounts

3

THE STORY OF JAMES HAY

William Loren Katz, Editor

❏

Stories and sayings related to slaves shed tremendous insight into the thought and practices of African Americans prior to the mid-nineteenth century. It has been assumed, for the most part, that these accounts and actions are framed by an embrace of Christian doctrine (as the dominant mode of religious expression) and practice. However, as the story of James Hay indicates, the thought and life of African American slaves was not always premised upon acceptance of Christian principles and frameworks, or of other dominant forms of religious expression. To the contrary, some slaves acted through reliance on human activity and ingenuity.

According to the following story, James Hay received harsh treatment from the plantation overseer as a result of his inability to meet work expectations. In response to this, Aunt Patience suggested that Hay recognize that the Lord will help him to fulfill his assigned task. Taking Aunt Patience seriously and literally, Hay awaits the assistance of the Lord with his work. When this does not occur, and his work remained incomplete, Hay was punished. As a result, Hay voices distrust in the Lord and rejects Christianity. What readers will find here is an example of the suspicion concerning divine beings that marks much of humanism, and in this way it serves as an example of the early presence of humanist attitudes within African American communities.

For additional evidence of this perspective, readers should see, for example, Lura Beam, He Called Them by the Lightning; A Teacher's Odyssey in the Negro South, 1908–1919 *(Indianapolis, Bobbs-Merrill, 1967),* 63–65. *More general statements that bring into question the theistic assumptions of Christianity, and that, as a result, relate to African American humanism can be found, for example, in the following folktale sources: "Brer Rabbit's Hankering for a Long Tail," in Abraham D. Roger,* African Folktales: Selected and Retold by Abraham Rogers *(New York: Pantheon Books, 1983),* 55, *and "Ole Massa and John Who Wanted to Go to Heaven," in Zora Neale Hurston,* Mules and Men *(Philadelphia: J. B. Lippincott, 1935; reprint, New York Perennial Library, 1990), 70–72. An analysis of these stories is found in Anthony Pinn,* Why, Lord? Suffering and Evil in Black Theology *(New York: Continuum, 1995), 139–146. Readers interested in general studies concerning African American thought during this period should see, for example, Ira Berlin, Marc Favreau, and Steven F. Miller, eds.,* Remembering Slavery *(New York: New Press in association with the Library of Congress, 1998); John W. Blassingame, ed.,* Slave Testimony: Two Centuries of Letters, Speeches, Interviews, and Autobiographies *(Baton Rouge: Louisiana State University Press, 1977); Eugene Genovese,* Roll, Jordan, Roll: The World the Slaves Made *(New York: Pantheon Books, 1974); and James O. Horton and Lois E. Horton,* In Hope of Liberty: Culture, Community and Protest among Northern Free Blacks, 1700–1860 *(New York: Oxford University Press, 1977).*

❏

There was a slave named James Hay, who belonged to a neighbor of master's; he was punished a great many times because he could not get his task done. The other slaves pitied him because he seemed unable to perform his task. One evening he got a severe whipping; the next morning as the slaves were having their tasks assigned them, an old lady by the name of Aunt Patience went by, and said, "Never mind, Jim, my son, the Lord will help you with your task today;" he answered, "Yes, ma'am." He began his work very faithfully and continued until it was half done, then he lay down under a tree; the others, not understanding his motive, thought he was tired and was taking a rest, but he did not return to his task until the overseer called him and asked him why he did not have his work nearer done. He said, "Aunt Patience told me dis morning that the Lord would help me today, and I thought as I did half of the task, the Lord might have finished the other half if he intended to help me at all." The overseer said "You see that the Lord did not come to help you and we shall not wait for him, but we will help you;" so Jim got a severe punishment. Sometime after this, Jim Hay was called upon by some professors of religion; they asked him if he was not tired of serving the devil, and told him that the Lord was good and had helped many of his people, and would help all who asked him and then take them home to heaven. Jim said that if the Lord would not do half an acre of his task for him when he depended on him, he did not think he could trust him, and Jim never became a Christian to my knowledge.

4

AN UNPUBLISHED
FREDERICK DOUGLASS LETTER

Herbert Aptheker

❏

Frederick Douglass (1818–1895) was a central figure in the efforts of African Americans to achieve freedom and equality within the context of the United States. Douglass was an abolitionist who knew the horrors of slavery firsthand. Born into slavery in Maryland, he eventually escaped and made his way north. Within a short period of time after arriving Douglass began lecturing against slavery. He spoke with force against an institution that belittled and dehumanized those of African descent. Although many who were involved in efforts to destroy the institution of slavery asserted the importance of basic Christian beliefs as backing for their efforts, it was not always clear where Douglass personally stood on key elements of Christian doctrine. For example, after one speech, Sojourner Truth is said to have asked Douglass if God was dead, the question deriving from his inattention to God as the source of liberation.

Douglass's connections to free thought and humanist notions become clearer through the following letter and commentary provided by Aptheker. In the letter Douglass hints at the difficulties he is having with religious leaders and

75

others who are troubled by his unwillingness to acknowledge the role of God in the progress of African Americans. Aptheker notes that Douglass's perspective concerning this becomes more forceful with each critique he addresses. The thrust of his position entails, in some instances, what resembles a deism of sorts. On other occasions, it entails a lack of concern with notions of God, preferring to give attention and priority to the efforts of humans to bring about their own liberation. In this way, his thought seems to be in keeping with basic principles of humanism.

The article by William L. Van Deburg provides additional insight into Douglass's liberal religious views. He argues that Douglass's perspective on God, shaped in part by the apathy of the churches, results in his ultimate rejection of the Supreme Being and his dependence upon humanity to bring about social transformation.

For more information on Frederick Douglass, see, for example, Michael Meyer, ed., Frederick Douglass: The Narrative and Selected Writings *(New York: Random House/Modern Library, 1984); John W. Blassingame, ed.,* The Frederick Douglass Papers *(New Haven: Yale University Press, 1979–); William S. McFeely,* Frederick Douglass *(New York: W. W. Norton & Company, 1991). For a general study of the abolitionist movement, see James Stewart,* Holy Warriors: The Abolitionists and American Slavery *(New York: Hill and Wang, 1976, 1996). For the reference to the Sojourner Truth question mentioned above, see Nell I. Painter,* Sojourner Truth: A Life, A Symbol *(New York: W. W. Norton & Company, 1996), 160–161. In addition to autobiographical materials related to Douglass, readers may also find the following autobiographical writings by African Americans interesting: Linda Brent,* Incidents in the Life of a Slave Girl *(New York: Harcourt Brace Jovanovich, 1973); Olaudah Equiano,* The Life of Olaudah Equiano, or Gustavus Vassa the African Written by Himself, *edited with an introduction by Paul Edwards (Harlow, Great Britain: Longman, 1989).*

❏

I have come into possession recently of a four-page, hand-written letter written by Frederick Douglass. It contains material of more than formal interest; the letter, in its entirety and exactly as written, reads:

Rochester. June 14.

Private.

Dear Friend:

Unlike yourself I have a better impression of Senator Revels since seeing him. He is not an able man but he is an amiable man and a modest man. I found in him no swelling sense of his own importance. There was nothing in his bearing that said "I am an American Senator."

Is there no mistake about his drinking champagne with his Boston friends? I was at a wedding with him a few weeks ago and found him more exemplary in this respect than his Master: for you know that Jesus himself preferred wine to water on such occasions—that is if he has not been misrepresented by his Biographers.

I have no doubt that the avowal of my liberal opinions will drive many from me who were once my friends and even exclude me from many platforms upon which I was a welcome speaker, but such is the penalty which every man must suffer who admits a new truth into his mind. I am sensitive to the good opinions of men and shall suffer— but I am in a measure prepared for whatever may come to me in this respect.

As to my not going far enough, I have to say, that while I am free to follow my convictions wherever they may lead— I deem it wise to avow those which are perfectly formed, clearly defined, and about which I am entirely undisturbed by doubts of any sorts. I bow to no priests either of faith or of unfaith. I claim as against all sorts of people, simply perfect freedom of thought.

Talk not of boring me with letters for though you have the dangerous talent of a good letter writer, you are in no danger of boring me, unless you require me to write as well as you do. Miss Assing informed me of the marriage of your cousin, Clementina. All happiness to her and her husband.

It seems very long since I saw you and dear Mrs Koehler and the children, yet you are all very fresh in my memory.

I found it very easy to like all your Free thinking circle.

Beside the letter which I send herewith to be used by the firm of Prang and Co. I shall send a brief notice of the portrait to the New Era at Washington—and perhaps to one or two other papers. If you can improve the wording of the letter (as is very likely for I do not know anything about art) do so.

I am expected Miss Assing in Rochester in the course of the next ten days. She evidently has much pleasure in seeing me in hot water with my old religious friends, and if she could have her way—the water would be a great deal hotter than it now is for my friend is a genuine image smasher.

I reciprocate all your kind wishes to you and all who are dear to you.

Very truly yours,
s/ Frdk. Douglass

Though the year of this letter is not given in the original, internal evidence makes it certain that it was written in 1870. Hiram R. Revels, the first Negro to be a United States Senator, took his seat on February 25, 1870 and served as a Senator only during 1870. The newspaper, the *New National Era* was started, with Douglass as a contributing editor, in January, 1870, and in August, 1870, Douglass left Rochester for Washington in order to take over the active editorship of the already-faltering newspaper. Furthermore, as we shall see below, the difficulties involving religious views, to which Douglass refers, arose early in 1870.

Precisely who the Mr. Koehler was to whom Douglass is writing, is not yet established. The Miss Assing mentioned in the letter undoubtedly is Ottilia Assing, of Rochester, who was a friend of many years, and had been a staunch Abolitionist; Douglass, in his autobiography, mentions particularly her help in the stormy days that followed immediately after John Brown's raid.

The whereabouts of the enclosure mentioned in the letter is not known, nor is it known what portrait Douglass is referring to.

The religious controversy to which Douglass refers is not mentioned in his autobiography, but there are references to it in the fourth volume of Philip S. Foner's, *The Life and Writings of Frederick Douglass* (N.Y., 1955, International Publishers, especially pages 45–50).

The difficulties arose as the result of remarks made by Douglass in the course of meetings celebrating President Grant's proclamation, on March 30, 1870, of the adoption of the Fifteenth Amendment. On April 19, 1870, what remained of the American Anti-Slavery Society convened for its last time in New York City. Douglass shared the platform with such stalwarts of the struggle as Wendell Phillips, Henry Highland Garnet, Lucretia Mott, Robert Purvis, Julia Ward Howe, and others. In his speech, Douglass noted that many had thanked God for the successful conclusion of the Abolitionist effort, but as for himself, said Douglass:

> I like to thank men. . . . I want to express my love to God and gratitude to God, by thanking those faithful men and women, who have devoted the great energies of their soul to the welfare of mankind. It is only through such men and such women that I can get a glimpse of God anywhere.

A few days later Douglass spoke again in celebration of the adoption of the Fifteenth Amendment—this time in Albany, New York—and once again, while he thanked by name the work of Phillips, Brown, Lovejoy, Lincoln, etc., he did not thank God. Rumblings began to appear from some of the clergy, and not least, quite naturally, from the Negro clergy. Speaking in Philadelphia on April 26, 1870, at a particularly well-attended meeting—again celebrating the Fifteenth Amendment—Douglass chose to deal even more clearly, and at some length, with his religious views. He explicitly affirmed, "I dwell here in no hackneyed cant about thanking God for this deliverance." He chose this course, he explained, for too often in the heat of the battle against slavery was he told to leave it all to God; there were some "always holding us back by telling us that God would abolish slavery in his own good time."

Not so, said Douglass. God has endowed man with great powers, but man "is to work out his own salvation." Therefore, he continued, he wanted to thank those men and women, and only those men and women, who "labored in the beginning, amid loss of reputation, amid insult and martyrdom, and at imminent peril of life and limb."

Nor was Douglass yet finished with the public avowal of his religious views, for at that moment the question of whether or not the Bible should be used in public schools was a matter of heated discussion. Douglass stated he was opposed to this because he believed in the complete and absolute separation of church and state: ". . . my command to the church, and all denominations of the church whether Catholic or Protestant is, hands off this Government. And my command to the Government is hands off the church."

Of course, this challenge could not go unanswered. Under the leadership of Bishop Campbell of the Philadelphia Colored Methodist Episcopal Church, a meeting was called by several Negro clergymen—the Reverend James Wilson, the Reverend J. Frisby Cooper, and others—for May 18, to protest these views. At this meeting a resolution was adopted taking views exactly opposite to those announced by Douglass: (1) there was a need to thank God above all for deliverance; and (2) the Bible must be an integral part of instruction in all public schools. If this were not sufficiently pointed, the Resolution closed with this sentence:

> That we will not acknowledge any man as a leader of our people who will not thank God for the deliverance and enfranchisement of our race, and will not vote to retain the Bible, the book of God, in our public schools.

Douglass was not one to leave a battle-field, however, as the previous thirty years of his life had demonstrated. He replied with an open letter in the *Philadelphia Press* reaffirming his position, denouncing bigotry and religious intolerance and declaring that he would not yield to ministerial pressure. And he would not, "because," he wrote:

> I would not stultify myself. During forty years of moral effort to overthrow slavery in this country, this system with all its hell-black horrors and crimes, found no more secure shelter anywhere than amid the popular religious cant of the day. One honest Abolitionist was a greater terror to slaveholders than whole acres of camp-meeting preachers shouting glory to God.

And, in case this was not enough, Douglass challenged Bishop Campbell to debate with him, publicly, the issues involved in this dispute. So far as the record shows, no such debate occurred, though it is not likely that it was Douglass who was the obstacle.

It is in the midst of this situation that Douglass wrote the letter dated June 14 that has been quoted above in full.

5

FREDERICK DOUGLASS

Maryland Slave to Religious Liberal

William L. Van Deburg

❏

> Do not class me with those who despise religion—do not
> identify me with the infidel.
> —Frederick Douglass at Market Hall, New York City,
> October 22, 1847

On April 26, 1870, black abolitionist Frederick Douglass addressed a
gathering assembled at Philadelphia's Horticultural Hall to celebrate
the recent ratification of the Fifteenth Amendment to the United
States Constitution. In a powerful speech, Douglass refused to follow
the views of the city's black clergy on the subject of God's role in the
successful anti-slavery crusade. "I dwell here in no hackneyed cant
about thanking God for this deliverance. . . ." he intoned, "my thanks
tonight are to willing hearts and willing hands that labored in the
beginning, amid loss of reputation, amid insult and martyrdom, and
at imminent peril of life and limb." Wendell Phillips, Elijah Lovejoy,

John Brown, and Abraham Lincoln were lauded for their contributions to the abolitionist cause. The Deity was shunned.[1]

Douglass' speech, marking the degree to which he had abandoned the beliefs of his youth, was an important milestone in his lifelong journey toward and through religious liberalism. This gradual shift in perception of the Godhead is certainly not unique among Christians, but the events which furthered the liberalization of his theology could be experienced by only one group of nineteenth-century Americans—the Negro slave turned freedman. Furthermore, it must be remembered that Douglass was definitely not a "common" freedman. His unique experiences as a chattel, abolitionist, and author necessitate an individual examination of his changing conception of God.

Young Douglass was exposed to the Biblical concept of a Supreme Being in the mid-1820's. One source of information was "Uncle" Isaac Copper, who taught a group of thirty slave youngsters the Lord's Prayer, encouraging the pupils' attention by the liberal use of a hickory switch. Douglass later wrote. "There was in my mind, even at that time, something a little inconsistent and laughable in the blending of prayer with punishment." The youngsters were also led to believe that God was good and knew what was best for everyone. White people were made to be rulers, while blacks were created as slaves.[2]

Sophia Auld, his master's wife, was a more important influence than "Uncle" Isaac. Douglass was fascinated by his mistress' mastery of the printed word and delighted in hearing her read the Holy *Bible.* Quickly denied access to this channel of knowledge by Hugh Auld, he became an avid seeker of clandestine printed matter. By converting neighborhood white boys into teachers, Douglass learned to read, but soon developed a deep loneliness and melancholy.

When he was thirteen years old, a white Methodist minister caused him to feel that he had a friend in God. The young slave did not know exactly what was required of a Christian, but he professedly realized that all men were sinners who must repent and be reconciled to God. Recalling this conversion experience in later years he noted:

"I finally found my burden lightened, and my heart relieved. . . . I saw the world in a new light, and my great concern was to have everybody converted."[3] Supported in his worship by a devout Negro acquaintance who lived near the Aulds, Douglass surrendered himself completely to this new faith in God, eventually establishing a Sunday School for fellow bondsmen.

His reliance on an other-worldly Being could not, however, erase the evidence of the slave master's apparent supremacy in purely physical matters. Various owners and overseers were at times vicious and brutal. Captain Aaron Anthony savagely whipped a young slave woman who had been secretly meeting with her lover. Colonel Edward Lloyd laid stripes on a slave mother of five for the heinous crime of "impudence." Douglass was deeply moved by "one of the most heart-saddening and humiliating scenes" that he had ever witnessed when "Old Barney" was given thirty lashes.[4] Descriptions of such observed physical punishments abound in Douglass' writings and are too well documented in studies of the plantation system to attribute them to a fertile imagination encouraged by the requirements of the anti-slavery lecture circuit.

He was most disheartened by the blatant hypocrisy exhibited by his two most avowedly Christian masters, Thomas Auld and Edward Covey. Captain Auld's conversion to Christianity did not modify his treatment of the slaves. "If religion had any effect at all on him," Douglass wrote, "it made him more cruel and hateful in all his ways."[5] No improvement was made in the chattels' swill-like food. Disobedient slaves were still whipped, except now Auld quoted *Bible* verses to justify his deeds. After a second Negro Sabbath School was broken up by a group of white Christians, Douglass noted that "this conduct, on the part of class-leaders and professedly holy men, did not serve to strengthen my religious conviction."[6]

Covey was an expert slave breaker as well as a class-leader in the Methodist Church. It was certainly not Christian love that enabled Covey to break Douglass in body and spirit in the summer of 1834.

After his terrifying experiences on the Covey farm, the future abolitionist could only reflect that "of all slaveholders with whom I have
ever met, religious slaveholders are the worst."[7]

It was only the freer rein allowed Douglass by William Friedland,
an unbeliever, that enabled him to reassert his belief in the Christian
God. After conducting a Sabbath School at the house of a free Negro
near the Friedland estate, he was allowed to return to Baltimore as an
apprentice in the ship-building trade. Douglass promptly took advan-
tage of this new freedom and joined the Sharp Street Methodist
Church. After fleeing to the North in 1838, the twenty-one-year-old
ex-slave continued to be "religiously inclined," soon becoming a class-
leader and licensed preacher in the Negro New Bedford Zion Methodist Church. Nevertheless, as Benjamin Quarles has written, the slave
whippings and deprivations left "a lasting impression on his
plastic mind."[8]

An extensive analysis of Black Methodism is beyond the scope of
this study. For the purpose of ascertaining Douglass' acceptance of
mainstream Christian doctrine in the 1840's and 1850's it is sufficient
to note that most black Christians viewed God as an omnipotent
Being who was the final judge of all human actions and the just,
loving force, ever on the side of oppressed peoples.[9]

During the pre-Civil War years, Douglass displayed an awareness
of an incredible number of doctrinal issues. His opinions on these
issues clearly showed a devotion to and a reverence of the Christian
God. That God created the earth and then allowed sinful man to
inhabit its surface was a foregone conclusion in Douglass' mind. In
1852, at the National Free Soil Convention in Pittsburgh, he asserted
his belief in the Supreme Being's omnipotence by declaring, "The
earth is God's, and it ought to be covered with righteousness, and not
slavery."[10]

The Creator was also the Supreme Judge of the Universe. Even as a
child, Douglass attributed an approaching cholera epidemic to a God
who was "angry with the white people because of their slaveholding

wickedness" and therefore, sought to punish the wrongdoers.[11] In an 1847 letter to aged slaveholder-statesman Henry Clay, Douglass reminded him that he must soon appear before God to "render up an account" of his stewardship. The abolitionist asked Clay if he thought that God would hold him guiltless if he died without freeing his chattels.[12] Again in January 1848, Douglass noted the power of his God, when, in a protest against the Mexican War, he pleaded for an end of hostilities and the recall of American troops. If such action was not taken, "so sure as there is a God of justice," the entire nation would be punished for their acceptance of the cruel "slaveholding crusade".[13] Slaveholders supporting the war would be held responsible "at the judgement, in the sight of a just God."[14]

Douglass believed that God created all men as equals and endowed them with strength and intellect through the workings of his grace and wisdom. Before he began his extensive search for Christian knowledge, the young chattel became perplexed and worried over the contradiction in plantation theology which posited the existence of a "good" God who allowed the "bad" institution of slavery to prosper. Not until he overheard one of his co-laborers explaining how blacks were captured and brought to America in chains did he realize that inequality was a man-made condition.[15] In an 1849 newspaper article Douglass encouraged fellow Negroes to continue their upward climb out of the intellectual and spiritual darkness imposed by slavery. Clearly championing human equality, he echoed the words in *The Acts of the Apostles* by noting that God was "no respecter of persons, and hath made of one blood all nations for to dwell upon all the face of the earth."[16]

In exposing white America's fear of Negro equality in an 1850 article, Douglass exhibited his belief in the ability of God to strengthen and rehabilitate a depressed people. The Negro "stands erect," he wrote, "upon his brow he bears the seal of manhood, from the hand of the living God."[17]

Not only did Douglass believe in a God-given physical strength, but he also ascribed the molding of man's mental capabilities to the Supreme Being. In an 1846 speech at Moorfields, England, the fiery abolitionist urged British Christians to condemn slavery in the United States because it destroyed the chattel's intellect, a faculty which was given to all people by the God of Creation.[18]

Douglass held that all of these gifts were made possible by God's grace, which was "sufficient" to enable him to escape slavery's shackles, and by the workings of the Creator's own powers of intellect as revealed in the Scriptures.[19] Heavenly wisdom was pure, peaceable, gentle, easily entreated, full of mercy and without partiality or hypocrisy.[20] He often compared these characteristics of God's rule to the popular slaveholding interpretation of the Holy *Bible* which "makes God a respecter of persons, denies his fatherhood of the race, and tramples in the dust the great truth of the brotherhood of man."[21]

The most important theological issue raised by Douglass was his attempt to show that a wise God invariably entered into the thoughts and actions of men, allying with the forces of right against the powers of evil. Douglass was certain of God's support when he proclaimed, "He who has God and conscience on his side, has a majority against the universe."[22] The Supreme Rule would "bring to naught" the councils of the ungodly and "confound the wisdom of the crafty."[23] Moreover, it was quite simple to enlist God in a noble cause. In a letter to Henry Clay, he used the ideas expressed in Isaiah 58:9 to support his case for emancipation.[24]

Without supernatural aid, slavery would be a continuing menace to the black man. God, decreeing that America should have no peace until she repented, was responsible for supporting the abolitionists in their crusade.[25] Indeed, it was "a happy interposition of God" that Douglass was able to "burst up through the dark incrustation of malice and hate" to become an anti-slavery lecturer.[26] He confidently believed that the "forces" of Heaven would eventually destroy the chattel system. "The arm of the Lord is not shortened and the doom of slavery is certain."[27] Certainly nothing but God's truth and love could "cleanse the land" of its most despicable institution.[28]

In addition to this deep faith in God's ability to further the abolitionist cause, he also mirrored mainstream black Christianity in his condemnation of those who relied on the powers of reason instead of on a just Creator. In 1852, Douglass condemned the writings of Voltaire, Bolingbroke, and Thomas Paine as infidelic.[29] A year later, he blasted a group of fellow reformers for their questioning of the Holy *Bible*'s authority. The *Bible* was a sacred text. To disregard its power would be as foolish as it would be "to fling away the Constitution."[30]

It would be a mistake, however, to portray Douglass as a piously conservative Christian. His biographers have correctly noted that he was not orthodox in his doctrine. His belief that religion should be used as an instrument for social reconstruction led him to despise the passive attitude shown by many Negro ministers.

As he progressed in his abolitionist career, Douglass was influenced by those champions of Reason, Transcendentalism, and Unitarianism whose doctrines he had condemned. In an 1848 essay, he noted that the destiny of the Negro race was committed to human hands. God was not wholly responsible for freeing those in bondage.[31] By 1853, he was willing to criticize Henry Ward Beecher's reliance on God to end slavery. If Beecher had been a slave, Douglass noted, he would have been "whipped . . . out of his willingness" to wait for the power of Christian faith to break his chains.[32]

Increasingly, enlightenment terminology crept into Douglass' writings and speeches. Negroes were adjudged to be "free by the laws of nature."[33]

The slaves' claim to freedom was "backed up by all the ties of nature, and nature's God."[34] Man's right to liberty was self-evident since "the voices of nature, of conscience, of reason, and of revelation, proclaim it as the right of all rights."[35]

An important factor acting to liberalize Douglass' theological views was his association with fellow abolitionist William Lloyd Garrison. The turbulent editor of *The Liberator* had been an orthodox Baptist who looked to the Church as God's appointed instrument for ending slavery. The Holy *Bible* was both a source of spiritual power and the arsenal from which he selected his anti-slavery weapons. Garrison broke violently with the clergy after they criticized his methodology.[36] In denouncing the churches as a hindrance to abolitionism and true Christianity, he undoubtedly influenced his young black protégé who believed the abolitionists to be the "most pure, enlightened and benevolent" people in the country.[37]

Douglass was also affected by the words of transcendentalist preacher Theodore Parker. The minister's ideas on the perfectibility of man and the sufficiency of natural religion were eventually incorporated in the abolitionist's epistemology. In 1854, Douglass noted, "I heard Theodore Parker last Sabbath. No man preaches more truth than this eloquent man, this astute philosopher."[38]

Another outstanding influence on his increasingly liberal conception of God was Robert Ingersoll, a militant agnostic who befriended him on a trip to Illinois. Appalled by the lack of compassion shown him by Midwest Christians. Douglass wrote, "to be an infidel no more proves a man to be selfish, mean, and wicked, than to be evangelical proves him to be honest, just, and humane."[39] This charge was to be repeated time and again in his writings.

By April 1870, and his speech at Horticultural Hall, Douglass held a much different concept of God than he had as a young man. As he explained the reasons for his break with the Garrisonians in March 1860, Douglass spoke of such a change:

> I have been very much modified both in feeling and opinion within the last fourteen years. Subsequent experience and reading have led me to examine [opinions] for myself. This has

brought me to other conclusions. When I was a child, I thought and spoke as a child.[40]

His faith in God's ability to destroy the slave system was weakened by the passage of the Fugitive Slave Act in 1850 and by the Dred Scott decision of 1857, both of which appeared to end all hope of speedy emancipation. With this abandonment of God, Douglass came to the conclusion that only man, aided by the laws of nature, could solve earthly problems. Furthered in this belief by the Civil War's seemingly godless brutality, he asserted that even if the Confederacy defeated the Union Army, "nature with the aid of free discussion would set herself right in the end. Great is truth, great is humanity, and they must prevail."[41]

Douglass took another large step toward a humanistic theology just one week before the Philadelphia address. On April 19, 1870, he spoke at the American Anti-Slavery Society convention in New York City. Noting that many others had thanked God for the success of the abolition movement, he thanked "those faithful men and women, who have devoted the great energies of their soul to the welfare of mankind," for the victory over slavery. It was only through such individuals that he could "get a glimpse of God anywhere."[42] This oration, along with the Philadelphia ratification speech mirrored the change that had been wrought in Douglass' thinking. Man had become the prime mover in his life.

Philadelphia's black Christian leadership raged at Douglass' seemingly blatant apostasy. A group of the city's leading ministers met at Bethel Colored Methodist Episcopal Church to formulate an appropriate answer to this doctrinal challenge, lest his observations gain widespread acceptance. Reverend James Williams sorrowfully rebuked the abolitionist, declaring, "We admire Frederick Douglass, but we love God more." He was confident that the errant one would change his views when shown the new creed's inherent falsity. Reverend Isaac C. Weir believed that Douglass had received so many ego-building honors and compliments that it was "not surprising that he has fallen."

The fifty-year-old ex-slave was also condemned for his stand in opposing the retention of Bible study in the public schools. Douglass believed that the use of the King James version was unfair to Roman Catholics and that church and state should be completely separated. In addition to registering his amazement at Douglass' support of a man-centered theology, Reverend J. Frisby Cooper asserted that barring the *Bible* from the schools would be the first step in its removal from the nation's churches and courts. Without God's word, the land would be subjected to an age of crime and lawlessness. Surely Douglass' quest for "notoriety" and "popularity" was a "fatal mistake" since it led him to support such a godless position.[43]

The final list of resolutions agreed upon by the ministers contained a damning condemnation of Douglass' views. In brusque language the clerics wrote, "We will not acknowledge any man as a leader of our people who will not thank God for the deliverance and enfranchisement of our race, and will not vote to retain the Bible, the book of God in our public schools."[44]

In a blistering open letter to the *Philadelphia Press,* Douglass answered the critics by reaffirming his position, denouncing religious intolerance and stating that he would not yield to ministerial pressure. He accused the black ministers of conducting a sham trial, rooted in religious malice that was reminiscent of the Middle Ages. If the ministers would work to reform the "character, manners, and habits" of the "festering thousands" of Philadelphia Negroes, they would do more to prove their churches sound than by "passing any number of worthy resolutions about thanking God."[45]

By June 1870, Douglass appeared to be resigned to his role of "infidel" and perfectly convinced that his man-centered beliefs were correct. He wrote,

I have no doubt that the avowal of my liberal opinions will drive many from me who were once my friends and even exclude me from many platforms upon which I was a welcome speaker, but such is the penalty which every man must suffer who admits a new truth into his mind. . . . I deem it wise to avow those [convictions] which are perfectly formed, clearly defined, and about which I am entirely undisturbed by doubts of any sorts.[46]

Near the end of his life, a final echo of reliance upon man's power was heard. In a convincing address on the "self-made man," Douglass criticized those who believed the laws of God to be perfect and unchangeable. In fact, he asserted that individuals who ascribed "success and failure, wealth and poverty, intelligence and ignorance, liberty and slavery" to a Supreme Being's actions were superstitious believers in a hoax akin to fortune-telling or divination.[47] Faith, in the absence of works, was "worth little."[48] Self-made men were "indebted to themselves for themselves. . . . If they have ascended high, they have built their own ladder."[49] There is little doubt that he considered himself to be in this category—a struggling, yet confident mortal who felt no need of super-natural assistance.

Since Douglass' biographers have neglected to analyze, and to a considerable extent, even to record such a change in his religious views, it is necessary to ascertain the reasons for his drift toward a liberal concept of God.

He certainly despised those "religious" slaveholders of his youth, but his continuing faith in God and his active church life in New Bedford contradict any assumption that the slavery experience was an exclusive liberalizing force.

The influence of Garrison, Parker, and Ingersoll was great, but none of these men remained in close and continual contact with Douglass in the post-Civil War years, the time of his greatest theological change.

The Dred Scott decision, the Fugitive Slave Act and the Civil War undoubtedly caused Douglass much heartache. They were influential in modifying his concept of a just Creator who was working convincingly and completely to destroy the ungodly. Nevertheless, other aspects of Douglass' experience must be analyzed before we can find a satisfactory explanation for his gradual abandonment of the traditional Godhead.

As he traveled abroad, the ex-chattel discovered that the poverty and destitution of slavery was in many respects a universal condition of the world's lowest classes. This observed contrast between the world's rich and poor deepened Douglass' belief in a religion that best served the interests of mankind to the exclusion of doctrinal complexity and rigidity in the puritanical sense.

After viewing Dublin's wretched masses in 1846, he asked, "Where is your religion that takes care for the poor. . . . Where are its votaries —what are they doing?" Douglass answered his own question by noting that believers were "wasting their energies in useless debate on hollow creeds and points of doctrine." Wrongs and sufferings "of any part of the great family of man" could not be allowed. "I am not only an American slave," he wrote, "but a man, and as such, am bound to use my powers for the welfare of the whole human brotherhood."[50]

On a visit to England he could not refrain from criticizing the clergy who had appealed to Liverpool authorities to break up the local soup kitchen. A footpath used by parishoners was continually crowded with multitudes of starving Irish, thus causing "inconvenience" to those on their way to worship.[51]

Douglass was also depressed by the backwardness of Dominicans and Haitians in the Caribbean. Haiti "was the first to be invaded by the Christian religion. . . . She was the first to see a Christian church and to behold the cross of Christ. She was also the first to witness the bitter agonies of the North bending under the blood-stained lash of Christian slave-holders."[52]

These thoughts, along with the continual recitation of slavery's evils that his abolitionist career demanded: combined with an ever-present feeling of anti-clericalism, were furthered by the Reconstruction era's generally broader view of religious orthodoxy. Together they changed Douglass' mind as to the power of God. In sum, Douglass became more liberal in his view of the Godhead because he was discouraged over the contradiction between Christian theory and practice.[53]

Constantly recounting the hypocrisy shown by the slaveholder who could "pray at morning, pray at noon, and pray at night" and still "lash up my poor cousin by his two thumbs and inflict stripes and blows upon his bare back, till the blood streamed to the ground! all the time quoting scripture, for his authority," Douglass convinced himself that "prejudice goes into the church of God." According to the pious white Christian, the kingdom of heaven was like a fisherman's net. When the net was drawn ashore, the Christians sat down to cull out the fish. Some of the fish had "rather black scales, so these were sorted out and packed by themselves."[54]

Even in New Bedford, Douglass encountered hypocrisy among God's servants. When he attempted to attend a revival meeting in a white church, he was met by a deacon who told him "in a pious tone, 'we don't allow niggers in here!' "[55] While in Scotland he directed his efforts toward exposing the conduct of the Free Church in holding fellowship with slaveholders and in "taking Slave money to build free churches."[56]

In the 1840's Douglass decided that slavery had "no champions so bold, brave and uncompromising" as the ministers of religion. The Church was "beyond all question, the chief refuge of slavery."[57]

By 1870, his belief in the contradiction between Christian theory and practice had developed into a rejection of the Supreme Being. The ministers had done nothing for the abolition of slavery but tell others that "God would abolish slavery in his own good time."[58] Too often, in the heat of anti-slavery battle he had been told to trust in God. Now that the struggle was ended, Douglass could not imagine an other-worldly force destroying slavery. He could only thank the men whom he had relied upon throughout the ante-bellum years, men who were not unmindful of the Negroes' plight.

In July 1886, Douglass summed up his post-war views of a Christianity whose central character was not now a viable part of his theology. "It is something to give the Negro religion," he wrote. "It is more to give him the ballot. It is something to tell him that there is a place for him in the Christian's heaven, it is more to let him have a place in this Christian country to live upon in peace."[59] Douglass' trip toward and through religious liberalism ended in the rejection of God's power and in the veneration of man and his reforms.

NOTES

1. *Philadelphia Press,* April 27, 1870: Herbert Aptheker, "An Unpublished Frederick Douglass Letter," *Journal of Negro History,* XLIV (July, 1959), pp. 278–280. See also Philip S. Foner, *Frederick Douglass* (New York, 1964), p. 269.

2. Frederick Douglass, *Life and Times of Frederick Douglass* (New York, 1962). p. 43.

3. *Ibid.,* p. 90. Charles Chesnutt wrote that Douglass had dreamed of liberty before becoming a Christian, but after his conversion he "prayed for it, and trusted in God." Booker Washington wrote that this new faith in God enlarged Douglass' mind, restrained his impatience, softened his disposition, and encouraged his hope for ultimate freedom. Charles Chesnutt, *Frederick Douglass* (Boston, 1899), p. 12; Booker T. Washington, *Frederick Douglass* (Philadelphia, 1906), p. 28.

4. Frederick Douglass, *My Bondage and My Freedom* (New York, 1855), p. 113.

5. Douglass, *Life and Times,* p. 109.

6. *Ibid.,* p. 111. Mrs. Rowena Auld nearly starved her slaves and yet, "with saintly air," she and her husband prayed daily that a merciful God would bless the chattels "in basket and store, and save them at last in His Kingdom." (p. 105).

7. Frederick Douglass, *Narrative of the Life of Frederick Douglass* (Cambridge, 1960), p. 110.

8. Benjamin Quarles, "Douglass' Mind in the Making," *Phylon,* VI, No. 1 (1945), p. 7: Samual J. May, *Some Recollections of Our Antislavery Conflict* (New York, 1869), p. 293. For a fascinating study of what Douglass was likely to hear on Sunday morning see William Pipes. Say *Amen. Brother! Old Time Negro Preaching: A Study in American Frustration* (New York, 1951).

9. Benjamin Mays, *The Negro's God as Reflected in His Literature* (New York, 1968), p. 126. For a more complete study of the black Methodists see Dwight Culver, *Negro Segregation in the Methodist Church* (New Haven, 1953), pp. 42–60: Joseph Hartzell, "Methodism and the Negro," *Journal of Negro History.* VIII (July, 1923), pp. 301–315: William Gravely, "Early Methodism and Slavery," *Wesleyan Quarterly Review,* 11 (May, 1965), pp. 84–100; Jeffrey Brackett, *The Negro in Maryland: A Study of the Institution of Slavery* (Baltimore: Johns Hopkins University Studies in Historical and Political Science, VI), pp. 205–206.

10. Speech at Pittsburgh, Pennsylvania, August 11, 1852, in Philip S. Foner, ed., *The Life and Writings of Frederick Douglas* (4 vols.: New York, 1950–1955), 11, p. 206.

11. Douglass, *Life and Times,* p. 89.

12. Douglass to Henry Clay, in *North Star,* Dec. 3, 1847.

13. *North Star,* Jan. 21, 1848.

14. Douglass, *My Bondage,* p. 191.

15. Douglass to Thomas Auld, in *Liberator,* Sept. 22, 1848.

16. *North Star,* Jan. 19, 1849.

17. *North Star,* June 13, 1850.

18. Speech at Moorfields, England, May 22, 1846, in *My Bondage,* Appendix, p. 408.

19. Douglass to Thomas Auld, in *Liberator,* Sept. 22, 1848.

20. Speech at Moorfields, England, May 22, 1846, in *My Bondage,* Appendix, p. 416.

21. Frederick Douglass, *Oration Delivered in Corinthian Hall* (Rochester, 1852), p. 29.

22. Speech at Pittsburgh, Pennsylvania. August 11, 1852, in Foner. *Life and Writings,* 11, p. 209.

23. Frederick Douglass, "The Folly of Our Opponents," in *The Liberty Bell* (Boston, 1845), p. 168, See also speech at New York City, Oct. 22, 1847, in *National Anti-Slavery Standard,* Oct. 28, 1847: *North Star,* Feb. 8, 1850.

24. Douglass to Henry Clay, in *North Star,* Dec. 3, 1847. Douglass cited God's promise by writing: "then shalt thou call and the Lord shall answer, thou shalt cry and he will say, Here I am."

25. Douglass to Samuel Hanson Cox, Oct. 30, 1846, in *Liberator,* Nov. 27, 1846.

26. Speech at New York City, May 11, 1847, in *National Anti-Slavery Standard,* May 20, 1847.

27. Douglass, *Oration,* p. 37.

28. Speech at New York City, Oct. 22, 1847, in *National Anti-Slavery Standard,* Oct. 28, 1847.

29. Douglass, *Oration,* p. 29.

30. Frederick Douglass, *Two Speeches* (Rochester, 1857), p. 45. See also speech at London, England, March 30, 1847, in Foner, *Life and Writings,* 1, p. 217: Benjamin Quarles, *Frederick Douglass* (Washington, D.C., 1948), p. 105.

31. *North Star,* July 14, 1848.

32. Benjamin Quarles, "Abolition's Different Drummer," in Martin Duberman, ed., *The Antislavery Vanguard* (Princeton, 1965), p. 127: *Annual Report of the American Anti-Slavery Society for 1853* (New York, 1853), pp. 51, 55.

33. Speech at Chicago, Nov., 1854, in Foner, *Life and Writings,* 11, p. 317.

34. *Douglass' Monthly,* Jan., 1859.

35. Douglass, *Two Speeches,* p. 32.

36. Goldwin Smith, *William Lloyd Garrison* (New York, 1892), p. 109; John Jay Chapman, *William Lloyd Garrison* (Boston, 1921), pp. 164–165; Oliver Johnson, *William Lloyd Garrison and His Times* (Boston, 1880), p. 67.

37. Douglass to Thomas Auld, in *Liberator,* Sept. 22, 1848. See also

Quarles, "Douglass' Mind," p. 5. Quarles noted that the ten-year association with the Garrisonian reformers "obviously entered into the fabric of his thinking."

38. J. R. Balme, *American States, Churches, and Slavery* (Edinburg, 1862), p. 221. See also Washington, *Frederick Douglass,* p. 321; *Douglass' Monthly,* July, 1860.

39. Douglass, *Life and Times,* p. 462; Quarles, *Frederick Douglass,* pp. 293 294.

40. Speech at Glasgow, Scotland, March 26, 1860, in Foner, *Life and Writings,* II, p. 480.

41. Speech at New York City, Feb., 1863, in *Douglass' Monthly,* March, 1863.

42. Aptheker, "Letter," p. 279.

43. Foner, *Frederick Douglass,* pp. 270–271; *Philadelphia Press,* May 19, 1870.

44. Aptheker, "Letter," pp. 280–281; *Philadelphia Press,* May 19, 1870.

45. *Philadelphia Press,* May 30, 1870; Foner, *Frederick Douglass,* p. 272.

46. Aptheker, "Letter," p. 278.

47. Speech on self-made men, n.d., Douglass Papers, Library of Congress. See also Frederic May Holland, *Frederick Douglass: The Colored Orator* (New York, 1969. Reprint of 1895 edition), p. 250; Foner, *Frederick Douglass,* p. 405.

48. Speech on self-made men, n.d., Douglass Papers; Holland, *Colored Orator,* p. 252.

49. Holland, *Colored Orator,* p. 251; Speech on self-made men, n.d., Douglass Papers.

50. Douglass to William Lloyd Garrison, in *Liberator,* March 27, 1846.

51. Balme, *American States,* p. 218.

52. Speech at Chicago, January 2, 1893, in Foner, *Life and Writings,* IV, p. 478.

53. For a more complete discussion of post-Civil War religious thought see Aaron I. Abbell, *The Urban Impact on American Protestantism, 1865–1900* (Cambridge, 1943); Frank H. Foster, *The Modern Movement in American Theology* (New York, 1939); Charles H. Hopkins, *The Rise of the Social Gospel in American Protestantism, 1865–1915* (New Haven, 1940).

54. Speech at Plymouth County Anti-Slavery Society, Dec., 1841, in *National Anti-Slavery Standard,* Dec. 23, 1841.

55. Douglass to William Lloyd Garrison, in *Liberator,* Jan. 30, 1846.

56. Douglass to Maria Chapman, March 29, 1846, in Foner, *Life and Writings,* I, p. 144.

57. Speech at London, March 30, 1847, in Foner, *Life and Writings,* I, p. 214. For Douglass' exceptions to this blanket condemnation see Douglass, *Oration,* p. 31.

58. Aptheker, "Letter," p. 280.

59. Douglass to W. H. Thomas, July 16, 1886, in Foner, *Life and Writings,* IV, p. 444.

C

Observations

6

NEGRO FOLK EXPRESSION

Spirituals, Seculars, Ballads, and Work Songs

Sterling Brown

❑

The thought of enslaved Africans in North America is first expressed through the creation of music. As some scholars have noted, the development of this musical tradition, beginning with spirituals and "secular" songs, is sparked by the emergence of the first Africans from slave ships.

Within these songs enslaved Africans wrestled with existential questions forced by the absurdity of slavery. Through this music, they sought to make sense of the world and provide a framework for life. Within the spirituals, the manner in which traditional religious doctrine dominated this rationale for life is apparent. However, as this article by Sterling Brown indicates, there were other forms of musical expression that did not embrace the basic doctrine of the Christian church, or other traditional forms of religious expression. In the words of Brown: "The slaves had many other moods and concerns than the religious; indeed some of these ran counter to the spiritual." Instead, these songs gave primary attention to humanity as the "measure of all things." On one level, these songs critique the doctrine of Christian churches and, on another level, these songs assert the importance of human activity both as a source of oppression and liberation—without reference to divine assistance. Through these songs, some African Americans embraced a form of thought running contrary to dominant expressions as housed in the religious music known as spirituals. In this way, the seculars—work songs, blues, and the like— provide additional clarity to the presence of humanistic leanings within early African American communities.

For more information on musical expression within African American communities in the pre-twentieth-century United States, see, for example, John Lovell, Jr., Black Song: The Forge and the Flame; The Story of How the Afro-American Spiritual Was Hammered Out *(New York: Macmillan, 1972); Dena J. Epstein,* Sinful Tunes and Spirituals: Black Folk Music to the Civil War *(Urbana: University of Illinois Press, 1977); Paul Oliver,* Blues Fell This Morning: The Meaning of the Blues *(New York: Cambridge University Press, 1979; 2d rev. ed. 1990). Lawrence W. Levine,* Black Culture and Black Consciousness: Afro-American Folk Thought from Slavery to Freedom *(New York: Oxford University Press, 1977), gives particular attention to the "non-religious" form of expression found in "secular" songs. This type of information is also found in Benjamin E. May,* The Negro's God as Reflected in His Literature *(New York: Negro Universities Press, 1969). Anthony Pinn's* Why, Lord? Suffering and Evil in Black Theology *(New York: Continuum, 1995) also provides information on the humanist leaning of certain types of African American music.*

❏

Seculars and Ballads

The slaves had many other moods and concerns than the religious; indeed some of these ran counter to the spirituals. Irreverent parodies of religious songs, whether coming from the black-face minstrelsy or from tough-minded cynical slaves, passed current in the quarters. Other-worldliness was mocked: "I don't want to ride no golden chariot; I don't want no golden crown; I want to stay down here and be, Just as I am without one plea." "Live a humble to the Lord" was changed to "Live a humbug." Bible stories, especially the creation, the fall of Man, and the flood, were spoofed. "Reign, Master Jesus, reign" became "Rain, Mosser, rain hard! Rain flour and lard and a big hog head, Down in my back yard." After couplets of nonsense and ribaldry, slaves sang with their fingers crossed, or hopeless in defeat: "Po' mourner, you shall be free, when de good Lord set you free."

Even without the sacrilege, many secular songs were considered "devil-tunes." Especially so were the briskly syncopated lines which, with the clapping of hands and the patting of feet, set the beat for swift, gay dancing. "Juba dis, Juba dat; Juba skin a yeller cat; Juba, Juba!" Remnants of this syncopation are today in such children's play songs as

> "Did you feed my cow?" "Yes, Maam."
> "Will you tell-a me how?" "Yes, Maam."
> "Oh, what did you give her?" "Cawn and hay."
> "Oh, what did you give her?" "Cawn and hay."

Verses for reels made use of the favorite animals of the fables. "Brer Rabbit, Brer Rabbit, yo' ears mighty long; Yes, My Lord, they're put on wrong; Every little soul gonna shine; every little soul gonna shine!" Often power and pomp in the guise of the bullfrog and bulldog have the tables turned on them by the sassy blue-jay and crow:

> A bullfrog dressed in soldier's clothes
> Went in de field to shoot some crows,
> De crows smell powder and fly away,
> De bullfrog mighty mad dat day.

Even the easy-going ox or sheep or hog acquired characteristics:

De ole sow say to de boar
I'll tell you what let's do,
Let's go and git dat broad-axe
And die in de pig-pen too.
Die in de pig-pen fighting,
Die wid a bitin' jaw!

Unlike Stephen Foster's sweet and sad[1] songs such as "Massa's in the Cold, Cold Ground," the folk seculars looked at slavery ironically. And where Foster saw comic nonsense, they added satiric point. Short comments flash us back to social reality: "Ole Master bought a yaller gal, He bought her from the South"; "My name's Ran, I wuks in de sand, I'd rather be a nigger dan a po' white man." Frederick Douglass remembers his fellow slaves singing "We raise de wheat, dey gib us de corn; We sift de meal, de gib us de huss; We peel de meat, dey gib us de skin; An dat's de way dey take us in."[2] Grousing about food is common: "Milk in the dairy getting mighty old, Skippers and the mice working mighty bold. . . . A long-tailed rat an' a bowl of souse, Jes' come down from de white folk's house." With robust humor, they laughed even at the dread patrollers:

Run, nigger, run, de patrollers will ketch you
Run, nigger, run; its almost day.
Dat nigger run, dat nigger flew;
Dat nigger tore his shirt in two.

The bitterest secular begins

My ole Mistis promise me
Fo' she died, she'd set me free;
She lived so long dat her head got bald,
And she give out de notion dyin' at all.

Ole marster also failed his promise. Then, with the sharp surprise of the best balladry: "A dose of poison helped him along, May de devil preach his funeral song!"

Under a certain kind of protection the new freedmen took to heart the songs of such an abolitionist as Henry C. Work, and sang exultantly of jubilo. They sang his lines lampooning ole master, and turned out their own:

> *Missus and mosser a-walkin' de street,*
> *Deir hands in deir pockets and nothin' to eat.*
> *She'd better be home a-washin' up de dishes,*
> *An' a-cleanin' up de ole man's raggitty britches.*[3]

But when the protection ran out, the freedmen found the following parody too true:

> *Our father, who is in heaven,*
> *White man owe me eleven and pay me seven,*
> *Thy kingdom come, they will be done,*
> *And if I hadn't took that, I wouldn't had none.*

Toward the end of the century, there was interplay between the folk-seculars and the vaudeville stage, and the accepted stereotypes appeared. "Ain't no use my working so hard, I got a gal in the white folks yard." From tent shows and roving guitar players, the folks accepted such hits as the "Bully Song" and the "coon-songs." "Bill Bailey, Won't You Please Come Home," and "Alabama Bound" shuttled back and forth between the folk and vaudeville. In the honky-tonks ribald songs grew up to become standbys of the early jazz: "Make Me a Pallet on The Floor," "Bucket Got A Hole In It," "Don't you leave me here; if you must go, baby, leave me a dime for beer." "Jelly Roll" Morton's autobiography, now released from the Library of Congress Archives, proves this close connection between the rising jazz and the old folk seculars. In the honky-tonks, songs handled sex freely, even licentiously; and obscenity and vituperation ran rampant in songs called the "dirty dozens."

One of the heroes of secular balladry is Uncle Bud, who was noted for his sexual prowess, a combination Don Juan and John Henry. His song is perhaps as uncollected as it is unprintable. Appreciative tales are told of railroading, of crack trains like The Cannon Ball and The Dixie Flyer, and The Rock Island Line, which is praised in rattling good verses. Such folk delights as hunting with the yipping and baying of the hounds and the yells and cheering of the hunters are vividly recreated. "Old Dog Blue" has been memorialized over all of his lop-eared kindred. The greatest trailer on earth, Old Blue keeps his unerring sense in heaven; there he treed a possum in Noah's ark. When Old Dog Blue died,

> *I dug his grave wid a silver spade*
> *I let him down wid a golden chain*
> *And every link I called his name;*
> *Go on Blue, you good dog, you!*

The above lines illustrate a feature of Negro folksong worth remarking. Coming from an old sea-chantey "Stormalong," their presence in a song about a hunting dog shows the folk habit of lifting what they want and using it how they will. Like southern white groups, the Negro has retained many of the old Scotch-English ballads. Still to be found are Negroes singing "In London town where I was born" and going on to tell of hard-hearted Barbara Allen. John Lomax found a Negro mixing up "Bobby Allen" with the cowboy song "The Streets of Laredo," burying "Miss Allen in a desert of New Mexico with six pretty maidens all dressed in white for her pallbearers."[4] But Negroes hand down fairly straight versions of "Lord Lovel," "Pretty Polly," and "The Hangman's Tree," which has special point for them with its repetend: "Hangman, hangman, slack on the line." The Elizabethan broadside "The Frog Went A-Courtin'" has long been a favorite Negro lullaby. From "The Lass of Roch Royal" two stanzas beginning "Who's gonna shoe yo' little feet" have found their way into the ballad of John Henry. The famous Irish racehorse Stewball reappears in Negro balladry as Skewball and Kimball. English nonsense refrains appear in songs like "Keemo-Kimo" and "Old Bangum." Even the Gaelic "Schule Aroon" has been found among Negroes, though the collector unwarily surmises it to be Guinea or Ebo. Similarly the Negro folk singer lends to and borrows from American balladry. "Casey Jones," though about an engineer, is part of the repertory; it has been established that a Negro engine-wiper was the first author of it. "Frankie and Johnnie," the most widely known tragedy in America, is attributed to both white and Negro authorship. It could come from either; it probably comes from both; the tenderloin cuts across both sections. Current singers continue the trading of songs: Leadbelly sings cowboy songs, yelling "Ki-yi-yippy-yippy-yay" with his own zest; and Josh White sings "Molly Malone" and "Randall, My Son" with telling power. But it is in narratives of their own heroes that Negro ballad makers have done best.

Prominent among such heroes are fugitives who outtrick and outspeed the law. "Travelin' Man" is more of a coon-song than authentically folk, but the hero whom the cops chased from six in the morning till seven the next afternoon has been warmly adopted by the people. Aboard the Titanic he spied the iceberg and dove off, and "When the old Titanic ship went down, he was shooting crap in Liverpool." More genuine is "Long Gone, Lost John" in which the hero outmatches the sheriff, the police, and the bloodhounds: "The hounds ain't caught me and they never will." Fast enough to hop the Dixie Flyer—"he missed the cowcatcher but he caught the blind"—Lost John can even dally briefly with a girl friend, like Brer Rabbit waiting for Brer Tortoise. But when he travels, he goes far: "the funniest thing I ever seen, was Lost John comin' through Bowlin' Green," but "the last time I seed him he was jumping into Mexico."

When Lost John "doubled up his fist and knocked the police down" his deed wins approval from the audience as much as his winged heels do. With bitter memories and suspicion of the law, many Negroes admire outlaws. Some are just tough killers; one is "a bad, bad man from bad, bad land"; another is going to start "a graveyard all of his own"; another, Roscoe Bill, who sleeps with one ear out because of the rounders about, reports to the judge blandly that

I didn't quite kill him, but I fixed him so dis mornin'
He won't bodder wid me no mo'
Dis mornin', dis evenin', so soon.

But the favorites, like such western desperadoes as Jesse James, Billy the Kid, and Sam Bass, stand up against the law. Railroad Bill (an actual outlaw of southern Alabama) "shot all the buttons off the sheriff's coat." On the manhunt, "the policemen dressed in blue, come down the street two by two." It took a posse to bring him in dead. Po' Lazarus also told the deputy to his face that he had never been arrested "by no one man, Lawd, Lawd, by no one man." Unlike his Biblical namesake in nature, Po' Lazarus broke into the commissary. The high sheriff sent the deputy to bring him back, dead or alive. They found him "way out between two mountains" and they "blowed him down."

They shot Po' Lazarus, shot him with a great big number
Number 45, Lawd, Lawd, number 45.

They laid Po' Lazarus on the commissary counter, and walked away. His mother, always worrying over the trouble she had with Lazarus, sees the body and cries.

Dat's my only son, Lawd, Lawd, dat's my only son.

In contrast "Stackolee" ends on a hard note. At Stack's murder trial, his lawyer pleads for mercy because his aged mother is lying very low. The prosecutor states that.

Stackolee's aged mammy
Has been dead these 'leven years.

Starting from a murder in Memphis in a dice game (some say over a Stetson hat), Stackolee's saga has traveled from the Ohio River to the Brazos; in a Texas version, Stack goes to hell, challenges the devil to a duel—pitchfork versus forty-one revolver—and then takes over the lower world.

One of America's greatest ballads tells of John Henry. Based on the strength and courage of an actual hammer-swinging giant, though in spite of what folk-singers say, his hammer cannot be seen decorating the Big Bend Tunnel on the C. & O. Road, John Henry reflects the struggle of manual labor against the displacing machine. The ballad starts with ill omens. Even as a boy John Henry prophesies his death at the Big Bend Tunnel. But he stays to face it out. Pitting his brawn and stamina against the new-fangled steam drill, John Henry says to his captain:

> *A man ain't nothing but a man.*
> *But before I'll let that steam driver beat me down*
> *I'll die with my hammer in my hand.*

The heat of the contest makes him call for water (in one variant for tom-cat gin). When John Henry is momentarily overcome, his woman, Polly Ann, spelled him, hammering "like a natural man." At one crucial point, John Henry gave "a loud and lonesome cry," saying, "A hammer'll be the death of me." But the general tone is self-confidence. John Henry throws the hammer from his hips on down, "Great gawd amighty how she rings!" He warns his shaker (the holder of the drill) that if ever he misses that piece of steel, "tomorrow'll be yo' burial day." His captain, hearing the mighty rumbling, thinks the mountain must be caving in. John Henry says to the captain: "It's my hammer swinging in the wind." Finally, he defeats the drill, but the strain kills him. The people gather round, but all he asks is "a cool drink of water 'fo I die." Polly Ann swears to be true to the memory (although in another version she turns out to be as fickle as Mrs. Casey Jones). John Henry was buried near the railroad where

Every locomotive come a-roarin' by
Says, "There lies a steel-drivin' man, Lawd, Lawd;
There lies a steel-drivin' man."

The topical nature of American balladry is seen in "Boll Weevil," a ballad that grew up almost as soon as the swarm of pests descended. "Come up from Mexico, they say."

The first time I seed the boll weevil
He was sitting on the square—

(The folk poet puns on the "square" of cotton boll, and the familiar southern town square.) A tough little rascal is celebrated who, when buried in the hot sand, says "I can stand it like a man"; when put into ice, says: "This is mighty cool and nice," and thrives and breeds right on, until finally he can take over:

You better leave me alone
I done et up all your cotton,
And now I'll start on your corn.

The ballad has grim side glances; the boll weevil didn't leave "the farmer's wife but one old cotton dress"; made his nest in the farmer's "best Sunday hat"; and closed the church doors since the farmer couldn't pay the preacher.

Oh, de Farmer say to de Merchant
I ain't made but only one bale
An' befo' I bring you dat one
I'll fight an' go to jail
I'll have a home
I'll have a home.

The stanzaic forms and general structure of "John Henry" and "The Boll Weevil" are fairly developed. One of the best folk ballads, however, is in the simpler, unrhymed African leader-chorus design. This is

"The Grey Goose," a ballad about a seemingly ordinary fowl who becomes a symbol of ability to take it. It is a song done with the highest spirits; the "Lord, Lord, Lord" of the responding chorus expressing amazement, flattery, and good-humored respect for the tough bird:

> *Well, last Monday mornin'*
> *Lord, Lord, Lord!*
> *Well, last Monday mornin'*
> *Lord, Lord, Lord!*

They went hunting for the grey goose. When shot "Boo-loom!" the grey goose was six weeks a-falling. Then it was six weeks a-finding, and once in the white house, was six weeks a-picking. Even after the great feather-picking he was six months parboiling. And then on the table, the forks couldn't stick him; the knife couldn't cut him. So they threw him in the hog-pen where he broke the sow's jawbone. Even in the sawmill, he broke the saw's teeth out. He was indestructible. Last seen the grey goose was flying across the ocean, with a long string of goslings, all going "Quank-quink-quank." Yessir, it was one hell of a grey goose. Lord, Lord, Lord!

Work Songs and Social Protest

More work songs come from the Negro than from any other American folk group. Rowing the cypress dug-outs in Carolina low-country, slaves timed their singing to the long sweep of the oars. The leader, a sort of coxswain, chanted verse after verse; the rowers rumbled a refrain. On the docks Negroes sang sailors' chanteys as metronomes to their heaving and hauling. Some chanteys, like "Old Stormy," they took over from the white seamen; others they improvised. Along the Ohio and Mississippi waterfronts Negro roustabouts created "coon-jine" songs, so-called after the shuffling dance over bucking gangplanks in and out of steamboat holds. Unless the rhythm was just right a roustabout and his bale or sack of cottonseed might be jolted into the brown waters. The singers cheered the speed of the highballing paddlewheelers: "left Baton Rouge at half pas' one, and got to Vicksburg at settin of de sun." But they griped over the tough captains "workin' hell out of me" and sang

> Ole Roustabout ain't got no home
> Makes his livin' on his shoulder bone.

For release from the timber and the heavy sacks there was always some city around the bend—Paducah, Cairo, Memphis, Natchez, and then

> Alberta let yo' hair hang low . . .
> I'll give you mo' gold
> Than yo' apron can hold . . .
> Alberta let yo' hair hang low.

These songs flourished in the hey-day of the packets; today they are nearly lost.

Another type of work song was chanted as a gang unloaded steel rails. Since these rails weighed over a ton apiece and were over ten yards long, any break in the rhythm of lifting them from the flat cars to the ground was a good way to get ruptured, maimed, or killed. So a chanter was employed to time the hoisting, lowering, and the getting away from it. He was a coach, directing the teamwork, and in self-protection the men had to learn his rhythmic tricks. In track-lining, a similar chanter functioned to keep the track straight in line. As he called, the men jammed their bars under the rails and braced in unison:

> Shove it over! Hey, hey, can't you line it!
> Ah shack-a-lack-a-lack-a-lack-a-lack-a-lack-alack. (Grunt)
> Can't you move it? Hey, hey, can't you try.[5]

As they caught their breath and got a new purchase, he turned off a couplet. Then came the shouted refrain as the men strained together.

More widely spread and known are the Negro work songs whose rhythm is timed with the swing back and down and the blow of broadaxe, pick, hammer, or tamper. The short lines are punctuated by a grunt as the axe bites into the wood, or the hammer finds the spike-head.

> *Dis ole hammer—hunh*
> *Ring like silver—hunh (3)*
> *Shine like gold, baby—hunh*
> *Shine like gold—hunh.*

The leader rings countless changes in his words and melody over the unchanging rhythm. When he grows dull or forgets, another singer takes over. The song is consecutive, fluid; it is doubtful if any one version is ever exactly repeated. Ballads, blues, even church-songs are levied on for lines, a simple matter since the stanzas are unrhymed. Some lines tell of the satisfaction of doing a man's work well:

> *I got a rainbow—hunh*
> *Tied 'round my shoulder—hunh—(3)*
> *Tain't gonna rain, baby—hunh*
> *Tain't gonna rain.*

(The rainbow is the arc of the hammer as the sunlight glints on the moving metal.) Sometimes a singer boasts of being a "sun-down man," who can work the sun down without breaking down himself. Lines quite as popular, however, oppose any speed-up stretch-out system:

> *Dis ole hammer—hunh*
> *Killt John Henry—hunh—(3)*
> *Twon't kill me, baby—hunh*
> *Twon't kill me.*

Some lines get close to the blues: "Every mail day / Gits a letter / Son, come home, baby / Son, come home." Sometimes they tell of a hard captain (boss):

Told my captain—hunh
Hands are cold—hunh—(3)
Damn yo' hands—hunh
Let de wheelin' roll.

The new-fangled machine killed John Henry; its numerous off-spring have killed the work songs of his buddies. No hammer song could compete now with the staccato roaring drill even if the will to sing were there. The steamboat is coming back to the Mississippi but the winches and cranes do not call forth the old gang choruses. A few songs connected with work survive such as the hollers of the lonely worker in the fields and woods, or the call boy's chant to the glory-hole.

Sleeping good, sleeping good,
Give me them covers, I wish you would.

At ease from their work in their bunkhouses, the men may sing, but their fancies ramble from the job oftener than they stay with it. Song as a rhythmic accompaniment to work is declining. John and Alan Lomax, whose bag of Negro work songs is the fullest, had to go to the penitentiaries, where laborsaving devices were not yet numerous, in order to find the art thriving. They found lively cotton-picking songs:

A-pick a bale, a-pick a bale
Pick a bale of cotton
A-pick a bale, a-pick a bale
Pick a bale a day.[6]

Slower songs came from gangs that were cutting cane or chopping weeds or hewing timber. Prison work is of course mean and tough:

"You oughta come on de Brazo in nineteen-fo'; you could find a dead man on every turn-row." So the convicts cry out to the taskmaster sun:

> Go down, Ol' Hannah, doncha rise no mo'
> Ef you rise any mo' bring judgment day.

They grouse about the food: ever "the same damn thing," and at that the cook isn't clean. An old evangelical stand-by, "Let the Light of the Lighthouse Shine On Me," becomes a hymn of hope that the Midnight Special, a fast train, will some day bring a pardon from the governor. They sing of their long sentences:

> Ninety nine years so jumpin' long
> To be here rollin' an' cain' go home.

If women aren't to be blamed for it all, they are still to be blamed for a great deal:

> Ain't but de one thing worries my min'
> My cheating woman and my great long time.

One song, like the best balladry, throws a searchlight into the darkness:

> "Little boy, what'd you do for to get so long?"
> Said, "I killed my rider in the high sheriff's arms."

From these men—long termers, lifers, three-time losers—come songs brewed in bitterness. This is not the double-talk of the slave seculars, but the naked truth of desperate men telling what is on their brooding minds. Only to collectors who have won their trust—such as the Lomaxes, Lawrence Gellert and Josh White—and only when the white captain is far enough away, do the prisoners confide these songs. Then they sing not loudly but deeply their hatred of the brutality of the chain-gang:

If I'd a had my weight in lime
I'd a whupped dat captain, till he went stone blind.
If you don't believe my buddy's dead
Just look at that hole in my buddy's head.[7]

A prisoner is told: "Don't you go worryin' about forty [the years of your sentence]. Cause in five years you'll be dead."

They glorify the man who makes a crazy dare for freedom; Jimbo for instance, who escapes almost under the nose of his captain, described as "a big Goliath," who walks like Samson and "totes his talker." They boast: "Ef ah git de drop / Ah'm goin' on / Dat same good way / Dat Jimbo's gone / Lawd Lawd, Lawd."[8] They reenact with graphic realism the lashing of a fellow-prisoner; the man-hunting of Ol' Rattler, "fastest and smellingest bloodhound in the South"; and the power of Black Betty, the ugly bull-whip. They make stark drama out of the pain, and hopelessness, and shame.

All I wants is dese cold iron shackles off my leg.

It is not only in the prison songs that there is social protest. Where there is some protection or guaranteed secrecy other *verboten* songs come to light. Coal miners, fortified by a strong, truculent union, sing grimly of the exorbitant company stores:

What's de use of me working any more, my baby? (2)
What's de use of me working any more,
When I have to take it up at de company store,
My baby?[9]

Or they use the blues idiom with a new twist:

Operator will forsake you, he'll drive you from his do' . . .
No matter what you do, dis union gwine to stand by you
While de union growing strong in dis land.[10]

And the sharecroppers sharply phrase their plight:

> *Go in the store and the merchant would say,*
> *'Your mortgage is due and I'm looking for my pay.'*
> *Down in his pocket with a tremblin' hand*
> *'Can't pay you all but I'll pay what I can,'*
> *Then to the telephone the merchant made a call,*
> *They'll put you on the chain-gang, an' you don't pay at all.*[11]

Big Bill Broonzy is best known as a blues singer, but in the cotton belt of Arkansas he learned a great deal that sank deep. His sharp "Black, Brown, and White Blues" has the new militancy built up on the sills of the old folksong. In an employment office, Big Bill sings. "They called everybody's number / But they never did call mine." Then working side by side with a white man:

> *He was getting a dollar an hour*
> *When I was making fifty cents.*

Onto this new protest he ties an old vaudeville chorus, deepening the irony:

> *If you's black, ah brother,*
> *Git back, git back, git back.*[12]

Such songs, together with the blues composed by Waring Cuney and Josh White on poverty, hardship, poor housing and jim crow military service, come from conscious propagandists, not truly folk. They make use of the folk idiom in both text and music, however, and the folk listen and applaud. They know very well what Josh White is talking about in such lines as:

> *Great gawdamighty, folks feelin' bad*
> *Lost everything they ever had.*

Prospect

It is evident that Negro folk culture is breaking up. Where Negro met only with Negro in the black belt the old beliefs strengthened. But when mud traps give way to gravel roads, and black tops and even concrete highways with buses and jalopies and trucks lumbering over them, the world comes closer. The churches and schools, such as they are, struggle against some of the results of isolation, and the radio plays a part. Even in the backwoods, aerials are mounted on shanties that seem ready to collapse from the extra weight on the roof, or from a good burst of static against the walls. The phonograph is common, the television set is by no means unknown, and down at the four corners store, a jukebox gives out the latest jive. Rural folk closer to towns and cities may on Saturday jaunts even see an occasional movie, where a rootin'-tootin' Western gangster film introduces them to the advancements of civilization. Newspapers, especially the Negro press, give the people a sense of belonging to a larger world. Letters from their boys in the army, located in all corners of the world, and the tales of the returning veterans, true Marco Polos, also prod the inert into curiosity. Brer Rabbit and Old Jack no longer are enough. Increasingly in the churches the spirituals lose favor to singing out of the books or from broadsides, and city-born blues and jive take over the jook-joints.

The migration of the folk Negro to the cities, started by the hope for better living and schooling, and greater self-respect, quickened by the industrial demands of two world wars is sure to be increased by the new cotton picker and other man-displacing machines. In the city the folk become a submerged proletariat. Leisurely yarn-spinning, slow-paced aphoristic conversation become lost arts; jazzed-up gospel hymns provide a different sort of release from the old spirituals; the blues reflect the distortions of the new way of life. Folk arts are no longer by the folk for the folk; smart businessmen now put them up for sale. Gospel songs often become show-pieces for radio slummers, and the blues become the double-talk of the dives. And yet, in spite of the commercializing, the folk roots often show a stubborn vitality. Just as the transplanted folk may show the old credulity, though the sophisticated impulse sends them to an American Indian for nostrums, or for fortune-telling to an East Indian "madame" with a turban around her head rather than to a mammy with a bandanna around hers; so the folk for all their disorganization may keep something of the fine quality of their old tales and songs. Assuredly even in the new gospel songs and blues much is retained of the phrasing and the distinctive musical manner. Finally, it should be pointed out that even in the transplanting, a certain kind of isolation—class and racial—remains. What may come of it, if anything, is unpredictable, but so far the vigor of the creative impulse has not been sapped, even in the slums.

Whatever may be the future of the folk Negro, American literature as well as American music is the richer because of his expression. Just as Huckleberry Finn and Tom Sawyer were fascinated by the immense lore of their friend Jim, American authors have been drawn to Negro folk life and character. With varying authenticity and understanding, Joel Chandler Harris, Du Bose Heyward, Julia Peterkin, Roark Bradford, Marc Connelly, E. C. L. Adams, Zora Neale Hurston and Langston Hughes have all made rewarding use of this material. Folk Negroes have themselves bequeathed a wealth of moving song, both religious and secular, of pithy folk-say and entertaining and wise folktales. They have settled characters in the gallery of American heroes; resourceful Brer Rabbit and Old Jack and indomitable John Henry. They have told their own story so well that all men should be able to hear it and understand.

NOTES

1. Thomas Talley, *Negro Folk Rhymes* (New York, 1922), p. 39.
2. Frederick Douglass, *Life and Times* (Hartford, Conn., 1882), p. 39
3. Talley, *op. cit.,* p. 97

4. John Lomax, *Adventure of A Ballad Hunter* (New York, 1947), p. 179.

5. Zora Neale Hurston, *Mules and Men* (Philadelphia, 1935), p. 322.

6. The Library of Congress, Music Division. Archive of American Folk Song for this and the following quotations.

7. Josh White, *Chain Gang Songs* (Bridgeport, Conn., Columbia Recording Corporation), Set C-22.

8. Willis James, "Hyah Come De Cap'n," from Brown, Davis, and Lee, *The Negro Caravan* (New York, 1948), p. 469.

9. John and Alan Lomax, *Our Singing Country* (New York, 1941), pp. 278–288.

10. Ibid.

11. Ibid.

12. *People's Songs,* Vol. 1, No. 10 (November, 1940), 9.

7

DANIEL PAYNE'S PROTESTATION
OF SLAVERY

Daniel Payne

❑

Some African Americans could not reconcile notions of a good, loving, kind, compassionate God—who breaks into human history—with the disproportionate and sustained oppression they encountered. For some who experienced this dilemma, a rejection of God proved the logical conclusion. Daniel A. Payne (1811–1893), one of the central figures in the growth of the African Methodist Episcopal Church, encountered slaves who held this perspective. Prior to joining the first independent Black denomination (the African Methodist Episcopal Church), Payne belonged to the Lutheran Church. While a Lutheran, Payne wrote an attack on the institution of slavery on religious grounds, arguing that it resulted in many African Americans' rejection of the existence of God. Although Payne does not describe in detail the "belief" structure of these areligious slaves, this article does provide further evidence for the existence of humanist perspectives within a portion of the slave population.

For additional information on African Americans during this period, see the sources listed for the first article in this section. For additional information on Daniel Payne and the African Methodist Episcopal Church, see, for example: Bishop Daniel Alexander Payne, Recollections of Seventy Years *(New York: Arno Press and The New New York Times, 1968); William E. Montgomery,* Under Their Own Vine and Fig Tree: The African-American Church in the South, 1865–1900 *(Baton Rouge: Louisiana State University Press, 1993); James T. Campbell,* Songs of Zion: The African Methodist Episcopal Church in the United States and South Africa *(New York: Oxford University Press, 1995); and Clarence E. Walker,* A Rock in a Weary Land: The African Methodist Episcopal Church During the Civil War and Reconstruction *(Baton Rouge: Louisiana State University Press, 1982).*

❏

For the Lutheran Herald.

Speech of Brother Daniel A. Payne, delivered at the last session of the Franckean Synod, June, 1839, in favor of the adoption of the Report on Slavery. Written out by himself.

Mr. President—I move the adoption of the Report, because it is based upon the following propositions:

American Slavery brutalizes man—destroys his moral agency, and subverts the moral government of God.

Sir—I am opposed to slavery, not because it enslaves the black man, but because it enslaves *man.* And were all the slave-holders in this land men of color, and the slaves white men, I would be as thorough and uncompromising an abolitionist as I now am; for wherever and whenever I may see a being in the form of a man, enslaved by his fellow man, without respect to his complexion, I shall lift up my voice to plead his cause, against all the claims of his proud oppressor; and I shall do it not merely from the sympathy which man feels towards suffering man, but because *God, the living God,* whom I dare not disobey, has commanded me to open my mouth for the dumb, and to plead the cause of the oppressed.

Slavery brutalizes man.—We know that the word man, in its primitive sense, signifies————. But the intellectual and moral structure of man, and the august relations which he sustains to the Deity, have thrown around the name, and the being designated by it a halo of glory, brightened by all the ideas, that are ennobling on earth, and blessed in eternity. This being God created but a little lower than the angels, and crowned him with glory and honor; but slavery hurls him down from his elevated position, to the level of brutes! strikes this crown of glory from his head, and fastens upon his neck the galling yoke! and compels him to labor like an ox, through summer's sun and winter's snow, without remuneration. Does a man take the calf from the cow and sell it to the butcher? So slavery tears the child from the arms of the reluctant mother, and barters it to the soul-trader for a young colt, or some other commodity! Does the bird-catcher tear away the dove from his mate? So slavery separates the groaning husband from the embraces of his distracted and weeping wife! And are the beasts of the forest hunted, tortured and slain at the pleasure of the cruel hunter? So are the slaves hunted, tortured and slain by the cruel monster slavery! To treat a man like a brute is to brutalize him. We have seen that slavery treats man like a brute, therefore slavery brutalizes man! But does slavery stop here? Is it content with merely treating the external man like a brute? No, sir, it goes further, and with a heart as brazen as that of Belshazzar, and hands still more sacrilegious, it lays hold of the *immortal mind, seizes the will, and binds that which Jehovah did not bind—fetters that which the Eternal made as free to move and act as the breath of Heaven! It destroys moral agency!* To destroy moral agency is to fetter or obstruct the will of man. Now let us see if slavery is innocent of this. The very moment that a man conceives the diabolic design of enslaving his brother's body, that very moment does he also conceive the still more heinous design of fettering his will, for well does he know that in order to make his dominion supreme over the body, he must fetter the living spring of all its motions. Hence the first lesson the slave is taught is to yield his will unreservedly and exclusively to the dictates of his master. And if a slave desire to educate himself or his children, in obedience to the dictates of reason, or the laws of God, he does not, he cannot do it without the consent of his master. Does reason and circumstances and the Bible command a slave to preach the gospel to his brethren? Slavery arises, and with a frown, and oath and a whip, fetters or obstructs the holy volition of his soul! I knew a pious slave in Charleston, who was a licensed exhorter in the M. E. C.; this good man was in the habit of spending his Saturday nights on the surrounding plantations, preaching to the slaves. One night, as usual, he got into a canoe, sailed across the river, and began to preach to the slaves on a certain plantation upon James' Island. While in the very act of preaching the unsearchable riches of Christ to dying men, the patroles seized him and whipped him in the most cruel manner, and compelled him to promise that he would never return to preach again to those slaves. In the year 1834, several colored brethren, who were also exhorters in the M. E. C. commenced preaching to several *destitute white families,* who gained a subsistence by cultivating some poor lands about three or four miles from Charleston. The first Sunday I was present; the house was nearly filled with these poor white farmers. The master of the house was awakened to a sense of his lost condition. During the following week he was converted. On the third Sunday from the day he was convinced of sin he died in the triumphs of faith, and went to heaven. On the fourth Sunday from the time the dear brethren began to preach, the patroles scented their track, and put them on the chase. Thus an end was put to their labors. Their willing souls were fettered, and the poor whites constrained to go without the preaching of the gospel. In a word, it is in view of man's moral agency that God commands him to shun vice, and practice virtue. But what female slave can do this? I lived 24 years in the midst of slavery, and never knew but six female slaves who were reputedly virtuous! What profit is it to the female slave that she is disposed to be virtuous? Her will, like her body, is not her own; they are both at the pleasure of her master; and he brands them at his will. *So it subverts the moral government of God.*

In view of the moral agency of man, God has most wisely and graciously given him a code of laws, and certain positive precepts, to control and regulate moral actions. This code of laws, and these positive precepts, with the divine influence which they are naturally calculated to exert on the mind of man, constitutes his moral government.

Now, to nullify these laws—to weaken or destroy their legitimate influence on the human mind, or to hinder man from yielding universal and entire obedience to them is to subvert the moral government of God.

Now, slavery nullifies these laws and precepts—weakens and destroys their influence over the human mind, and hinders men from yielding universal and entire obedience to them; therefore slavery subverts the moral government of God. This is the climax of the sin of slavery! This is the daring *Monster!* He stretcheth out his hand against God, and strengtheneth himself against the Almighty—he runneth on him, even on his neck, upon the thick bosses of his buckler. Thus saith the Lord, "Thou shalt not commit adultery." But does the man who owns a hundred females obey the law? Does he not nullify it, and compel the helpless woman to disobey God? Concerning the religious instruction of children, thus saith the Lord, "Bring them up in the nurture and admonition of the Lord." But what saith slavery? "They are my property, and shall be brought up to serve me. They shall not *even learn to read his word,* in order that they may be brought up in his nurture and admonition." If any man doubts this, let him read the slave code of Louisiana, and see if it is not death to teach slaves. Thus saith the Lord, "Remember the Sabbath day, to keep it holy." Does not slavery nullify this law, and compel the slave to work on the Sabbath? Thus saith the Lord, "Obey thy father and thy mother." Can the slave children obey this command of God? Does not slavery command the children to obey the master, and him alone? Thus saith the Son of God, "What God hath joined together let no man put asunder." Does not slavery nullify this law, by breaking the sacred bands of wedlock, and separating the husband and the wife forever? Thus saith the Son of God, "Search the Scriptures." Does not slavery seal up the word of God, and make it criminal for the slave to read it? In 1834, the legislature of South Carolina enacted a law prohibiting the instruction of any slave; and Mr. Lawrence, in a pamphlet which he published in 1835, to defend this law, declared, that if the slaves were permitted to read the Bible, ninety of them would become infidels, like Voltaire, where ten would become christians." "Go ye into all the world, and preach the gospel unto every creature," saith the Son of God. Does slavery permit it? In 1835, a minister of the Episcopal Church, in the city of Charleston, appealed to the civil authority for permission to preach to the free population of an evening, but they would not permit him.

The objector may reply, that at the present moment there are four Methodist missionaries, and one Lutheran, laboring among the slave population of South Carolina. We answer, that this is true, and we are glad of it; but this fact does not overthrow our proposition, nor falsify what we have stated, for although a few planters have permitted the gospel to be preached to their slaves, the majority of them prohibit it, and this permission is extraneous to slavery, and is no part of its creed nor code. Slavery never legislates for the religious instruction of slaves, but, on the contrary, legislates to perpetuate their ignorance; and there are laws this very moment in the statute-books of South Carolina and other states, prohibiting the religious instruction of slaves. But this is not all that slavery does to subvert the moral government of God. The slaves are sensible of the oppression exercised by their masters; and they see these masters on the Lord's day worshipping in his holy Sanctuary. They hear their masters professing christianity; they see these masters preaching the gospel; they hear these masters praying in their families, and they know that oppression and slavery are inconsistent with the christian religion; therefore they scoff at religion itself— mock their masters, and distrust both the goodness and justice of God. Yes, I have known them even to question his existence. I speak not of what others have told me, but of what *I have both seen and heard from the slaves themselves.* I have heard the mistress ring the bell for family prayer, and I have seen the servants immediately begin to sneer and laugh; and have heard them declare they would not go in to prayers; adding, if I go in she will only just read, "Servants obey your masters;" but she will not "break every yoke, and let the oppressed go free." I have seen colored men at the church door, *scoffing at the ministers,* while they were preaching, and saying, you had better go home, and set your slaves free. A few nights ago between 10 and 11 o'clock a runaway slave came to the house where I live for safety and succor. I asked him if he was a christian; "no sir," said he, "white men treat us so bad in Mississippi that we can't be christians."

Sir, I taught school in Charleston five years. In 1834 the legislature of our state enacted a law to prohibit colored teachers. My school was filled with children and youth of the most promising talents; and when I looked upon them, and remembered that in a few more weeks this school shall be closed, and I be permitted no more to teach them, notwithstanding I had been a professor-seven years, I began to question the existence of the Almighty, and to say, if indeed there is a God, does he deal justly? Is he a just God? Is he a holy Being? If so, why does he permit a handful of dying men thus to oppress us? Why does he permit them to hinder me from teaching these children, when nature, reason and Revelation command me to teach them? Thus I began to question the Divine government, and to murmur at the administration of his providence. And could I do otherwise, while slavery's cruelties were pressing and grinding my soul in the dust, and robbing me and my people of those privileges which it was hugging to its breast, and giving thousands to perpetuate the blessing which it was tearing away from us? Sir, the very man who made the law alluded to, did that very year, and at that very session of the legislature, give 20,000 dollars to increase the property of South Carolina College.

In a word, slavery tramples the laws of the living God under its unhallowed feet—weakens and destroys the influence which those laws are calculated to exert over the mind of man; and constrains the oppressed to blaspheme the name of the Almighty. For I have often heard them sneeringly say, that *"The Almighty made Charleston on a Saturday night, when he was weary, and in a great hurry." O, Brethren of the Franckean Synod! awake! AWAKE! to the battle, and hurl the hottest thunders of divine truth at the head of this cruel monster, until he shall fall to rise no more; and the groans of the enslaved are converted into the songs of the free!*

PART II

TWENTIETH-CENTURY HUMANISM

Twentieth-Century African American History

AS MENTIONED EARLIER, by the end of the nineteenth century, stories of opportunity in a "more hospitable" environment were drawing African Americans away from rural southern realities and into the big cities, as part of the Great Migration. What they found did not meet their expectations. There were some jobs, for example, but they still faced discrimination that kept them out of the more desirable jobs; poverty persisted, only the environment had changed. Economic hardship would heighten in the 1930s because of the Great Depression. In addition, discrimination placed—often by law—African Americans in the less desirable neighborhoods, where poor conditions increased the likelihood of ill health, poor education opportunities, few social outlets, and high levels of frustration. Much of their frustration matched the hardships faced by African Americans who remained in the South. Jim Crow regulations that restricted the multileveled mobility of African Americans took various shapes, based upon region, but remained a force that circumscribed possibilities. The power of Jim Crow regulations would have this type of effect for more than fifty years, and what these regulations failed to accomplish the Klu Klux Klan and other organizations attempted to achieve. Some political leaders, Woodrow Wilson, for one, gave U.S. citizens hope through his attention to the problems fostered by the industrial age. Yet banking reforms and other such programs had little impact on African Americans. Efforts to bring discriminatory bills before Congress, combined with attacks upon African Americans in popular culture (for example, the film *Birth of a Nation*) and the scientific racism espoused by figures such as Harvard's Louis Agassiz, continuously challenged the standing of African Americans. Wilson was not alone in his questionable commitment to African Americans; Theodore Roosevelt, for example, had shown that helping African Americans would occur only when it was politically expedient. Despite the circumstances, African American leaders such as Booker T. Washington and W. E. B. Du Bois continued to fight for the advancement of African Americans.

There were, however, what many African Americans considered glimmers of hope; one entailed the move away from a position of neutrality with respect to World War I (1917). Advocates for social transformation and the progress of African Americans believed that the war would bring to the forefront the struggles of African Americans for equality in keeping with the democratic vision. Some believed that the participation of African Americans in the war effort would result in enfranchisement. As a result, African Americans were encouraged to volunteer for active service. Despite racism within the armed forces, African Americans were present in large numbers. Yet, even this service at home and abroad did not eradicate discrimination.

For some, after World War I, the Communist Party's rhetoric concerning social transformation was appealing; others gave attention to the establishing of unions and other labor mechanisms that would help African Americans achieve success. Some responded to the ongoing poor treatment through an embrace of Black nationalism. For some, this entailed a desire to relocate to Africa. Relocation was a relatively old idea, having had advocates in the 1800s, but what differed now was the strong leadership of figures such as Marcus Garvey. As often happens, cultural production—literature, the visual arts, music, and so on—provided a creative outlet for response to sociopolitical circumstances. Through the emergence of the two phases of the Harlem Renaissance, African American writers and artists expressed the angst of African Americans and chronicled the failures and successes of African Americans to forge meaning in the world. They gave expression, through fictional depictions as well as autobiographical treatments, to the struggle of African Americans to find support for their efforts through political affiliations, cultural affiliations, and the like. Possibilities for envisioning this new life moved in various directions, from vehement Black nationalism to integration.

Black nationalism would take a variety of forms during the first half of the twentieth century, one being the Honorable Elijah Muhammad's Nation of Islam. With time, this movement would, using the personality of Malcolm X, gain a great deal of attention and provide a voice to many African Americans wrestling with a seemingly absurd world. In part, they responded to the damage done to African American communities throughout the Great Depression, and the failure of African American patriotism, demonstrated through participation in war efforts, to bring about the wholesale betterment of life options for African Americans.

The Nation of Islam's stance on social transformation was at odds with the dominant approach, the civil rights movement, which developed in the late 1950s, and with its major spokesperson—Martin Luther King, Jr. The civil rights movement, with the support of the Southern Christian Leadership Conference and earlier "freedom fighters" such as the Reverend Pauli Murray, sought to gain civil rights for African Americans based upon a reclaiming of the nation's own rhetoric and recorded aims. With time, King and other members of the movement's Christian arm would bring their critique of U.S. society to bear on the country's involvement in the Vietnam War, as well as on class stratification and poverty. The efforts of civil rights activists were met with hostility in the South, as southerners attempted to maintain the separation "between the races" and the inequities growing from this. Yet, gains were made. In other parts of the United States the message of Black Power, advocated by the Black Panthers and the Student

Nonviolent Coordinating Committee after its break with the Christian wing of the civil rights movement, had more appeal.

Many gains were made because of the struggles of "freedom fighters" both within and outside the mainstream civil rights movement. New legislation was not enough to induce permanent attitudinal changes. As a result, many of the advances eroded during the presidencies of Ronald Reagan and George Bush. Yet, there are those who continue the struggle started generations ago with the hope of transforming the United States. Some are affiliated with recognized religious bodies and their work is based upon the principles of overtly religious doctrine. Others labor toward transformation without this framework; they do not depend upon theistically constructed understanding of praxis. It is to these workers—humanists—that our attention now turns.

SUGGESTED READING

Stokely Carmichael and Charles V. Hamilton, *Black Power: The Politics of Liberation in America* (New York: Vintage Books, 1967).

Harold Cruse, *The Crisis of the Negro Intellectual: A Historical Analysis of the Failure of Black Leadership* (New York: Quill, 1984).

W. E. B. Du Bois, The *Souls of Black Folk* (New York: Vintage Books/The Library of America, 1990).

John Hope Franklin, *From Slavery to Freedom: A History of Negro Americans,* 5th ed. (New York: Alfred A. Knopf, 1980).

David J. Garrow, *Bearing the Cross: Martin Luther King, Jr., and the Southern Christian Leadership Conference* (New York: Random House, 1986).

Vincent Harding, *There Is a River: The Black Struggle for Freedom in America* (New York: Harcourt Brace Jovanovich, 1981).

Leon F. Litwack, *Trouble in Mind: Black Southerners in the Age of Jim Crow* (New York: Alfred A. Knopf, 1998).

Cornel West, *Prophesy Deliverance: An Afro-American Revolutionary Christianity* (Philadelphia: Westminster Press, 1982).

A

History, Culture, and Politics

8

THE NEGRO'S GOD AS REFLECTED IN HIS LITERATURE

Ideas of God Involving Frustration, Doubt, God's Impotence, and His Non-Existence

Benjamin E. Mays

❏

Benjamin E. Mays (1894–1984) received his Ph.D. from the University of Chicago in 1935. Yet, prior to that point, Mays had already distinguished himself as a minister and intellectual. Employed by the Institute of Social and Religious Research in New York City, Mays directed a study of Black churches that resulted in the important book (coauthored by J. W. Nicholson) The Negro's Church *(1933). With the much deserved recognition that text received, Mays moved into the academy as the dean of the School of Religion at Howard University (1934). Later, Mays distinguished himself as president of Morehouse College, in Atlanta (1940). It was there that his intellectual abilities and connection to the Black church informed future leaders such as Martin Luther King, Jr.*

*Prior to taking the position at Morehouse, Mays wrote the text we are concerned with here—*The Negro's God as Reflected in His Literature. *This text was and continues to be important because of the insight it provides with respect to African American doctrines of God. For the purposes of this anthology, it is important because of the light it sheds on the presence of* *humanism within cultural production, giving attention to the influential period of literary (and canon) formation known as the Harlem Renaissance. As I have noted elsewhere, with the development of the Harlem Renaissance and its exploration of uncomfortable and raw life questions, as well as the "deradicalization of churches," the increase in alternate responses to oppression made space available for humanist interpretations. The literature of the Harlem Renaissance provides insights that not only inform theological reflection because of their concern with religious themes and imagery but also provides, when personal positions are considered, a much needed challenge to ideas of religious normality within Black communities. In this way, it affords license to advocate humanism.*

The following excerpt from The Negro's God *chronicles the development and content of what can be termed humanist thought within African American cultural production.*

For general information on the Harlem Renaissance, see Alain Locke, ed., The New Negro *(New York: Atheneum, 1968); David L. Lewis,* When Harlem Was in Vogue *(New York: Knopf/distributed by Random House, 1981); Nathan Irvin Huggins,* Harlem Renaissance *(New York: Oxford University Press, 1971); James Weldon Johnson,* Black Manhattan *(New York: Arno Press, 1930); Jon Michael Spencer,* The New Negroes and Their Music: The Success of the Harlem Renaissance *(Knoxville: University of Tennessee Press, 1997). Works of individual members of the Harlem Renaissance are noted in some of the following personal accounts and general observations. For additional information on Mays and his work, see his* Seeking to Be a Christian in Race Relations *(New York: Friendship Press, 1957);* Born to Rebel: An Autobiography *(New York: Scribner, 1971); and* Disturbed about Man *(Richmond: John Knox Press, 1969).*

❏

In the development of the idea of God in Negro literature there is a tendency or threat to abandon the idea of God "as a useful instrument" in social adjustment, as evidenced by the following facts:

1. There is a strong tendency to doubt God's value to the Negro in his struggle to gain a stable economic, social, and political foothold in America.
2. God is described as having outlived His usefulness. Historically, when gods have outlived their usefulness, either they have been abandoned or a new conception of God has been developed to meet the new experiences. The younger Negro writers seem to be inclined to abandon the idea rather than develop new conceptions.
3. There is a denial of the existence of God.

It is clear that this third development does not mean that the idea of God is unrelated to the growing demand for social change—not that at all. Rather, it seems to mean that these heretical ideas of God develop because in the social situation the "breaks" seem to be against the Negro, and the authors are unable to harmonize this fact with the God pictured by Christianity. Perhaps the most expressive of these doubts, ending in denial of the existence of God, is to be found in *Quicksand.* The novel is built around Helga Crane, a Chicago girl, whose father was a Negro and whose mother was a white immigrant. Quite early her father deserted her mother, and when she was six years old, her mother married again—this time a white man. Helga's mother died when she was fifteen. Her uncle, Peter Nilssen, took care of her for awhile and educated her. . . . Since she was a Negro, her step-father, her step-brothers and sisters, her numerous cousins, aunts, and uncles—all repudiated her and shunned her. . . . In [a] letter her uncle sent her five thousand dollars and suggested that she visit her Aunt Katrina in Copenhagen. Finally, she accepted the suggestion and went to Denmark. No prejudice greeted her in Denmark and she had the opportunity to marry in high circles but refused. . . . Finally, she began to hunger for America, not so much for America, but for association and companionship with Negroes. . . . The author says that this experience of yearning to be with Negroes caused Helga Crane, for the first time, to feel sympathy for her father rather than feel contempt and hatred, which she had often felt, because he deserted her mother. Helga returned to America, partially determined never to marry because she felt that it was a sin to bring black children into the world. . . . But in spite of this attitude toward marriage, she finally married the Reverend Mr. Pleasant Green and became the mother of five children. It was at the Reverend Mr. Green's revival she became converted. Later on, she repudiated this simple religious faith during a period of convalescence when she had time to think through the racial situation. It is here that she revolts against the white man's God and denies the existence of God.

God Does Not Exist

In that period of racking pain and calamitous fright Helga had learned what passion and credulity could do to one. In her was born angry bitterness and an enormous disgust. The cruel, unrelieved suffering had beaten down her protective wall of artificial faith in the infinite wisdom, in the mercy, of God. For had she not called in her agony on Him? And He had not heard. Why? Because she knew now, He wasn't there. Didn't exist. Into that yawning gap of unspeakable brutality had gone, too, her belief in the miracle and wonder of life. Only scorn, resentment, and hate remained—and ridicule. Life wasn't a miracle, a wonder. It was, for Negroes at least, only a great disappointment. Something to be got through with as best one could. No one was interested in them or hyped them. God! Bah! . . . (*Quicksand,* 291, 292)

. . . Helga Crane gives us ideas of God that not only involve doubt, frustration, and bewilderment; but primarily, she repudiates the validity of the idea of God and denies His existence. The personal, physical suffering through which she had passed, the mental agony and torture which she had suffered, owing to race, had not only caused her to cast aside the white man's God, but these experiences had led her to the conclusion that God did not even exist. In Helga Crane, there is complete abandonment of the idea that God is helpful in personal, social, and racial adjustment. Even before she expressed flat denial, she doubted God, as shown by her belief that Negroes should not bring children into the world. Her denial of the existence of God is due not only to her personal rebuffs, suffering, and disappointment but also to the social situation of her people. The idea that God loves all people, regardless of race, is nonsense because there are ten million Negroes who see nothing in daily practice to sustain the belief. . . .

The next quotation is taken from one of James Weldon Johnson's most recent and widely read books, *Along This Way.* The idea of God presented here differs greatly from the idea presented in Mr. Johnson's poem, "Fifty Years," in which the view is expressed that the Negro is a part of some great plan. In that poem, Mr. Johnson does not doubt God. He believes that there is purpose in the universe. In this quotation, Mr. Johnson presents his views of religion and future life, in addition to his idea of God.

Doubting Purpose and a Personal God

My glance forward reaches no farther than this world. I admit that through my adult life I have lacked religiosity. But I make no boast of it; understanding, as I do, how essential religion is to many, many people. For that reason, I have little patience with the zealot who is forever trying to prove to others that they do not need religion; that they would be better off without it. Such a one is no less a zealot than the religionist who contends that all who "do not believe" will be consigned to eternal hell fires. It is simply that I have not felt the need of religion in the commonplace sense of the term. I have derived spiritual values in life from other sources than worship and prayer. I think that the teachings of Jesus Christ embody the loftiest ethical and spiritual concepts the human mind has yet borne. I do not know if there is a personal God; I do not see how I can know; and I do not see how my knowing can matter. What does matter, I believe, is how I deal with myself and how I deal with my fellows. I feel that I can practice a conduct toward myself and toward my fellows that will constitute a basis for an adequate religion, a religion that may comprehend spiritually {sic} and beauty and serene happiness.

As far as I am able to peer into the inscrutable, I do not see that there is any evidence to refute those scientists and philosophers who hold that the universe is purposeless; that man, instead of being the special care of a Divine Providence, is a dependent upon fortuity and his own wits for survival in the midst of blind and insensate forces. But to stop there is to stop short of the vital truth. For mankind and for the individual this state, what though it be accidental and ephemeral, is charged with meaning. Man's sufferings, his joys, his aspirations, his defeats, are just as real and of as great moment to him as they would be if they were part of a mighty and definite cosmic plan. . . . (James Weldon Johnson, *Along This Way* [New York: Viking Press, 1933], 431, 414)

Whatever the nature of the God Mr. Johnson believes in, it is clear that this God does not operate in some future place called Heaven, and his God does not consign one to Hell. With respect to the idea that God is personal, Mr. Johnson is an agnostic, admitting that there may be a God of some sort. Johnson's inclination to accept the idea of a purposeless universe, his idea that man is not under the special care of a Divine Providence, and his inclination to accept the view that man is dependent upon chance and his own ability for survival, imply that God does not exist. The author's conviction that "man's sufferings, his joys, his aspirations, his defeats" are not parts of any definite cosmic plan, and his strong implication that man's state here is accidental and ephemeral also infer the non-existence of God. The last paragraph of the excerpt, however, insists that man needs a God if he is to possess sufficient faith to enable him to face life with fortitude. The logic of this paragraph might easily lead one to conclude that there is a plurality of gods and that whatever it is that enables one "to continue to hope and struggle on" is God. If this is true, there would be as many gods as there are things that stimulate man to live courageously in a world of blind chance. On the other hand, Mr. Johnson may intend to say that for the brave and strong of heart, there is no need of a belief in God; but for the weak and frail, the "so-called" masses, the belief in God is a necessity; otherwise, life for them would have no meaning. . . .

George S. Schuyler, who for twenty years has been in the public eye as a writer, lecturer, and critic of American social life, also presents an interesting view substantiating the third main contention of this study. In an unpublished statement, he writes:

> It is well of course, that I am an atheist. I have said so time
> and again, and long before any of my literary contemporaries
> in Senegambia began to be assailed with doubts and said so
> in public.

In some respect Schuyler's statement coincides with that of James Weldon Johnson previously quoted. Both agree that belief in God is necessary for many people and that if they find comfort and solace in the belief, they should not be ridiculed or criticized. Both find something noble and beautiful in religion. There is no effort on Schuyler's part nor in Johnson's recent statement to molest or deride the simple faith of the masses. Though critical of institutionalized religion, there is a profound appreciation for the church. The attitude expressed by

Schuyler is in striking contrast to that revealed by the editors of the *Messenger* and Langston Hughes. In one sentence Schuyler implies that religion is compensatory; but he also implies that compensatory religion has value for those who believe in God and religion.

When the *Messenger* magazine was in operation, it served as an outstanding critic of the Negro Church and religion. The editors believed that the Negro ministry should center its attention on economics, history, sociology, and physical science—less on Bible. In a Thanksgiving editorial in 1919, the *Messenger* denied allegiance to the traditional God. It said:

> We do not thank God for anything nor do our thanks include gratitude for which most persons usually give thanks at this period. With us we are thankful for different things and to a different Deity. Our Deity is the toiling masses of the world and the things for which we thank are their achievement. (*Messenger*, Dec., 1919, p. 4.)

In the next poem, Langston Hughes turns Communist and repudiates Christ. This selection is also a repudiation of God and religion, which is a radical departure from the faith implicit in his earlier writings. It appeared in the November–December issue of the *Negro Worker*, 1932, a thirty-six page bi-monthly magazine published by Reds in Hamburg, Germany.

GOOD-BYE CHRIST
Listen Christ,
You did all right in your day I reckon
But that day's gone now.
They ghosted you up a swell story, too,
Called it Bible—
But its dead now
The popes and the preachers've
Made too much money from it
They've sold you to too many

Kings, generals, robbers, and killers—
Even to the Tzar and the Cossacks
Even to Rockefeller's church,
Even to the Saturday Evening Post.
You ain't no good no more.
They've pawned you
Till you've done wore out
Goodbye.
Christ Jesus Lord God Jehovah,
Beat it on away from here now.
Make way for a new guy with no religion at all.
A real guy named
Marx Communist Lenin Peasant Stalin,
Worker ME—
I said, ME
Go ahead on now.
You're getting in the way of things Lord.

According to [Hughes] Christ and perhaps God have all outlived their usefulness. The world must be left for reconstruction in the hands of Communists. Christ is not only of no use in perfecting social change, but He is a decided handicap. He gets in the way of things.

9

HUMANISM IN POLITICAL ACTION

Norm R. Allen, Jr.

❑

In this original piece, Allen (the executive director of African Americans for Humanism) provides a summary of humanist ideals and activism in political and social movements, during the twentieth century. Throughout history, he argues, human-centered thought and action have been influential in reforming and transforming society. Though many humanist thinkers and activists have kept their nonreligious views in the closet, their contributions to humanity must be understood and recognized by all who are serious about gaining a true understanding of human struggles and resistance to oppression. That is to say, much has been said and written about the role that religion and religious leaders have played in Black political life and culture. Indeed, some scholars and intellectuals argue that religion is inextricably linked to Black political action and progress. But what has been downplayed or ignored is the influential role that humanism and humanist ideals have played in Black political ideals and movements.

For additional information, see Norm R. Allen, Jr., African-American Humanism: An Anthology *(Buffalo: Prometheus Books, 1991); Fred*

Whitehead, Freethought on the American Frontier *(Buffalo: Prometheus Books, 1992); and Norm Allen, Jr., "Religion and the New African American Intellectuals,"* Nature, Society, and Thought *9, no. 2 (May 1996): 159–187.*

❏

One of the most easily recognizable political movements in U.S. history is the civil rights movement. Many see it primarily as a religious movement conceived and headed by religious leaders. It is generally known that civil disobedience is a method of protest most thoughtfully articulated by Henry David Thoreau. But it is not widely known that, ironically, his theory became influential after his death largely because it is secular and tied to no particular religion. Indeed, Thoreau's earliest protest centered on a church/state separation issue. In 1838, the state demanded that he pay a tax to a minister whose church Thoreau did not even attend. (He never went to church and associated mostly with unchurched individuals.) Thoreau believed that, if anything, it should be the duty of the clergyman to support the school financially. He therefore refused to pay the tax, though another man paid it unbeknownst to him. In 1846, Thoreau was arrested and jailed for refusing to pay a poll tax. After his first night in jail, relatives paid his fine (again, without his knowledge or permission.) For Thoreau, to pay the tax would have given him a guilty conscience. In his philosophy, it was important that an individual refuse to perform an action that went against his or her conscience. He believed that an individual's belief—and not blind obedience to God—was the main criterion for determining a course of action.

Thoreau was a fierce opponent of slavery and of the Mexican-American War. Moreover, he was opposed to funding slavery and the war with his taxes. He wrote antislavery essays. In his most famous essay, "Civil Disobedience," he argued that people have the right to disobey unjust laws. He did not, however, suggest that they have a duty—divine or secular—to do so. Moreover, he argued that though the U.S. Constitution defended slavery, those who opposed slavery had the right to do so. In the final analysis, government oppression will flow only from individuals who allow it. Often, a powerful minority will act unjustly in the name of the majority, and with the latter's tacit consent. In this case, the people have the right to oppose the government.

The most famous adherents of Thoreau's philosophy were Gandhi and Martin Luther King, Jr. King led one of the most important and influential social justice movements in history. Ironically, both King and Gandhi were religionists who wedded a secular philosophy to their cause. Furthermore, unlike Gandhi and King, Thoreau was not a pacifist. Indeed, Thoreau enthusiastically supported John Brown's raid on Harper's Ferry, and chastised Brown's critics. Thoreau opposed the notion of Manifest Destiny and the annexation of Texas, which became a slave state. He helped slaves escape to freedom by way of the Underground Railroad. He was opposed to missionaries, and he was a strong critic of organized religion. His humanistic contributions to social justice have been a boon to humankind.

In the twentieth century, some Black humanist leaders were less reluctant to remain in the closet. A. Philip Randolph is regarded as "the grandfather of the civil rights movement." He was one of the most important labor leaders of the century. He organized the Brotherhood of Sleeping Car Porters. In his early days, Randolph was a socialist who strongly opposed Marcus Garvey and other authoritarian leaders with reactionary agendas. He and the Black humanist activist Chandler Owen eventually started the *Messenger,* a socialist magazine that carried strong critiques of religion. In 1941—when the United States entered World War II—Randolph led a march on Washington in opposition to segregation in businesses that received government contracts. In 1963 he spoke at the March on Washington during the civil rights movement, and had a major part in organizing it.

It was not always easy for Randolph to express his distaste for religion. Because he often worked with religious leaders, there were times when he felt obligated to conceal his atheism, socialism, and pacifism. In many Black circles, these positions were frowned upon. Randolph even had an honorary membership in a Black church, though he remained an atheist.

In his later years, Randolph abandoned socialism but never abandoned progressive politics. In 1973, he signed *Humanist Manifesto II,* which offered humanistic suggestions for the future of humankind. Randolph and Owen were among the early soapbox, street orators of Harlem. Another—Hubert Henry Harrison—was among the best and might have been the first. Harrison was an outspoken atheist, socialist, and activist. Like Randolph and Owen, he was involved with the International Workers of the World (the "Wobblies") and other labor movements. He influenced both Marcus Garvey's Universal Negro Improvement Association (U.N.I.A.) and the *Messenger* group. According to atheist activist John Ragland, in June 1917 Harrison "introduced Marcus Garvey to the United States."[1]

Harrison profoundly influenced one of his admirers—Joel Augustus Rogers. Rogers spent fifty years researching Black history, focusing largely on personages. His books included the three-volume *Sex and Race,* in which he examined the history of "race" mixing. Rogers—a secular humanist—spoke at U.N.I.A. meetings and influenced numerous Black leaders, including Malcolm X.

An examination of Malcolm's ideas provides another good example of how humanist ideals have influenced Black political activism. Though Malcolm was a Sunni Muslim, his worldview was secular. Indeed, after his departure from the Nation of Islam (NOI), he founded the secular Organization of Afro-American Unity (OAAU) and the religious Muslim Mosque, Inc. Most of Malcolm's time, thought, and energy went into developing the secular organization. Moreover, he consistently maintained that religion and politics should not be mixed. He believed that religion was personal, and that it did more to divide than to unite humanity.

After Malcolm's break with the NOI, he was freed from the shackles of religious dogma, which he despised. He examined new ideas— including those of white, nonreligious socialists. He spoke at forums hosted by the Socialist Workers Party and deemed their official newspaper, *The Militant,* one of the best in the United States. He openly invited Black atheists, agnostics, Confucianists, and others to join his organization. He continued his verbal assaults upon Christianity and stressed the importance of human thought and action.

Malcolm was highly impressed by Roger's *Sex and Race* and *Africa's Gift to America.* Rogers stressed the importance of history in human rights struggles and persuaded millions of people to challenge traditional historical scholarship.

Many religionists have asserted that Malcolm had become a humanist or had embraced a humanistic worldview.[2] He was primarily interested in fostering critical thinking and calling upon the best human minds to find solutions to the many problems afflicting people of African descent. He had become increasingly political and rejected Elijah Muhammad's admonition to leave everything in the hands of God. In his estimation, religion might have utilitarian value, but a mutually agreed upon theology was unnecessary and needlessly problematic and divisive. He agreed with his colleague Albert Cleage of the Shrine of the Black Madonna in Detroit, that nothing is more sacred than the liberation of Black people, but his outlook was international, and he was concerned with human rights struggles throughout the world.

James Farmer—who also signed *Humanist Manifesto II*—was a major leader of the civil rights movement. He was born January 12, 1920, in Marshall, Texas, where his father had been the state's first Black Ph.D. For three years, his father was a pastor at Black Methodist churches in Texarkana, Texas, and, later, in Galveston.[3] As a

"Preacher's Kid" (PK), Farmer endured many pressures growing up. He writes:

> PK's are generally distrusted by their peers: they are fashioned in the goody-goody mold. Naturally, rebellion is a most common response to the unnatural life-style of PK's—rebellion of all sorts. Adam Clayton Powell, Jr. wore the cloth with an impudent nonchalance. Malcolm X moved from Harlem vice-lordship to militant black nationalism. Deviation from society's accepted conventions has high incidence among PK's—alcoholism, homosexuality, profligacy, promiscuity, protest action.[4]

Farmer experienced a world in which preachers were highly privileged. They were admired and respected throughout their communities. They were viewed as saints who could do no wrong—the ultimate role models. But Farmer adds:

> This world of preachers and preachments is, in a sense, a world of endemic hypocrisy. No one can be as good as the preacher's aura would make believe. It is also a breeding ground for politicians; the Machiavellian thrust of black church politics would make Democratic and Republican Party shenanigans look like a Boy Scout jamboree.[5]

In April 1942, Farmer cofounded the secular Committee of Racial Equality (later changed to Congress of Racial Equality) in Chicago. Originally, the group advocated nonviolent action to combat racial discrimination. In May 1942, CORE led an organized sit-in to desegregate the Jack Spratt restaurant in Chicago. The protest—which might have been the first of its kind in the United States—was successful. Despite the victory, however, Farmer, like Randolph, learned that many Blacks still disapproved of the idea of meeting violence with nonviolence.

Farmer's views were profoundly influenced by the humanist Melvin B. Tolson. Before he was a published author, Tolson was an instructor at Wiley College, a Methodist school in Marshall, Texas. Farmer, who had entered the college on a four-year scholarship at the age of fourteen, was enrolled in a course taught by Tolson. One day during Farmer's first semester, Tolson told Farmer to read Marx, Freud, and Darwin, instructing him to examine their views and defend his ideas. Tolson—who served as the school's debate coach—informed Farmer that critical thinking and debate were crucial to one's success and understanding. Farmer, incidentally, had won his scholarship through a series of public speaking contests.

At Wiley, debaters often discussed segregation. Tolson once reprimanded Farmer for condemning segregation yet watching a movie in a segregated theater. Tolson then suggested that Farmer read Thoreau's essay on civil disobedience. Farmer reflected deeply upon racism in the South. Moreover, he wanted to put his knowledge into action and decided to dedicate his life to eradicating racism. He heard the great orators Mordecai Johnson, Ralph Bunche, Randolph, and others. He studied the ideas of Marx, Eugene Debs, and other socialist thinkers. He continued to sharpen his debating skills and to grow in knowledge. He graduated from the Howard University School of Religion, and he wrote a thesis on religion and racism. But he did not become ordained.

On May 3, 1961, Farmer took part in the first great Freedom Ride. It was successful, and Farmer—a pacifist—won over more people to the cause of passive resistance. CORE became one of the most influential civil rights organizations in the United States, and Farmer became one of the "Big Four" civil rights leaders (along with Martin Luther King, Jr., Roy Wilkins, and Whitney Young). Members of CORE bravely endured beatings, death threats, verbal abuse, imprisonment, and the like. The organization supported sit-ins, rent strikes, education, legal defense, scholarships, and other activities.

Farmer's training and experience as a debater served him well. Indeed, he and the Black conservative and atheist George Schuyler were regarded as the only spokespersons capable of effectively debating

Malcolm X. Most civil rights leaders avoided Malcolm like the plague. Farmer, however, had confidence in his movement and understood many of the weaknesses in Malcolm's position. Farmer writes of a revealing photocopy of a letter from George Lincoln Rockwell of the American Nazi Party:

> I have just had a meeting with the most extraordinary black man in America: The Honorable Elijah Muhammad, leader of the Nation of Islam. I was amazed to learn how much they agree on things; they think that blacks should get out of this country and go back to Africa or to some other place and so do we. They want to get black men to leave white women alone; and so do we . . . The Honorable Elijah Muhammad and I have worked out an agreement of mutual assistance in which they will help us on some things and we will help them on others . . . Can you imagine a rally of the American Nazis in Union Square protected from Jewish hecklers by a solid phalanx of Elijah Muhammad's stalwart black stormtroopers? Oi, oi, oi![6]

Malcolm said he was unaware of the meeting, and he thanked Farmer for not mentioning it during a debate between the two of them. This, however, was not the first time a reactionary Black nationalist group formed an alliance with white supremacists, nor was it the last. Marcus Garvey's Universal Negro Improvement Association formed an alliance with the Ku Klux Klan in the '20s. In the '80s, Louis Farrakhan's Nation of Islam formed an alliance with the racist White Aryan Resistance. In the '90s, the Nation has worked with neofascist Lyndon LaRouche. On September 10, 1996, the Nation's Fruit of Islam paramilitary group provided security for the British pro-Nazi author David Irving at a speech in Oakland, California.

Conversely, progressive humanistic organizations like CORE have consistently opposed white supremacist organizations and movements. After Farmer resigned on March 1, 1966, however, the leadership of CORE and other organizations grew increasingly militant.

Floyd McKissick, who assumed leadership of the group after Farmer's departure, embraced Black Power, as did many other progressive organizations. Today, CORE is a conservative organization headed by Roy Inniss. His son, Niger, is a major spokesperson for the group.

The African Pioneer Nationalist Movement (APNM) made its presence known in Harlem during the '50s and '60s. Headed by Carlos Cooks, the organization was explicitly atheistic. They advocated African redemption, as did Marcus Garvey. Cooks, his lieutenant Charles Peeker, and other members excited Harlemites and other observers with their street oratory. They drew crowds at 125th Street and 7th Avenue, across the street from the famed Theresa Hotel, where Malcolm X was assassinated. Legally, street speakers in Harlem were required to display an American flag. APNM speakers complied, using a small American flag and a huge African liberation flag bearing the colors red, black, and green. The APNM supported the unsuccessful drive to take the United States before the United Nations on the charge of human rights violations. The organization advocated Black pride, unity, and the teaching of Black history. There was much anger directed toward whites, and as in most Black nationalist organizations, homophobia was condoned and encouraged. The organization was small, but it strongly influenced the thinking of many Black nationalists.

Humanism has played a major role in many political movements in the United States. The Western world, however, has not cornered the market on humanism. Indeed, humanist ideals and organizations can be found around the globe, including Africa. The late Tai Solarin was one of Nigeria's leading educators, social critics, and prodemocracy activists. He was the chairman of the People's Bank of Nigeria and a writer for such leading Nigerian newspapers as *The Guardian.* An outspoken atheist, on January 27, 1956, he founded the Mayflower School—perhaps the only secular high school in Nigeria.

Though "Uncle Tai," as he was affectionately known, had been educated in a Methodist mission school, he held that mission schools could not effectively provide students with a proper education. Moreover, he saw no positive correlation or causality between religious education and public morality. He believed that education could be valuable only when it was secular and free from sectarian influences. He thought it a civic duty of Nigerian adults to save their children from the negative influences of religious education, which has been part of Nigeria's history for more than 150 years. He regarded attempts by Western missionaries to convert and "civilize" Africans as misguided and harmful. Moreover, he deemed unethical attempts by missionaries to use schools to convert African children to Christianity. To him, Roman Catholicism was the most oppressive religion, the one most likely to suppress children's critical thinking skills.

According to Solarin, not only did Western religious education not only harmed children but trained Nigerians to do the bidding of the British government. Africans were taught to revere European culture and customs and to denigrate their own. Furthermore, in some cases, mission school officials stole government money earmarked for education. Therefore, Solarin contended that Africans must be responsible for making education secular and relevant to the needs of African societies. The Mayflower School is one of Nigeria's finest. Secular messages emphasizing the importance of education are found on the school's walls. Solarin, who idolized Robert Ingersoll, regularly wore a white cap bearing one of Ingersoll's favorite sayings: "KNOWLEDGE IS LIGHT." The students are serious, well-mannered, and eager to learn.

Solarin, a great humanitarian, spent much of his life condemning Nigeria's military rulers, and went to jail for his efforts. He always played a major role in Nigeria's prodemocracy movements. Indeed, fellow Nigerian and Nobel Laureate Wole Soyinka dedicated his book *The Open Sore of a Continent* to Solarin. In the words of Soyinka, Solarin participated in a protest march against the military dictatorship of Sani Abacha. Solarin said that he planned to "walk a step or two. . . ."

Soyinka relates that Solarin fought for democracy until the day he died:

> Tai Solarin walked the entire distance with a small group, at his own measured pace, hailed by crowds as he passed, some of whom fell in step with him over different sections. He was accompanied by, separated from, then reunited with [his wife] Sheila, as Abacha's goons hauled off the old man and his wife in separate wagons to nearby police stations, only to be compelled by besieging crowds to release and return them exactly where they had picked them up. They offered to give him a ride to the march's destination, but Tai was resolved to go out on his feet. Tai Solarin's "step or two" took him all the way to the rendezvous on Lagos Island, but he had a much further destination at hand, and I insist to myself till this day that I read it in his eyes that dawn. The following morning, he took the final step going up the stairs in his Sagamu home, missed it, and fell backwards to his death.[7]

The *New York Times* ran an obituary on Solarin, reporting that he died on July 27, 1994, at the age of seventy-two. Many Nigerians have called him "the conscience of the nation," and he credited humanism for much of his success, popularity, and influence.

Soyinka is one of Nigeria's most famous human rights activists. Like Solarin, he had spent time in jail for his human rights activism. He fled Nigeria for his life in 1994. In 1997, while still in exile, he and eleven other dissidents were charged with treason in connection with a series of bombings of army installations. Following the dictator Sani Abacha's death, the new Nigerian government withdrew the treason charge against Soyinka. Soyinka—a laureate of the International Academy of Humanism—is a strong secularist. He has opposed theocracy and religious fanaticism relentlessly. He immediately rushed to the defense of author Salman Rushdie when the Ayatollah Khomeini charged him with blasphemy and called for his death in 1989:

Following the outbreak of the Rushdie affair Wole Soyinka, the Nigerian dramatist and Nobel laureate, issued a characteristically combative statement calling on writers around the world to bombard Iran with pastiches of *The Satanic Verses;* and added: "If Salman Rushdie is unnaturally and prematurely silenced, the creative world will launch its own jihad." According to unconfirmed reports Soyinka himself received a death sentence within twenty-four hours of his statement. The arrow of (divine) retribution in this instance was said to have been fired, not from Tehran, but from the ancient Islamic city of Kano in northern Nigeria.[8]

Far from being deterred by death threats, Soyinka later defended the outspoken atheist Taslima Nasrin of Bangladesh. Like the atheist Rushdie, Nasrin was threatened with death after she was accused of offending Islam with her book *Lajja!* (Shame!). Soyinka wrote to the prime minister of Bangladesh, insisting that the Bangladesh government do everything in its power to protect Nasrin.

Soyinka is a staunch critic of despotic African governments. He believes that all forms of injustice should be opposed in the strongest terms. To those, like Minister Farrakhan, who assert that Westerners must have patience as oppressive African governments struggle to bring forth democracy, he has this to say:

> Nigerians fly the latest jets, we have some of the finest pilots in the world. Technology and cyberspace are not strange to Nigerians, they are used on a daily basis. Faxes and cellular phones abound everywhere. The Nigerians didn't say that they were going to wait 1,000 years before they caught up with modern technology. The latest cars, like the Lexus, are already cruising in Nigeria. I don't believe that mental apprehension of democracy is beyond those who acquire a more complicated facility for operating the latest gadgets. I think it's a very condescending statement, and should be deplored.[9]

Soyinka has long been critical of Blacks in the United States who labor under the illusion that injustice wears only a white face, and that the crimes of Black oppressors should be ignored or downplayed. He has returned to Nigeria to help the nation make the transition back to democracy. Largely because of his efforts, the international community has backed Nigeria's call for democracy and human rights.

Humanism has been very influential in the history of progressive political action. But what will be the role of humanism in the future? What major contributions will Blacks make to humanist theory and activism? And will there ever be peace between religion and humanism in political action?

Black humanists can continue to make important contributions to humanist theory by challenging many of the assumptions made by Eurocentric, middle-class humanists. For example, many white humanists embrace a dogmatic scientism. They believe that scientists are without biases, and they scoff at "conspiracy theories." Progressive Black humanists, however, are not so quick to scoff. Black humanists are much more likely to take note of the infamous Tuskegee experiment—*a genuine government conspiracy*—in which men were infected with syphilis and allowed to go untreated. They will discuss the fact that President Clinton recently apologized for the thousands of radiation experiments that the U.S. government carried out on Americans in the 1940s. There are numerous instances of the use of science for evil purposes. Black humanists are likely to be aware of this fact, and are less likely to rush blindly to the defense of science whenever controversial problem arise. Good science must be viewed as a means to an end—genuine progress—and not an end in itself.

Humanism will continue to be a force in human affairs. Human thought and human action have been the only true agents of positive change. Theism and humanism will have areas of agreement, but there will probably always be conflict between the two, though the conflict need not be violent. Contrary to the views of Stephen Jay Gould and other reputable scientists, science—and its offspring, humanism—and religion make claims about the natural world. Science and religion are used to make predictions about the natural world. Both areas of thought have much to say about human behavior. Disagreements will inevitably arise between the two. Politically active humanists, however, must come out of the closet and command respect. As the twenty-first century opens, Black humanists must not be afraid to let theists know that humanism is a valuable life stance with much to offer the world. If this happens, humanism will grow by leaps and bounds. If it does not happen, humanism will continue to exist on the margins, and will continue to be grossly misunderstood, feared, and despised.

NOTES

1. John Ragland, "Atheists of a Different Color," *American Atheist* (February 1987): 25.

2. Michael Eric Dyson, *Making Malcolm: The Myth and Meaning of Malcolm X* (New York: Oxford University Press, 1995), 65.

3. James Farmer, *Lay Bare the Heart: An Autobiography of the Civil Rights Movement* (New York: Plume, 1985), 34, 35.

4. Ibid., 34.

5. Ibid.

6. Ibid., 226.

7. Wole Soyinka, *The Open Sore of a Continent: A Personal Narrative of the Nigerian Crisis* (New York: Oxford University Press, 1996), 54–55.

8. Adewale Maja-Pearce, *Who's Afraid of Wole Soyinka?: Essays on Censorship* (London: Heinemann, 1991), 62.

9. Norm R. Allen, Jr., interview with Wole Soyinka, "Why I Am a Secular Humanist," *Free Inquiry* 17, no. 4 (fall 1997): 49.

B

Personal Accounts

10

ON A CERTAIN CONSERVATISM
IN NEGROES

Hubert H. Harrison

❏

Hubert Henry Harrison (1883–1927) was born in the U.S. Virgin Islands (St. Croix). In 1890, at the age of seven, the family moved to New York City where later Harrison held various jobs. At a fairly early age, he developed an attachment to the Socialist Party and embraced a form of humanism. He would eventually work for the party. His studies in history and literature informed his writings and speeches given between 1911 and 1914 as a major orator for the party.

Harrison argued that socialism provided African Americans with a means by which to improve their current socioeconomic and political situation. To convince African Americans of this, he fought to have the Socialist Party devote sustained attention to the race issue. Part of his effort resulted in the development of the Colored Socialist Club, a pioneering effort to "organize" African Americans around the central issues of socialism.

As time passed, however, Harrison realized that the Socialist Party would never give race issues the needed attention, the party's concern being the class issue. He eventually left the party and began independent efforts to address the socioeconomic and political needs of African Americans. In part, Harrison sought to achieve his agenda while connecting African Americans to international concerns through the formation of his Liberty League of Negro-Americans. His efforts impressed nationalists such as Marcus Garvey, who offered Harrison the editorship of the Negro World. *Although he continued to write for the* Negro World, *Harrison eventually became a primary speaker for the New York City Board of Education. He also became a U.S. citizen in 1922. Harrison's activities during the 1920s also included helping to establish the New York City Public Library's collection of African American materials. Harrison devoted a great deal of time to labor issues as well, as they related to African Americans.*

The following excerpt will provide the reader with Harrison's perspective concerning progressive politics and the Black church. His argument, in summation, entails a rejection of the church as a liberating force because religion keeps African Americans submissive and trapped within oppressive circumstances. Within this piece, one gets a sense of Harrison's commitment to humanistic principles.

For additional information on African American involvement in progressive politics see, for example, Robin D. G. Kelley, " 'Afric's Sons with Banner Red': African-American Communists and the Politics of Culture, 1919–1934," 35–54, in Robin D. G. Kelley and Sidney Lemelle, ed., Imagining Home: Class, Culture and Nationalism in the African Diaspora *(New York: Verso; 1994); Mark Naison,* Communists in Harlem during the Depression *(Urbana: University of Illinois Press, 1983); and Philip Foner,* American Socialism and Black Americans: From the Age of Jackson to World War II *(Westport, Conn.: Greenwood Press, 1977). For additional information on Harrison, see Hubert Henry Harrison,* When Africa Awakes *(Baltimore: Black Classic Press, 1920, 1997), and Harrison's articles in the* New York Call *(1911) and* International Socialist Review *(1912).*

❏

It would be a difficult task to name one line of intellectual endeavor among white men in America, in which the American Negro has not taken his part. Yet it is a striking fact that the racial attitude has been dominantly conservative. Radicalism does not yet register to any noticeable extent the contributions of our race in this country. In theological criticism, religious dissent, social and political heresies such as Single Tax, Socialism, Anarchism—in most of the movements arising from the reconstruction made necessary by the great body of that new knowledge which the last two centuries gave us—the Negro in America has taken no part. And today our sociologists and economists still restrict themselves to the compilation of tables of statistics in proof of Negro progress. Our scholars are still expressing the intellectual viewpoints of the eighteenth century. The glimmer of a change is perceptible only in some of the younger men like Locke of Howard University and James C. Waters, Jr.

It is easy to account for this. Christian America created the color line; and all the great currents of critical opinion, from the eighteenth century to our time, have found the great barrier impassible and well-nigh impervious. Behind the color line one has to think perpetually of the color line, and most of those who grow up behind it can think of nothing else. Even when one essays to think of other things, that thinking is tinged with the shades of the surrounding atmosphere.

Besides, when we consider what Negro education is to-day when we remember that in certain southern counties the munificent sum of 58 cents is spent for the annual education of a Negro child; that the "great leader" of his race decries "higher education for them; that Negro boys who get as far as "college" must first surmount tremendous special obstacles—we will cease to wonder at the dearth of thinkers who are radical on other than racial matters.

Yet, it should seem that Negroes, of all Americans, would be found in the Freethought fold since they have suffered more than any other class of Americans from the dubious blessings of Christianity. It has been well said that the two great instruments for the propagation of race prejudice in America are the Associated Press and the Christian Church. This is quite true. Historically, it was the name of religion that cloaked the beginnings of slavery on the soil of America, and buttressed its continuance. The church saw to it that the religion taught to slaves should stress the servile virtues of subservience and content, and these things have bitten deeply into the souls of black folk. True, the treasured music of these darker millions preserves, here and there, the note of stifled rebellion; but this was in spite of religion—not because of it. Besides, such of their "sorrow-songs" as have this note in them were brutally banned by their masters, and driven to the purlieus of the plantation, there to be sung in secret. And all through the dark days of slavery, it was the Bible that constituted the divine sanction of this "peculiar institution." "Cursed be Canaan," "Servants obey your masters" and similar texts were the best that the slaveholders' Bible could give of consolation to the brothers in black, while, for the rest, teaching them to read was made a crime so that whatever of social dynamite there might be in certain parts of the book, might not come near their minds.

Lowell, in his "Biglow Papers," has given a caustic but correct summary of the Christian slaveholders' theology in regard to the slavery of black working-people:

> "All things wuz gin to man for's use, his sarvice an' delight
> An' don't the Greek an' Hebrew words that mean a man mean white?
> Ain't it belittlin' the good book in all its proudes' features
> To think 't wuz wrote for black an' brown an' 'lasses-colored creatures.
> Thet couldn' read it ef they would—nor ain't by lor allowed to,
> But ought to take wut we think suits their naturs, an' be proud to?
>
> .   .   .   .
>
> Where'd their soles go ter, I'd like to know, ef we should let 'em ketch
> Freeknowledgism an' Fourierism an' Speritoolism an' sech?"

When the fight for the abolition of slavery was on, the Christian Church, not content with quoting scripture, gagged the mouths of

166

such of their adherents as dared to protest against the accursed thing, penalized their open advocacy of abolition, and opposed all the men like Garrison, Lovejoy, Phillips and John Brown, who fought on behalf of the Negro slave. The detailed instances and proofs are given in the last chapter of "A Short History of the Inquisition," wherein the work shows the relation of the church and slavery.

Yet the church among the Negroes today exerts a more powerful influence than anything else in the sphere of ideas. Nietzsche's contention that the ethics of Christianity are the slave's ethics would seem to be justified in this instance. Show me a population that is deeply religious, and I will show you a servile population, content with whips and chains, contumely and the gibbet, content to eat the bread of sorrow and drink the waters of affliction.

The present condition of the Negroes of America is a touching bit of testimony to the truth of this assertion. Here in America the spirit of the Negro has been transformed by three centuries of subjection, physical and mental, so that they have even glorified the fact of subjection and subservience. How many Negro speakers have I not heard vaunting the fact that when in the dark days of the South the Northern armies had the Southern aristocracy by the throat, there was no Negro uprising to make their masters pay for the systematic raping of Negro women and the inhuman cruelties perpetrated on Negro men. And yet the sole reason for this "forbearance" is to be found in the fact that their spirits had been completely crushed by the system of slavery. And to accomplish this, Christianity—the Christianity of their masters—was the most effective instrument.

A recent writer, Mr. E. B. Putnam-Weale, in his book, "The Conflict of Color," has quite naively disclosed the fact that white people are well aware of this aspect of Christianity and use it for their own ends. Mr. Putnam-Weale makes no pretense of believing in the Christian myth himself, but he wants it taught to the Negroes; and comparing it with Islam, he finds it a more efficient instrument of racial subjugation. The Mohammedan, he finds, preaches the equality of all true believers—and lives up to it. The white Christian preaches the brotherhood of man, but wants "niggers" to sit in the rear pews, to ride in "Jim Crow" cars, and generally to "keep in their place." He presents this aspect of the case under the caption of "The Black Samson and the White Delilah," and, with less fear than an angel, frankly advises the white-Lords of Empire not so much to civilize as to christianize Africa, so that Delilah's work may be well done.

Here in America her work has been well done; and I fear that many years must pass before the leaders of thought among my people in this country contribute many representatives to the cause of Freethought. Just now, there are a few Negro Agnostics in New York and Boston, but these are generally found to be West Indians from the French, Spanish, and English islands. The Cuban and Porto Rican cigar-makers are notorious Infidels, due to their acquaintance with the bigotry, ignorance and immorality of the Catholic priesthood in their native islands. Here and there one finds a Negro-American who is reputed to have Agnostic tendencies; but these are seldom, if ever, openly avowed. I can hardly find it in my heart to blame them, for I know the tremendous weight of the social proscription which it is possible to bring to bear upon those who dare defy the idols of our tribe. For those who live by the people must needs be careful of the people's gods; and

> "An up-to-date statesmen has to be on his guard,
> If he must have beliefs not to b'lieve 'em too hard."

Myself, I am inclined to believe that freedom of thought must come from freedom of circumstance; and so long as our "leaders" are dependent on the favor of our masses for their livelihood, just so long will they express the thought of the masses, which of itself may be a good thing or a bad according to the circumstances of the particular case. Still there is a terrible truth in Kipling's modern version of Job's sarcastic bit of criticism:

"No doubt but ye are the people—your throne is above the King's,
Whoso speaks in your presence must say acceptable things;
Bowing the head in worship, bending the knee in fear—
Bringing the word well-smoothen—such as a King should hear."

And until this rising generation of Negroes can shake off the trammels of such time-serving leaders as Mr. Washington, and attain the level of that "higher education" against which he solidly sets his face; until they, too, shall have entered into the intellectual heritage of the last two hundred years, there can be little hope of a change in this respect.

11

RELIGION, FROM *DUST TRACKS ON A ROAD*

Zora Neale Hurston

❑

Zora Neale Hurston (1891–1960) was born in Eatonville, Florida. After having been educated at Howard University, Barnard College, and Columbia University (with Franz Boas), Hurston combined her talent for writing with her interest in African American folk life. What resulted was pioneering work in the anthropological discussion of African American life. During the Harlem Renaissance (1919–1940), in works such as Mules and Men *(Philadelphia: J. B. Lippincott 1935), Hurston explored the religious and larger cultural world of African Americans through observation but also through personal involvement. Often inadequately appreciated by her contemporaries, Hurston's work has made an invaluable contribution to scholarship related to African Americans in particular and the cultural complex of the United States in general.*

Although Hurston's work gives a great deal of attention to the religiosity of African Americans, and often entailed personal involvement, there is reason to believe that her personal perspective was agnostic in nature. This being the case, her belief structure is in line with basic humanistic assumptions. The following piece provides the reader with a sense of Hurston's agnosticism, and her appeal to human accountability and responsibility for human life.

Additional writings by Hurston include Their Eyes Were Watching God *(New York: Negro Universities Press 1937);* Moses, Man of the Mountain *(Philadelphia: J. B. Lippincott, 1939); and* The Sanctified Church, *edited by Toni Cade Bambara (Berkeley: Turtle Island Foundation, 1981). Other sources related to the life and work of Hurston include Robert Hemenway,* Zora Neale Hurston *(Urbana: University of Illinois Press, 1977); Lillie P. Howard,* Zora Neale Hurston *(Boston: Twayne Publishers, 1980); and Henry L. Gates, Jr., and Anthony Appiah ed.,* Zora Neale Hurston: Critical Perspectives Past and Present *(New York: Amistad, 1993).*

❏

You wouldn't think that a person who was born with God in the house would ever have any questions to ask on the subject.

But as early as I can remember, I was questing and seeking. It was not that I did not hear. I tumbled right into the Missionary Baptist Church when I was born. I saw the preachers and the pulpits, the people and the pews. Both at home and from the pulpit, I heard my father, known to thousands as "Reverend Jno" (an abbreviation for John) explain all about God's habits, His heaven, His ways and means. Everything was known and settled.

From the pews I heard a ready acceptance of all that Papa said. Feet beneath the pews beat out a rhythm as he pictured the scenery of heaven. Heads nodded with conviction in time to Papa's words. Tense snatches of tune broke out and some shouted until they fell into a trance at the recognition of what they heard from the pulpit. Come "love feast"* some of the congregation told of getting close enough to peep into God's sitting-room windows. Some went further. They had been inside the place and looked all around. They spoke of sights and scenes around God's throne.

That should have been enough for me. But somehow it left a lack in my mind. They should have looked and acted differently from other people after experiences like that. But these people looked and acted like everybody else—or so it seemed to me. They plowed, chopped wood, went possum hunting, washed clothes, raked up back yards, and cooked collard greens like anybody else. No more ornaments and nothing. It mystified me. There were so many things they neglected to look after while they were right there in the presence of All-Power. I made up my mind to do better than that if ever I made the trip.

I wanted to know, for instance, why didn't God make grown babies instead of those little measly things that messed up didies and cried all the time? What was the sense in making babies with no teeth? He knew that they had to have teeth, didn't He? So why not give babies their teeth in the beginning instead of hiding the toothless things in hollow stumps and logs for grannies and doctors to find and give to people? He could see all the trouble people had with babies, rubbing their gums and putting wood-ice around their necks to get them to cut teeth. Why did God hate for children to play on Sundays? If Christ, God's son, hated to die, and God hated for Him to die and have everybody grieving over it ever since, why did He have to do it? Why did people die anyway?

It was explained to me that Christ died to save the world from sin and then, too, so that folks did not have to die any more. That was a

*The "Love Feast" or "Experience Meeting" is a meeting held either the Friday night or the Sunday morning before Communion. Since no one is supposed to take Communion unless he or she is in harmony with all other members, there are great protestations of love and friendship. It is an opportunity to reaffirm faith plus anything the imagination might dictate.

simple, clear-cut explanation. But then I heard my father and other preachers accusing people of sin. They went so far as to say that people were so prone to sin, that they sinned with every breath they drew. You couldn't even breathe without sinning! How could that happen if we had already been saved from it? So far as the dying part was concerned, I saw enough funerals to know that somebody was dying. It seemed to me that somebody had been fooled and I so stated to my father and two of his colleagues. When they got through with me, I knew better than to say that out loud again, but their shocked and angry tirades did nothing for my bewilderment. My head was full of misty fumes of doubt.

Neither could I understand the passionate declarations of love for a being that nobody could see. Your family, your puppy and the new bull-calf, yes. But a spirit away off who found fault with everybody all the time, that was more than I could fathom. When I was asked if I loved God, I always said yes because I knew that that was the thing I was supposed to say. It was a guilty secret with me for a long time. I did not dare ask even my chums if they meant it when they said they loved God with all their souls and minds and hearts, and would be glad to die if He wanted them to. Maybe they had found out how to do it, and I was afraid of what they might say if they found out I hadn't. Maybe they wouldn't even play with me any more.

As I grew, the questions went to sleep in me. I just said the words, made the motions and went on. My father being a preacher, and my mother superintendent of the Sunday School, I naturally was always having to do with religious ceremonies. I even enjoyed participation at times; I was moved, not by the spirit, but by action, more or less dramatic.

I liked revival meetings particularly. During these meetings the preacher let himself go. God was called by all of His praise-giving names. The scenery of heaven was described in detail. Hallelujah Avenue and Amen Street were paved with gold so fine that you couldn't drop a pea on them but what they rang like chimes. Halle-lujah Avenue ran north and south across heaven, and was tuned to sound alto and bass. Amen Street ran east and west and was tuned to "treble" and tenor. These streets crossed each other right in front of the throne and made harmony all the time. Yes, and right there on that corner was where all the loved ones who had gone on before would be waiting for those left behind.

Oh yes! They were all there in their white robes with the glittering crowns on their heads, golden girdles clasped about their waists and shoes of jeweled gold on their feet, singing the hallelujah song and waiting. And as they walked up and down the golden streets, their shoes would sing, "sol me, sol do" at every step.

Hell was described in dramatic fury. Flames of fire leaped up a thousand miles from the furnaces of Hell, and raised blisters on a sinning man's back before he hardly got started downward. Hell-hounds pursued their ever-dying souls. Everybody under the sound of the preacher's voice was warned, while yet they were on pleading terms with mercy, to take steps to be sure that they would not be a brand in that eternal burning.

Sinners lined the mourner's bench from the opening night of the revival. Before the week was over, several or all of them would be "under conviction." People, solemn of face, crept off to the woods to "praying ground" to seek religion. Every church member worked on them hard, and there was great clamor and rejoicing when any of them "come through" religion.

The pressure on the unconverted was stepped up by music and high drama. For instance I have seen my father stop preaching suddenly and walk down to the front edge of the pulpit and breathe into a whispered song. One of his most effective ones was:

Run! Run! Run to the City of Refuge, children!
Run! Oh, run! Or else you'll be consumed.

The congregation working like a Greek chorus behind him would take up the song and the mood and hold it over for a while even after he had gone back into the sermon at high altitude:

> *Are you ready-ee? Hah!*
> *For that great day, hah!*
> *When the moon shall drape her face in mourning, hah!*
> *And the sun drip down in blood, hah!*
> *When the stars, hah!*
> *Shall burst forth from their diamond sockets, hah!*
> *And the mountains shall skip like lambs, hah!*
> *Havoc will be there, my friends, hah!*
> *With her jaws wide open, hah!*
> *And the sinner-man, hah!*
> *He will run to the rocks, hah!*
> *And cry, Oh rocks! Hah!*
> *Hide me! Hah!*
> *Hide me from the face of an angry God, hah!*
> *Hide me, Ohhhhhh!*
> *But the rocks shall cry, hah!*
> *Git away! Sinner man git away, hah!*

(Tense harmonic chant seeps over the audience.)

>   *You run to de rocks,*
> CHORUS: *You can't hide*
> SOLOIST: *Oh, you run to de rocks*
> CHORUS: *Can't hide*
> SOLOIST: *Oh, run to de mountain, you can't hide*
> ALL: *Can't hide sinner, you can't hide.*
>   *Rocks cry " 'I'm burning too, hah!*
>   *In the eternal burning, hah!*
>   *Sinner man! Hah*
>   *Where will you stand? Hah!*
>   *In that great gittin'-up morning? Hah!*

The congregation would be right in there at the right moment bearing Papa up and heightening the effect of the fearsome picture a hundredfold. The more susceptible would be swept away on the tide and "come through" shouting, and the most reluctant would begin to waver. Seldom would there be anybody left at the mourners' bench when the revival meeting was over. I have seen my father "bring through" as many as seventy-five in one two-week period of revival. Then a day would be set to begin the induction into the regular congregation. The first thing was to hear their testimony or Christian experience, and thus the congregation could judge whether they had really "got religion" or whether they were faking and needed to be sent back to "lick de calf over" again.

It was exciting to hear them tell their "visions." This was known as admitting people to the church on "Christian experience." This was an exciting time.

These visions are traditional. I knew them by heart as did the rest of the congregation, but still it was exciting to see how the converts would handle them. Some of them made up new details. Some of them would forget a part and improvise clumsily or fill up the gap with shouting. The audience knew, but everybody acted as if every word of it was new.

First they told of suddenly becoming conscious that they had to die. They became conscious of their sins. They were Godly sorry. But somehow, they could not believe. They started to pray. They prayed and they prayed to have their sins forgiven and their souls converted. While they laid under conviction, the hell-hounds pursued them as they ran for salvation. They hung over Hell by one strand of hair. Outside of the meeting, any of the listeners would have laughed at the idea of anybody with hair as close to their heads as ninety-nine is to a hundred hanging over Hell or anywhere else by a strand of that hair. But it was part of the vision and the congregation shuddered and groaned at the picture in a fervent manner. The vision must go on. While the seeker hung there, flames of fire leaped up and all but destroyed their ever-dying souls. But they called on the name of Jesus and immediately that dilemma was over. They then found themselves walking over Hell on a foot-log so narrow that they had to put one foot right in front of the other while the howling hell-hounds pursued them relentlessly. Lord! They saw no way of rescue. But they looked on the other side and saw a little white man and he called to them to come there. So they called the name of Jesus and suddenly they were on the other side. He poured the oil of salvation into their souls and, hallelujah! They never expect to turn back. But still they wouldn't believe. So they asked God, if he had saved their souls, to give them a sign. If their sins were forgiven and their souls set free, please move that big star in the west over to the east. The star moved over. But still they wouldn't believe. If they were really saved, please move that big oak tree across the road. The tree skipped across the road and kept on growing just like it had always been there. Still they didn't believe. So they asked God for one more sign. Would He please make the sun shout so they could be sure. At that God got mad and said He had shown them all the signs He intended to. If they still didn't believe, He would send their bodies to the grave, where the worm never dies, and their souls to Hell, where the fire is never quenched. So then they cried out "I believe! I believe!" Then the dungeon shook and their chains fell off. "Glory! I know I got religion! I know I been converted and my soul set free! I never will forget that day when the morning star bust in my soul. I never expect to turn back!"

The convert shouted. Ecstatic cries, snatches of chants, old converts shouting in frenzy with the new. When the tumult finally died down, the pastor asks if the candidate is acceptable and there is unanimous consent. He or she is given the right hand of fellowship, and the next candidate takes the floor. And so on to the end.

I know now that I liked that part because it was high drama. I liked the baptisms in the lake, too, and the funerals for the same reason. But of the inner thing, I was right where I was when I first began to seek answers.

Away from the church after the emotional fire had died down, there were little jokes about some of the testimony. For instance a deacon said in my hearing, "Sister Seeny ought to know better than to be worrying God about moving the sun for her. She asked Him to move de tree to convince her, and He done it. Then she took and asked Him to move a star for her and He done it. But when she kept on worrying Him about the sun, He took and told her, says, 'I don't mind moving that tree for you, and I don't mind moving a star just to pacify your mind, because I got plenty of *them*. I ain't got but one sun, Seeny, and I aint going to be shoving it around to please you and nobody else. I'd like mighty much for you to believe, but if you can't believe without me moving my sun for you, you can just go right on to Hell.' "

The thing slept on in me until my college years without any real decision. I made the necessary motions and forgot to think. But when I studied both history and philosophy, the struggle began again.

When I studied the history of the great religions of the world, I saw that even in his religion man carried himself along. His worship of strength was there. God was made to look that way, too. We see the Emperor Constantine, as pagan as he could lay in his hide, having his famous vision of the cross with the injunction: *"In Hoc Signo Vinces,"* and arising next day not only to win a great battle, but to start out on his missionary journey with his sword. He could not sing like Peter, and he could not preach like Paul. He probably did not even have a good straining voice like my father to win converts and influence people. But he had his good points—one of them being a sword —and a seasoned army. And the way he brought sinners to repentance was nothing short of miraculous. Whole tribes and nations fell under conviction just as soon as they heard he was on the way. They did not wait for any stars to move, nor trees to jump the road. By the time he crossed the border, they knew they had been converted. Their testimony was in on Christian experience and they were all ready for the right hand of fellowship and baptism. It seems that Reverend Brother

Emperor Constantine carried the gospel up and down Europe with his revival meetings to such an extent that Christianity really took on. In Rome where Christians had been looked upon as rather indifferent lion-bait at best, and among other things as keepers of virgins in their homes for no real good to the virgins, Christianity mounted. Where before, emperors could scarcely find enough of them to keep the spectacles going, now they were everywhere, in places high and low. The arrow had left the bow. Christianity was on its way to world power that would last. That was only the beginning. Military power was to be called in time and time again to carry forward the gospel of peace. There is not apt to be any difference of opinion between you and a dead man.

It was obvious that two men, both outsiders, had given my religion its chances of success. First the Apostle Paul, who had been Saul, the erudite Pharisee, had arisen with a vision when he fell off of his horse on the way to Damascus. He not only formulated the religion, but exerted his brilliant mind to carry it to the most civilized nations of his time. Then Constantine took up with force where Paul left off with persuasion.

I saw the same thing with different details, happen in all the other great religions, and seeing these things, I went to thinking and questing again. I have achieved a certain peace within myself, but perhaps the seeking after the inner heart of truth will never cease in me. All sorts of interesting speculations arise.

So, having looked at the subject from many sides studied beliefs by word of mouth and then as they fit into great rigid forms, I find I know a great deal about form, but little or nothing about the mysteries I sought as a child. As the ancient tent-maker said, I have come out of the same door wherein I went.

But certain things have seemed to me to be true as I heard the tongues of those who had speech, and listened at the lips of books. It seems to me to be true that heavens are placed in the sky because it is the unreachable. The unreachable and therefore the unknowable always seems divine—hence, religion. People need religion because the great masses fear life and its consequences. Its responsibilities weigh heavy. Feeling a weakness in the face of great forces, men seek an alliance with omnipotence to bolster up their feeling of weakness, even though the omnipotence they rely upon is a creature of their own minds. It gives them a feeling of security. Strong, self-determining men are notorious for their lack of reverence. Constantine, having converted millions to Christianity by the sword, himself refused the consolation of Christ until his last hour. Some say not even then.

As for me, I do not pretend to read God's mind. If He has a plan of the universe worked out to the smallest detail, it would be folly for me to presume to get down on my knees and attempt to revise it. That, to me, seems the highest form of sacrilege. So I do not pray. I accept the means at my disposal for working out my destiny. It seems to me that I have been given a mind and will-power for that very purpose. I do not expect God to single me out and grant me advantages over my fellow men. Prayer is for those who need it. Prayer seems to me a cry of weakness, and an attempt to avoid, by trickery, the rules of the game as laid down. I do not choose to admit weakness. I accept the challenge of responsibility. Life, as it is, does not frighten me, since I have made my peace with the universe as I find it, and bow to its laws. The ever-sleepless sea in its bed, crying out "How long?" to Time; million-formed and never motionless flame; the contemplation of these two aspects alone, affords me sufficient food for ten spans of my expected lifetime. It seems to me that organized creeds are collections of words around a wish. I feel no need for such. However, I would not, by word or deed, attempt to deprive another of the consolation it affords. It is simply not for me. Somebody else may have my rapturous glance at the archangels. The springing of the yellow line of morning out of the misty deep of dawn, is glory enough for me. I know that nothing is destructible; things merely change forms. When the consciousness we know as life ceases, I know that I shall still be part and parcel of the world. I was a part before the sun rolled into shape and burst forth in the glory of change. I was, when the earth was hurled out from its fiery rim. I shall return with the earth to Father Sun, and still exist in substance when the sun has lost its fire, and disintegrated in infinity to perhaps become a part of the whirling rubble in space. Why fear? The stuff of my being is matter, ever changing, ever moving, but never lost; so what need of denominations and creeds to deny myself the comfort of all my fellow men? The wide belt of the universe has no need for finger-rings. I am one with the infinite and need no other assurance.

12

BLACK BOY

A Record of Childhood and Youth

Richard Wright

❑

Richard Wright (1908–1960) was born in the segregated South—Missis-sippi. Drawing from this background, most of his writings address the effects of racism upon the African American's psyche and physical actions. Guided by what some have referred to as a sense of realism, Wright provides a powerful analysis of the socioeconomic, political, and cultural consequences of life in both the northern and southern states. At certain points in his life, Wright drew on the Communist Party and existential thought (for example, The Outsider *{New York: Harper, 1953}) as a way of addressing his existential concerns. Books such as* Native Son *(New York: Harper Brothers, 1940) won him acclaim as a major literary voice.*

What is clear throughout all of his work is the manner in which literacy provides a means of "liberation." In addressing this point, Wright's depiction of Christianity's effect on African Americans is harsh and his personal rejection of the church clear. Wright's autobiographical text, Black Boy, *highlights his early move away from organized religions and his understanding of reading and writing as powerful tools for growth and development.*

Wright's grandmother, in particular, was concerned with his spiritual condition, and she did her best to bring him into the church. When her efforts failed, she attempted to bring him into a state of salvation through his friends. The following excerpt from Black Boy *presents Wright's conversation with a young friend. It is clear that Wright's position is in keeping with primary concerns of humanism—denouncement of supernaturalism and a central concern with humanity and human activity.*

Readers interested in additional work by and about Richard Wright might find the following sources useful. In addition to Wright's work noted above, see Richard Wright, Uncle Tom's Children *(New York: Harper & Brothers, 1938); and* American Hunger *(New York: Harper & Row 1977). Other writings by Wright include* 12 Million Black Voices: A Folk History of the Negro in the United States *(New York: Viking Press, 1941), and* White Man, Listen! *(Garden City, N.J.: Anchor Books, 1964). For biographical information on Wright, see Michel Fabre,* The Unfinished Quest of Richard Wright *(New York: Morrow, 1973). For critical essays on Wright, see Harold Bloom ed.,* Richard Wright: Modern Critical Views *(New York: Chelsea House, 1987); Ralph Ellison, "Richard Wright's Blues" from* Shadow and Act *(New York: Random Horse, 1964). As an additional note, readers can find a "milder" version of this humanism in others of this period, such as Margaret Walker (1915–). See, for example, Charles Rowell, "An Interview with Margaret Walker,"* Black World *25, no. 2 (1975).*

❏

Granny was an ardent member of the Seventh-Day Adventist Church and I was compelled to make a pre-tense of worshiping her God, which was her exaction for my keep. The elders of her church expounded a gospel clogged with images of vast lakes of eternal fire, of seas vanishing, of valleys of dry bones, of the sun burning to ashes, of the moon turning to blood, of stars falling to the earth, of a wooden staff being transformed into a serpent, of voices speaking out of clouds, of men walking upon water, of God riding whirlwinds, of water changing into wine, of the dead rising and living, of the blind seeing, of the lame walking; a salvation that teemed with fantastic beasts having multiple heads and horns and eyes and feet; sermons of statues possessing heads of gold, shoulders of silver, legs of brass, and feet of clay; a cosmic tale that began before time and ended with the clouds of the sky rolling away at the Second Coming of Christ; chronicles that concluded with the Armageddon; dramas thronged with all the billions of human beings who had ever lived or died as God judged the quick and the dead. . . .

While listening to the vivid language of the sermons I was pulled toward emotional belief, but as soon as I went out of the church and saw the bright sunshine and felt the throbbing life of the people in the streets I knew that none of it was true and that nothing would happen.

Once again I knew hunger, biting hunger, hunger that made my body aimlessly restless, hunger that kept me on edge, that made my temper flare, hunger that made hate leap out of my heart like the dart of a serpent's tongue, hunger that created in me odd cravings. No food that I could dream of seemed half so utterly delicious as vanilla wafers. Every time I had a nickel I would run to the corner grocery store and buy a box of vanilla wafers and walk back home, slowly, so that I could eat them all up without having to share them with anyone. Then I would sit on the front steps and dream of eating another box; the craving would finally become so acute that I would force myself to be active in order to forget. I learned a method of drinking water that made me feel full temporarily whether I had a desire for water or not; I would put my mouth under a faucet and turn the water on full force and let the stream cascade into my stomach until it was tight. Sometimes my stomach ached, but I felt full for a moment.

No pork or veal was ever eaten at Granny's, and rarely was there meat of any kind. We seldom ate fish and then only those that had scales and spines. Baking powder was never used; it was alleged to contain a chemical harmful to the body. For breakfast I ate mush and gravy made from flour and lard and for hours afterwards I would belch it up into my mouth. We were constantly taking bicarbonate of soda for indigestion. At four o'clock in the afternoon I ate a plate of greens cooked with lard. Sometimes on Sundays we bought a dime's worth of beef which usually turned out to be uneatable. Granny's favorite dish was a peanut roast which she made to resemble meat, but which tasted like something else.

My position in the household was a delicate one; I was a minor, an uninvited dependent, a blood relative who professed no salvation and whose soul stood in mortal peril. Granny intimated boldly, basing her logic on God's justice, that one sinful person in a household could bring down the wrath of God upon the entire establishment, damning both the innocent and the guilty, and on more than one occasion she interpreted my mother's long illness as the result of my faithlessness. I became skilled in ignoring these cosmic threats and developed a callousness toward all metaphysical preachments. . . .

In the home Granny maintained a hard religious regime. There were prayers at sunup and sundown, at the breakfast table and dinner table, followed by a Bible verse from each member of the family. And it was presumed that I prayed before I got into bed at night. I shirked as many of the weekday church services as possible, giving as my excuse that I had to study; of course, nobody believed me, but my lies were accepted because nobody wanted to risk a row. The daily prayers were a torment and my knees became sore from kneeling so long and often. Finally I devised a method of kneeling that was not really kneeling; I learned, through arduous repetition, how to balance myself on the toes of my shoes and rest my head against a wall in some convenient corner. Nobody, except God, was any the wiser, and I did not think that He cared.

Granny made it imperative, however, that I attend certain all-night ritualistic prayer meetings. She was the oldest member of her church and it would have been unseemly if the only grandchild in her home could not be brought to these important services; she felt that if I were completely remiss in religious conformity it would cast doubt upon the stanchness of her faith, her capacity to convince and persuade, or merely upon her ability to apply the rod to my backside.

Granny would prepare a lunch for the all-night praying session, and the three of us—Granny, Aunt Addie, and I—would be off, leaving my mother and Grandpa at home. During the passionate prayers and the chanted hymns I would sit squirming on a bench, longing to grow up so I could run away, listening indifferently to the theme of cosmic annihilation, loving the hymns for their sensual caress, but at last casting furtive glances at Granny and wondering when it would be safe for me to stretch out on the bench and go to sleep. At ten or eleven I would munch a sandwich and Granny would nod her permission for me to take a nap. I would awaken at intervals to hear snatches of hymns or prayers that would lull me to sleep again. Finally Granny would shake me and I would open my eyes and see the sun streaming through stained-glass windows.

Many of the religious symbols appealed to my sensibilities and I responded to the dramatic vision of life held by the church, feeling that to live day by day with death as one's sole thought was to be so compassionately sensitive toward all life as to view all men as slowly dying, and the trembling sense of fate that welled up, sweet and melancholy, from the hymns blended with the sense of fate that I had already caught from life. But full emotional and intellectual belief never came. Perhaps if I had caught my first sense of life from the church I would have been moved to complete acceptance, but the hymns and sermons of God came into my heart only long after my personality had been shaped and formed by unchartered conditions of life. I felt that I had in me a sense of living as deep as that which the church was trying to give me, and in the end I remained basically unaffected.

My body grew, even on mush and lard gravy, a miracle which the church certainly should have claimed credit for. I survived my twelfth year on a diet that would have stunted an average-sized dog, and my glands began to diffuse through my blood, like sap rising upward in trees in spring, those strange chemicals that made me look curiously at girls and women. The elder's wife sang in the choir and I fell in love with her as only a twelve-year-old can worship a distant and unattainable woman. During the services I would stare at her, wondering what it was like to be married to her, pondering over how passionate she was. I felt no qualms about my first lust for the flesh being born on holy ground; the contrast between budding carnal desires and the aching loneliness of the hymns never evoked any sense of guilt in me.

It was possible that the sweetly sonorous hymns stimulated me sexually, and it might have been that my fleshy fantasies, in turn, having as their foundation my already inflated sensibility, made me love the masochistic prayers. It was highly likely that the serpent of sin that nosed about the chambers of my heart was lashed to hunger by hymns as well as dreams, each reciprocally feeding the other. The church's spiritual life must have been polluted by my base yearning, by the leaping hunger of my blood for the flesh, because I would gaze at the elder's wife for hours, attempting to draw her eyes to mine, trying to hypnotize her, seeking to communicate with her with my thoughts. If my desires had been converted into a concrete religious symbol, the symbol would have looked something like this: a black imp with two horns; a long, curving, forked tail; cloven hoofs, a scaly, naked body; wet, sticky fingers; moist, sensual lips; and lascivious eyes feasting upon the face of the elder's wife. . . .

A religious revival was announced and Granny felt that it was her last chance to bring me to God before I entered the precincts of sin at the public school, for I had already given loud and final notice that I would no longer attend the church school. There was a discernible lessening in Aunt Addie's hostility; perhaps she had come to the conclusion that my lost soul was more valuable than petty pride. Even my mother's attitude was: "Richard, you ought to know God through *some* church."

The entire family became kind and forgiving, but I knew the motives that prompted their change and it drove me an even greater emotional distance from them. Some of my classmates—who had, on the advice of their parents, avoided me—now came to visit and I could tell in a split second that they had been instructed in what to say. One boy, who lived across the street, called on me one afternoon and his self-consciousness betrayed him; he spoke so naïvely and clumsily that I could see the bare bones of his holy plot and hear the creaking of the machinery of Granny's maneuvering.

"Richard, do you know we are all worried about you?" he asked.

"Worried about me? Who's worried about me?" I asked in feigned surprise.

"All of us," he said, his eyes avoiding mine.

"Why?" I asked.

"You're not saved," he said sadly.

"I'm all right," I said, laughing.

"Don't laugh, Richard. It's serious," he said.

"But I tell you that I'm all right."

"Say, Richard, I'd like to be a good friend of yours."

"I thought we were friends already," I said.

"I mean true brothers in Christ," he said.

"We know each other," I said in a soft voice tinged with irony.

"But not in Christ," he said.

"Friendship is friendship with me."

"But don't you want to save your soul?"

"I simply can't feel religion," I told him in lieu of telling him that I did not think I had the kind of soul he thought I had.

"Have you really tried to feel God?" he asked.

"No. But I know I can't feel anything like that."

"You simply can't let the question rest there, Richard."

"Why should I let it rest?"

"Don't mock God," he said.

"I'll never feel God, I tell you. It's no use."

"Would you let the fate of your soul hang upon pride and vanity?"

"I don't think I have any pride in matters like this."

"Richard, think of Christ's dying for you, shedding His blood, His precious blood on the cross."

"Other people have shed blood," I ventured.

"But it's not the same. You don't understand."

"I don't think I ever will."

"Oh, Richard, brother, you are lost in the darkness of the world. You must let the church help you."

"I tell you, I'm all right."

"Come into the house and let me pray for you."

"I don't want to hurt your feelings . . ."

"You can't. I'm talking for God."

"I don't want to hurt God's feelings either," I said, the words slipping irreverently from my lips before I was aware of their full meaning.

He was shocked. He wiped tears from his eyes. I was sorry.

"Don't say that. God may never forgive you," he whispered.

It would have been impossible for me to have told him how I felt about religion. I had not settled in my mind whether I believed in God or not; His existence or nonexistence never worried me. I reasoned that if there did exist an all-wise, all-powerful God who knew the beginning and the end, who meted out justice to all, who controlled the destiny of man, this God would surely know that I doubted His existence and He would laugh at my foolish denial of Him. And if there was no God at all, then why all the commotion? I could not imagine God pausing in His guidance of unimaginably vast worlds to bother with me.

Embedded in me was a notion of the suffering in life, but none of it seemed like the consequences of original sin to me; I simply could not feel weak and lost in a cosmic manner. Before I had been made to go to church, I had given God's existence a sort of tacit assent, but after having seen His creatures serve Him at first hand, I had had my doubts. My faith, such as it was, was welded to the common realities of life, anchored in the sensations of my body and in what my mind could grasp, and nothing could ever shake this faith, and surely not my fear of an invisible power.

"I'm not afraid of things like that," I told the boy.

"Aren't you afraid of God?" he asked.

"No. Why should I be? I've done nothing to Him."

"He's a jealous God," he warned me.

"I hope that He's a kind God," I told him.

"If *you* are kind to Him, He is a kind God," the boy said. "But God will not look at you if you don't look at Him."

During our talk I made a hypothetical statement that summed up my attitude toward God and the suffering in the world, a statement that stemmed from my knowledge of life as I had lived, seen, felt, and suffered it in terms of dread, fear, hunger, terror; and loneliness.

"If laying down my life could stop the suffering in the world, I'd do it. But I don't believe anything can stop it," I told him.

He heard me but he did not speak. I wanted to say more to him, but I knew that it would have been useless. Though older than I, he had neither known nor felt anything of life for himself; he had been carefully reared by his mother and father and he had always been told what to feel.

13

ON BEING NEGRO IN AMERICA

J. Saunders Redding

❑

J. Saunders Redding (1906–1988) was born in Wilmington, Delaware. Redding completed his education at Brown University (M.A. and Ph.D.) and also studied at Columbia University. He taught at several institutions, including Southern University, prior to writing such groundbreaking works as To Make a Poet Black *(Chapel Hill: University of North Carolina, 1939) and* No Day of Triumph *(New York: Harper and Brothers, 1942). These texts marked Redding as a scholar whose insights were sharp and profound. In 1943, he returned to the academy and held posts at institutions including Hampton University and Cornell University.*

In the following excerpt, the reader gains a sense of the religiophilosophical framework undergirding Redding's work. The bibliography contained in A Scholar's Conscience, *an edited volume, provides important information concerning works by Redding. Interested readers may find it useful to examine the following piece of fiction written by Redding:* Stranger and Alone *(Boston: Northeastern University Press, 1969, 1989). These nonfiction books might also be of interest:* They Came in Chains: Americans from Africa *(Phila-*

delphia: Lippincott, 1950); The Lonesome Road: The Story of the Negro's Part in America *(New York: Doubleday, 1958); and* The Negro *(Washington, D.C.: Potomac Books, 1967).*

❏

Although I am not a very religious person, I do not see how I can leave God out of consideration in these matters. God has been made to play a very conspicuous part in race relations in America. At one time or another, and often at the same time, He has been the protagonist for both sides. He has damned and blessed first one side and then the other with truly godlike impartiality. His ultimate intentions, revealed to inspired sages, are preserved in a thousand volumes. Anyone who reads the literature of race cannot but be struck by the immoderate frequency with which God is invoked, and by the painstaking consideration that is given, even by social scientists, to race relations as a problem of Christian ethics.

God, of course, is an implicit assumption in the thought of our age. He is one of those beliefs so spontaneous and ineluctable and taken so much as a matter of course that they operate with great effectiveness (though generally on a level of subconsciousness) in our society. He is a belief that operates just by being, like a boulder met in the path which must be dealt with before one can proceed on his journey. God is a complex composed entirely of simple elements—mediator, father, judge, jury, executioner, and also love, virtue, charity—each of which generates a very motley collection of often contradictory ideas. God is a catalyst, and He is also a formulated doctrine inertly symbolized in the ritual and the dogma of churches called Christian. God is the Absolute Reality, but this does not prevent His being ostentatiously offered as the excuse for our society's failure to come to grips with big but relative realities. God and the Christian religion must be reckoned with.

I do not know how long I have held both God and the Christian religion in some doubt, though it must have been since my teens. Nor do I know exactly how this came about. . . .

Sometime during my teens I became aware that for most Negroes God was a great deal more than a spirit to be worshiped on Sundays. He had a terrifying immediacy as material provider and protector. Once a group of us teen-agers went on a Sunday evening (our own church worshiped only in the morning) to a mission church deep in the Bridge District where the Negro population was concentrated. We went to mock, as some of us had heard our parents do, at the malapropisms of the illiterate minister and his ignorant flock, the crazy singing and shouting, and the uninhibited behavior of members in religious ecstasy. We did not remain to pray, but I was struck by what I saw and heard, and afterward my natural curiosity led me to go occasionally alone. The service did not resemble, either in ritual or content (both of which were created spontaneously), the service to which I was used. Any member of the church could stand up and pray. A whole evening might be given over to these impulsive outbursts. The prayers impressed me with their concreteness, their concern for the everyday.

Negroes made irrational claims on God which they expected Him to fulfill without any help from them and without any regard for the conditions under which they could be fulfilled, and I suppose that when their claims failed, there was some sort of psychological mechanism that produced satisfactory excuses. It was all very simple and direct, but God just did not work that way—not the white folk's God I was taught to worship. . . .

I do not know when I began to notice the white people. I suppose they had always been there. But along in my fourteenth or fifteenth year, I suddenly seemed to see them. Small phalanxes of them always seemed to be pushing or imperiously demanding passage through the crowds that fell away before them like grain before a scythe. The white people sneered—or so it seemed to me—and took pictures and made derisive comments. They looked down in laughing contempt from the windows, balconies and roofs of the buildings that lined the street. They came, also from miles around, to watch the show, not to be a part of it. I realized with deep shame that what the Negroes did on this holy day made a clowns' circus for the whites. The Negroes' God made fools of them. Worship and religiosity were things to be mocked and scorned, for they stamped the Negro as inferior.

There must have been many vague progressions of thought and many gradations of emotion between the premise and the conclusion. However little I was aware of them, my nerves, muscles and brain—conditioned by a thousand random and forgotten experiences—must have prepared me to accept the conclusion without outrage and shock. I simply rejected religion. I rejected God. Not my instincts, but my deepest feelings revolted compulsively—not because I was I, a sort of neutral human stuff reacting directly to experience, but because I was Negro. It is hard to make it clear; but there were two people sharing my physical existence and tearing me apart. One, I suppose, was the actual self which I wanted to protect and yet which I seemed to hate with a consuming hatred; and the other was the ideal self which tried compulsively to shape the actual self away from all that Negroes seemed to be. At what emotional and psychic cost this deep emotional conflict went on within me I do not know. It was years before I understood that what I had wanted then was to be white.

It was also years before I made a sort of armed truce with religion and with God. I stepped around God determinedly, gingerly, gloating that I was free of Him and that He could not touch me. Indeed, I had to step around Him, for He was always there. . . .

I moved around Him warily, laughing, mocking His pretensions, determined that He would not betray me into Negroness. If there lingered still in the deep recesses of my real self some consciousness of a religious spirit, then the ideal self—the Negro-hating me—did all it could to exorcise it.

How unmitigating and long-lasting this conflict was is proved for me in the fact that only in the last ten years have I been able to go to church without a feeling of indulging in some senseless necromantic ritual, and without feeling that my wanting to go—and I did many times *want* to go; if this seems contradictory, I cannot help it—was a mark of inferiority, the foolish expression of a weak and senseless wish to attain an impossible realm of being differing in its essential nature— that is, in its reality—from anything my experience has taught me can be attained. I do not believe in an afterlife; in otherworldliness. The experiences of this world are too potent and too much with me. I do not see how any Negro can believe in another world, and the religion which has inspired him to that belief, if it has saved him, has done so by making him content with the very degradation of his humanity that is so abhorrent to the principles of Christianity.

But it is not alone for the reasons outlined above that I have held religion suspect. Let us concede that the God of the Negroes has been largely a pagan god and largely stripped of the divinest attributes, interceding intimately and directly for man without man's help. They have fashioned a god to their need. But the whites also have fashioned a god to their need, and have believed in him, and have professed to follow him. He is a moral God, a God of truth and justice and love. I do not wish to carry this too far, for I have no capacity for philosophic speculation; but it seems to me that if the qualities attributed to God represent man's acknowledged needs, and if the principles of Christianity represent the universal source of man's social genius, then he has sacrificed the fulfillment of his basic needs (or "the good life") to the fulfillment of desires that run counter to the purpose of living. He has not given his religion a chance to help him effect that far-going social transformation and evolution which should be religion's end. Religion has become a disembodied sort of activity, when, to be effective, it should be a social function intimately linked up with man's fate on earth.

While there is almost no religion operating in race relations, there is plenty of God. I do not say this facetiously, nor with ironic intent;

and, anyway, it has at least been implied before. There is an extensive literature on the part God has played in race relations since the fifteenth century. Principally God and the word of God have been used to perpetuate the wicked idea of human inferiority. I need not go into this farther than to point out modern man's subtle modifications of the idea of God and the intellectual gymnastics that have made those modifications possible, even when, it seems to me, the environment has not made them necessary, and even though in the fundamental concept of the Godhead is the idea of immutability. But God has changed, and though man himself has wrought these changes, he has declared them God's own changes and therefore factors, equations, and of a piece with the mysterious and unknowable nature of God. Indeed, God's very supernaturalness, His mysteriousness and inscrutability ("God moves in mysterious ways His wonders to perform," *ergo* "we cannot know God's purpose in making the black race inferior to the white," and we cannot "fathom the repulsion which God has given one race for another, or one people for another") are largely modern attributions which confound the ancient knowledge and excuse modern sin. God was not always so.

And before the ancient concepts crashed under the onslaught of sophistication, of scientific materialism and the new philosophies it brought into being, Christianity had become a way of life. It had become a way of life to be striven for because it seemed to satisfy the needs of ordinary men. There is nothing mysterious about Christianity. Granted that mystery reposes in the life of Christ (as, let it be said, it did not originally repose in God)—but Christ's life and what he is reported to have done are one thing: what he is reported to have taught is another. What he taught is as clear and concrete and literal as the lead story in a good newspaper.

He was, for all the mystery surrounding him, a social engineer with a far and cosmic vision. The present age has not denied that he was right. Though there are those (and I among them) who reject the traditionally perpetuated events of his life as a factual record, his ministry remains the source of Christian religion. What has happened is that the age, while acknowledging Christianity as the highest way of life that man has thus far conceived, has denied the authority of God to make man live up to Christ's teachings. The dream of God and the reality of Christ have become separated. . . .

Theology quite aside, it seems to me that the bearing which the Christian religion should have on human relations throughout the world and on race relations in the Western world is simple enough and direct enough. . . .

It offers a mature approach to experience. Modern man's incredible good luck in escaping the direst consequences of conduct unlighted by luminous beliefs and uncontrolled by moral principles is fast running out. A third world war may destroy man altogether—if, that is, he does not destroy himself in more subtle and tortuous ways without war. It would be foolish optimism not to assume the possibility of this.

It is not the nobility of Christ's life that I would urge; it is the practicality of his injunctions. It is more a matter of being sensible than of being "good."

14

EXPERIENCES OF A CHIMNEY SWEEPER

Lyle Saxon, Editor

❏

Socioeconomic and political upheaval experienced during the 1910s and 1920s caused a rethinking of the relationship between African American religious organizations and social problems. For many Black churches, the increasing needs of African Americans—in both the North and the South—became a burden they were either unable or unwilling to shoulder. This change in outlook was often accompanied by a theological shift that placed emphasis on "other-worldly" rewards for difficulties encountered on earth. Scholars have documented that this change in activity and its accompanying theological rationale provided an impetus for a movement of African Americans into "extra-church," to use Charles Long's terminology, forms of orientation.[1] These new movements that developed during the 1920s and 1930s include the Moorish Science Temple and the Nation of Islam. Besides these possibilities, many African Americans rejected theistic orientations altogether, and placed their confidence in themselves and the importance of making gains in this world. Underlying the perspective of this group is an embrace of humanistic sensibilities and the placement of responsibility for world events squarely on the shoulders of humans.

An example of this perspective is found in the following account of John Montgomery, Jr., a chimney sweep. Within his conversation, Montgomery highlights the importance of pleasure and enjoyment on earth, and argues that African Americans' sense of self, by and large, is hampered by churches. Rather than a healthy concern for life in this world, churches spread an unhealthy preoccupation with the "other world." Although Montgomery's personal activities do not show strict adherence to ethics and morals promoting the welfare of the larger community, he does point to a basic notion of humanism: a lack of concern with the supernatural based upon a sense of the human as the measure of all things.

Readers interested in additional folklore that points to basic principles of humanism as a nontheistic lack of concern with the supernatural and as a recognition of humanity as the shaper of its destiny might see, for example, "Brother Gregg Identifies Himself" and "Sister Sadie Washington's Littlest Boy," in J. Massive Brewer, ed., American Negro Folklore *(Chicago: Quadrangle Books, 1968), 112–114, and 114–116; "The Preacher and His Farmer Brother," in Langston Hughes and Arna Bontemps, ed.* The Book of Negro Folklore *(New York: Dodd, Mead & Company, 1958, 1965), 141. The hermeneutic of suspicion and embrace of life's "rawness" evident in the "Experiences of a Chimney Sweeper," are also found in African American musical productions that feature the blues. For information related to this, see Jon Michael Spencer,* Blues and Evil *(Nashville: University of Tennessee Press, 1993). For general information on the blues, see Paul Oliver,* Blues Fell This Morning: The Meaning of the Blues *(New York: Horizon, 1960); Robert Palmer,* Deep Blues *(New York: Penguin Books, 1982); and Alan Lomax,* The Land Where the Blues Began *(New York: Delta Books, 1993).*

NOTE

1. Charles Long, Significations: Signs, Symbols and Images in the Interpretation of Religion *(Philadelphia: Fortress Press, 1986).*

❏

John Junior began to talk. "Me, I'm a chimney sweep from way back—
a chimney sweeper havin' a holiday. My pa was a chimney sweeper.
. . . my ma was a chimney sweeper. Ask Susie." He wanted to say more
about his mother and father but Emma interrupted him to remind
him that his mother wasn't a chimney sweeper, but was a washwoman.
"Shut up," John Junior said.

"I was born in Westwego. Took after my pa and ma. She born me
in whiskey. My pa drank whiskey like the tank that bottles it. He was
a laborer in the Round House of the T. P. My ma didn't work at all.
She was a good-time woman. But when she married my pa she settled
down. She got into an argument with some people and bore me to
prove she could have a baby. I'm sho glad of it. No, my ma didn't
have to work. She had enough to do takin' care of my pa when he
got drunk."

He moved away from the post and eased himself down on the step.
"I ain't got no education. Went to the third grade. That was enough
fo' me. My pa stopped me, made me get a job on a milk truck. I was
makin' two dollars a week. What I did with my money? I had a good
time, that's what. Sho, school is all right fo' them who wants it, but I
figures all you got to know is how to read and write, then nobody can
cheat you out of nothin'. Ain't figures enough?

"I believe my pa and ma liked large families, but they tell me—
now I don't know—but they tell me my ma had such a time bringin'
me she swore she wasn't goin' bring no more. She and pa drank so
much they don't even remember how it all started, to tell the truth.
Sho, I drank, too. Pa used to make me drunk, half the time. I've
always liked whiskey and who don't like the way I do, they know
what they can do.

"I quit the milk truck, couldn't have my fun like I wanted to. Had
to get up too early. I was only ten years old then. What I didn't like

about the milk truck was I couldn't be wid that sweet little gal next door long enough. Then, I got me a job ridin' a bike. Three-fifty a week. I went to work so I could buy the clothes I wanted. My pa and ma wouldn't give me nothin'. I always did like to be dressed up. I like it now but my money ain't right. That's all a po' man can do— dress up, and have a good time."

Susie reminded John Junior that he spent three hundred dollars of his bonus on clothes for himself and his women.

But John had a defense: "Ain't we got to look fine when we walk down the street?" Susie reminded him that he pawned most of his clothes for whiskey, which encouraged John Junior to shout back: "A good bottle of whiskey is worth a suit in pawn any day. Then agin, a man as ugly as me is got to spend money on women. Ain't that right? It ain't no need fo' me to fool myself. I always did spend money on women and I'm goin' to keep on doin' it.

"Sho, I done other jobs besides workin' on a milk truck and ridin' a bike. I worked at the Round House when I was a man. Made twenty-one fifty. Used every bit of it up, that's right. Man, I used to buy mo' fun than a chicken had feathers. They used to call me lil John Junior. A chip off his daddy's block. I was a mess. Had women shakin' down and doin' the Eagle Rock wid dollar bills in their hands. Have fun, live. You don't live but once. When you die, square up the Devil. No, indeed! There never was a Christian in my family, we don't believe in that stuff. My pa used to say, "Get me a bucket full of wine I'll join the church.' Spare time? Man, I ain't had no spare time. Don't have none now. In my spare time I have my fun!

"I came to this part of town when I was about twenty. Bought so much stuff I had to go back on the other side. The policeman says: 'Boy, go back where you b'long. You is got these womens jumpin' naked.'

"Well, I tell you. There ain't nothin' wrong with being a chimney sweeper. The work might be dirty but the money is sho clean and long. Yes suh! You get bucks when you clean chimneys! SWEEPER!

ROOAP, ROOAP, SWEEPER! CHIMNEY SWEEPER! GET 'UM CLEAN 'FORE YOU SCREAM. . . . FIRE! ROOAP! ROOAP! SWEEPER! I charge some people two dollars, and some two dollars and a half, mostly two and a half. I charge by the day and by the chimney. Jews make their own prices. You can't jew them up. The only thing I don't like about cleanin' chimneys is when them womens hang around me. They sho can give orders. What they know about cleanin' chimneys won't fill a book, but they hang around you. Sometimes I feel like tellin' um, 'Don't cry around me, lady, I'm not the fireman.'

"How I started cleanin' chimneys? Let me see. Say, you wants to know everything. Well, I was friendly with a fellow named Jeff Scott. He's dead. Jeff was makin' plenty money and needed help. So, me and him made up as partners. We used to make as high as twenty dollars a day fo' both of us. Wasn't bad, eh? Them was the days. Ain't no money in it now. Everybody is usin' gas and electric lights. And then again, nobody wants to pay. Can't make but about four or five dollars a day in the season . . . that in the winter time. Some say 'Let's get a union' but not me. I don't want no union. Fo' what? Fo' a bunch of black bastards to land in jail.

"How we get our jobs? Well, most of 'em is from our customers. They send us to people. And the fire stations send us lots of business too. But, we just go along the street hollerin'. The reason why the fire stations wants to give us work because it saves them from a lot of work. See?

"It feels all right to clean chimneys. It's a job. And a good job. Sho, I'm proud of it. All them people who laughs at us is crazy. I used to make mo' money in a day cleanin' chimneys than some people who laugh at us make in a week. Money was just that good. Then agin, there is a lot of places that feed you. Everybody likes a chimney sweeper. People think we is Mardi Gras. We don't care. We pick up a lot of tips like that.

"This is how we clean a chimney: We take them long corn vines and tie 'um together and sweep the soot down from top. It takes two men to do it. We draw down a small fire in the chimney by throwin' salt up the chimney. Salt is a strong-actin' agent fo' fire. It can't stand salt.

"I don't know why we wears beaver hats and them kind of clothes. I believes them is the uniforms because they don't look dirty. Nobody minds dirty clothes gettin' dirty. Does they? A white man gave me my beaver. The coat and pants is mine. We tie rope around our waist because we have to use it sometimes, to pull ourselves up and down the roof. We use that rope like a ladder. Man, sometimes we almost go down in one of them chimneys. I seen the time when I was in one of 'um like Santa Claus, reachin' down in there like a baby reachin' for candy. We take our pads, rags, salt and stuff and wrap them up in a bundle.

"The trouble with this business is that them bastards cuts the prices all the time. Some of them womens tell you, "The other man said he'd clean my chimney fo' fifty cents.' All that dust and stuff gets in your eyes. Man, that's dangerous. Suppose you get consumption? Cleanin' chimneys is bad on your lungs. I drink milk and liquor to keep from losin' my lungs. No, I ain't never been sick in my life.

"There ain't no mo' money in cleanin' chimneys, ain't nothin' to it. Everything is modern and streamline. I'm tryin' to be a streamline myself." He laughed and the women laughed with him. "I was so streamline I fell off a woman's roof one mornin'. The woman had done said, 'What you goin' do way up there?' I said, 'I'm goin' to examine things.' She had to examine my head.

"Say man, them chimneys make you so dirty that when you get home you got to take a bath in kerosene. Everything on you gets black. That work makes you nervous. A white man sho could never be no chimney sweeper. He would look like he was carryin' his shadow aroun'.

"Some white folks like to talk with you, especially them from the North. They say they ain't never seen nothin' like us. They wants to know where we live and how we live. One white lady ain't had nothin' fo' us to do, she just called us in and gave us wine and two dollars to talk with us. Man, we ain't told that woman nothin'. I ain't goin' to never let nobody know all my business. 'Specially no white folks. We get cigarettes, clothes and things from people. All in all we do all right. But, we don't take things instead of money. Some of them white folks try to get you to do that, but not me. I tells them to pay me money, sumpin' I can use. I can get bread, clothes, and what I wants with my money. It ain't coneyfit.

"I strictly haves my fun. No, I ain't tendin' bein' no Christian. That's the trouble with niggers now. They pray too damn much. Everytime you look around you see some nigger on his knees and the white man figurin' at his desk. What in the world is they prayin' fo'? Tryin' to get to heaven? They is goin' to get there anyhow. There ain't no other hell but this one down here. Look at me. I'm catchin' hell right now. I'm drunk and I ain't got no money.

"If I had some? Man, don't ask me no question like that. What else is I'm goin' to do but have my fun. I pay my rent, give my old lady what she takes to pay the insurance, buy food, and get her sumpin' and that's all. What I'm goin' to do? Ain't no need fo' me to save nothin'. I ain't never been able to save nothin' in my life. I don't want to save nothin'. You want me to have troubles?

"I went to war—didn't get killed. Come on back—got my bonus. And then got me a load of womens and threw it away. Ain't that bein' a sucker? When you spend your money you ain't got nothin' to show fo' it. When you spend your money on whiskey you got whiskey to show fo' it.

"My wife is a good woman. She ain't had to work in two years. I took her out the white folks' kitchen. She wasn't makin' but three dollars a week, anyhow. That ain't no money. Sho, she brought the pots and pans home. But what was in 'um? A lot of leftovers. Man, as long as I can make a dollar sweepin' chimneys I ain't goin' to eat nobody's leftovers. I can buy what I want and I'm my own boss. Do you know that I been sweepin' chimneys off and on fo' eighteen years? Before I did that I used to be a common laborer. If I can help it I'll never be a common laborer agin. I likes to be my own boss. Don't want no white folks hollerin' at me.

"I fo'got to tell you that sweepin' chimneys is a hard thing in the wintertime, it's mighty cold five o'clock in the mornin'. I'll never fo'get. Man, I went hollerin' under a politician's window one mornin'. ROOAP . . . ROO . . . AP . . . ROOO . . . OAP! CHIMNEY SWEEPER . . . RO . . . ROOAP . . . REEE . . . REE . . . ROOAP . . . CHIMNEY! Man, the politician poked his head out of his window and told me, 'Say, you black bastard, if you don't get the hell away from here I'm comin' out there and rope your damn neck to one of them trees!' His wife stuck her head out the window and just laughed. It was early in the mornin' too. She just laughed, and said, 'Darlin', leave him alone. I think he's cute.' The man looked at her and looked at me; I was ready to make haste. He started cussin' agin, 'You black bastard, if you don't get goin' you'll be cute. You won't have no damn head.' Then, he looked at his wife. 'Cute hell. You run your damn trap all night and here comes that chimney man runnin' his mouth early in the mornin' and you say he's cute. I'll kill that nigger.' Man, did I leave from away from there! That's why we don't go out early in the mornin' no mo'."

The man with the bottle said, "Come on, John, quit talkin' and let's go to that saloon on Washington Avenue."

Emma said, "John."

He looked at her and said: "Baby, get my dinner ready. I'll be back."

But the woman knew that he was off with his friends. Old Susie was angry; she shrugged her shoulders and said, "Damn fool, there he goes bummin' with rats when he has a nice gent'man to talk with."

A black man called to John Junior from a passing automobile, "Where you goin'?"

He flipped his fingers and shouted back, "I'm goin' make some women shake down and show their linen. Everybody is worrin' about John. Can't a man have a holiday?"

Emma was "plum digusted" with John. "All he knows is work, more work, fun and more fun. That fool has more holidays than the President. He ain't never had nothin' . . . ain't got nothin' and ain't goin' to never have nothin'. He's the best money-circulator in the whole round world."

15

THE AUTOBIOGRAPHY OF
W. E. B. DU BOIS

A Soliloquy on Viewing My Life from the Last Decade of Its First Century

William Edward Burghardt Du Bois

❏

W. E. B. Du Bois (1868–1963), born in Great Barrington, Massachusetts, was educated at Fisk University and Harvard University. He was the first African American to receive a Ph.D. from Harvard University, and his dissertation is considered a classic treatment of the slave trade. Du Bois is recognized as one of the key intellectuals of this century, breaking ground in a variety of areas including pragmatism and sociology. His writings are well known and widely used both inside and outside the academy. Du Bois was a pioneering figure in the efforts to achieve equality for African Americans in the United States but, faced with the prospects of a country unwilling to change, he left the United States and spent his last years in Ghana.

One of Du Bois's better known and most widely used books is Souls of Black Folk *(1903). In that text, he clearly outlines the problem that would plague the United States: the "color-line." In that text, Du Bois explores the ontological and epistemological consequences of slavery and continued oppression for both African Americans and the dominant society. His insights are sharp and they still demand attention. What is also of interest about this text is the manner in which Du Bois makes use of African American cultural production, for example, the spirituals, to frame his discussion. In using the spirituals, Du Bois draws heavily on the cornerstone of the Black church tradition, and he continues this process in other books, such as* Prayers for Dark People *(edited by Herbert Aptheker, 1980).*

One would assume, from his use of religiotheological language and symbols, that Du Bois had a personal attachment to the dominant form of religious expression in African American communities, the Black church. By extension, one would most likely assume that this attachment to the Black church and its theological foundation informed Du Bois's sociopolitical activities. However, writings by Du Bois point to another foundation for his work, one more in keeping with the humanist tradition. That is to say, within Du Bois's writings is evidence for a philosophical (or theological) framework that de-nounces supernatural orientations and gives primary attention to rational thought and human ingenuity. Gerald Horne provides one such account in Black and Red: W. E. B. Du Bois and the Afro-American Response to the Cold War, 1944–1963. *Drawing from Du Bois's personal correspon-dence, Horne records the following:*

> *I do not believe in the existence and rulership of the one God of the Jews. I do not believe in the miraculous birth and the miracles of the Christ of the Christians; I do not believe in many of the tenets of Mohammedanism and Buddhism; and frankly I do not believe that the Guardian of the Bahai' faith has any supernatural knowledge.*[1]

Du Bois's humanist leanings are also clearly articulated in the following passages from A Soliloquy. *The first selection is drawn from a portion of the book devoted to Du Bois's opinion of the Soviet Union. He notes, based upon his personal appreciation for socialism, that the Soviet Union has great poten-tial for teaching the world lessons related to proper human relations, if it is allowed to conduct its affairs without interference. Du Bois is convinced that economic restructuring is necessary if issues of injustice are to be effectively addressed.*

It is in his reflections on religion within the Soviet Union that readers get a sense of Du Bois's personal position. Beginning with a discussion of Marx's rejection of nonprogressive forms of religiosity, Du Bois applauds a rejection of superstition (an embrace of the supernatural) and stifling dogma. Throughout the other portions of the following material, Du Bois outlines his movement away from traditional forms of religiosity and his embrace of "freethought." At one point, this is done through a rehearsal of thoughts he had, at age sixty, concerning death. Du Bois says that it is "beautiful" to die for a cause one values. But he also remarks that death is the end, and we should learn to value this life and not fill our children with useless thoughts of heaven and hell. The final segment continues this line of reasoning by, once again, telling of his rejection of Christian dogma.

For additional information on Du Bois, the sources are numerous. Interested readers should give attention to the following works by Du Bois: The Suppression of the African Slave Trade to the United States of America, 1638–1870, *Harvard Historical Studies Number 1 (New York: Longmans, Green, 1896);* The Philadelphia Negro: A Social Study *(Philadelphia: University of Pennsylvania, 1899);* The Souls of Black Folk: Essays and Sketches *(Chicago: A. C. McClurg, 1903);* Black Reconstruction in America: An Essay Toward a History of the Part Which Black Folk Played in the Attempt to Reconstruct Democracy in America, 1860–1880 *(New York: Russell and Russell, 1935);* Dusk of Dawn: An Essay toward an Autobiography of a Race Concept *(New York: Harcourt, Brace, and World, 1940). Readers interested in a sampling of Du Bois writings should see David Levering Lewis, ed.,* W. E. B. Du Bois: A Reader *(New York: Henry Holt and Company, 1995). Interesting secondary treatments include David Levering Lewis,* W. E. B. Du Bois: Biography of a Race *(New York: Henry Holt and Company, 1993); V. P. Franklin,* Living Our Stories, Telling Our Truths: Autobiography and the Making of the African-American Intellectual Tradition *(New York: Oxford University Press, 1995), chap. 6; Cornel West,* The American Evasion of Philosophy: A Genealogy of Pragmatism *(Madison: University of Wisconsin Press, 1989), chap. 4.*

NOTE

1. *Gerald Horne,* Black and Red *(Albany: State University of New York Press, 1986), 16. This is taken from Du Bois to B. P. Moreno, November 15, 1948, Reel 62, #381, Du Bois Papers, University of Massachusetts, Amherst. I have attempted to secure a copy of this letter, but I have been unable to locate it on the named reel.*

❏

I leave one subject to the last, as I leave the Soviet Union—religion. I lived two months opposite the inscription on the Second House of the Soviets, written by Marx: "Religion is the opium of the people!" Whatever was true of other lands, this was certainly true in Russia in 1926 and before. Symbols of religion ruled Moscow, the vast five domes of the Cathedral of Christ and the 350 other churches of the city dominated the landscape, as they loomed and glowed. There were gems of beautiful bejewelled churches; hordes of priests intoning litanies, begging alms, forgiving sins. There were thousands of shrines. Only one who has heard the chant of a Russian service, seen its color and genuflections; only those who know the gorgeous litany and the beauty of Russian churches can realize what Lenin, agreeing with Marx, meant when he called the Russian religion "opium."

But is was worse than opium. It was a Russian priest, Father Petrov,[1] who said of Russia in 1908, "There is no Christian Tsar and no Christian government. Conditions of life are not Christian. The upper classes rule the lower classes. A little group keeps the rest of the population enslaved. This little group has robbed the working people of wealth, power, science, art and religion, which they have also subjected; they have left them only ignorance and misery. In the place of pleasure they have given the people drunkenness; in the place of religion, gross superstition; and beside the work of a convict, a work without rest or reward. The ruling clergy with its cold, heartless bony fingers, has stifled the Russian church, killed its creative spirit, chained the Gospel itself, and 'sold' the church to the government. There is not an outrage, no crime, no perfidy of the state authorities, which the monks who rule the church would not cover with the mantle of the church, would not bless, would not seal with their own hands."

The British Trade Union report of 1925 said: "A very strong propaganda in the Press, the schools, colleges and Trade Union clubs is, however, carried on against religion generally, and especially as practised by the old Orthodox Church. The former Government-controlled licensed houses of prostitution where girls were exposed for hire at recognized fee, have been closed. In Tsarist days these houses were a recognized government institution; the opening ceremony was undertaken by a police officer and the premises blessed by Russian Orthodox Priests."[2]

All this has gone and none regrets that the Russian Orthodox religion has been dethroned. But the Russian church remains and other churches still carry on in the Soviet Union. However, the Soviet Union does not allow any church of any kind to interfere with education, and religion is not taught in the public schools. It seems to me that this is the greatest gift of the Russian Revolution to the modern world. Most educated modern men no longer believe in religious dogma. If questioned they will usually resort to double-talk before admitting the fact. But who today actually believes that this world is ruled and directed by a benevolent person of great power who, on humble appeal, will change the course of events at our request? Who believes in miracles? Many folk follow religious ceremonies and services; and allow their children to learn fairy tales and so-called religious truth, which in time the children come to recognize as conventional lies told by their parents and teachers for the children's good. One can hardly exaggerate the moral disaster of this custom. We have to thank the Soviet Union for the courage to stop it.

The United States has moved from the hysteria of calling all Soviet women prostitutes, all Russian workers slaves and the whole Russian people ready for revolt, of regarding all Soviet rulers as criminals conspiring to conquer the United States and rule the world; of breaking every treaty they made. From this false and utterly ridiculous position, we have begun to recognize the Soviet Socialist Republic as giving its people the best education of any in the world, of excelling in science, and organizing industry to its highest levels. Our increasing number of visitors to Russia see a contented people who do not hate the United States, but fear its war-making, and are eager to cooperate with us. From such a nation we can learn. . . .

My religious development has been slow and uncertain. I grew up in a liberal Congregational Sunday School and listened once a week to a sermon on doing good as a reasonable duty. Theology played a minor part and our teachers had to face some searching questions. At 17 I was in a missionary college where religious orthodoxy was stressed; but I was more developed to meet it with argument, which I did. My "morals" were sound, even a bit puritanic, but when a hidebound old deacon inveighed against dancing I rebelled. By the time of graduation I was still a "believer" in orthodox religion, but had strong questions which were encouraged at Harvard. In Germany I became a freethinker and when I came to teach at an orthodox Methodist Negro school I was soon regarded with suspicion, especially when I refused to lead the students in public prayer. When I became head of a department at Atlanta, the engagement was held up because again I balked at leading in prayer, but the liberal president let me substitute the Episcopal prayer book on most occasions. Later I improvised prayers on my own. Finally I faced a crisis: I was using Crapsey's *Religion and Politics* as a Sunday School text. When Crapsey was hauled up for heresy, I refused further to teach Sunday School. When Archdeacon Henry Phillips, my last rector, died, I flatly refused again to join any church or sign any church creed. From my 30th year on I have increasingly regarded the church as an institution which defended such evils as slavery, color caste, exploitation of labor and war. I think the greatest gift of the Soviet Union to modern civilization was the dethronement of the clergy and the refusal to let religion be taught in the public schools.

Religion helped and hindered my artistic sense. I know the old English and German hymns by heart. I loved their music but ignored their silly words with studied inattention. Great music came at last in the religious oratorios which we learned at Fisk University but it burst on me in Berlin with the Ninth Symphony and its Hymn of Joy. I worshipped Cathedral and ceremony which I saw in Europe but I knew what I was looking at when in New York a Cardinal became a strike-breaker and the Church of Christ fought the Communism of Christianity.

I revered life. I have never killed a bird nor shot a rabbit. I never liked fishing and always let others kill even the chickens which I ate. Nearly all my schoolmates in the South carried pistols. I never owned one. I could never conceive myself killing a human being. But in 1906 I rushed back from Alabama to Atlanta where my wife and six-year old child were living. A mob had raged for days killing Negroes. I bought a Winchester double-barreled shotgun and two dozen rounds of shells filled with buckshot. If a white mob had stepped on the campus where I lived I would without hesitation have sprayed their guts over the grass. They did not come. They went to south Atlanta where the police let them steal and kill. My gun was fired but once and then by error into a row of *Congressional Records,* which lined the lower shelf of my library.

My attitude toward current problems arose from my long habit of keeping in touch with world affairs by repeated trips to Europe and other parts of the world. I became internationally-minded during my four years at Harvard, two in college and two in the graduate school. Since that first trip in 1892, I have made 15 trips to Europe, one of which circled the globe. I have been in most European countries and traveled in Asia, Africa and the West Indies. Travel became a habit and knowledge of current thought in modern countries was always a part of my study, since before the First World War when the best of American newspapers took but small account of what Europe was thinking.

I can remember meeting in London in 1911 a colored man who explained to me his plan of leading a black army out of Africa and across the Pyrenees. I was thrilled at his earnestness! But gradually all that disappeared, and I began building a new picture of human progress.

This picture was made more real in 1926 when it became possible for me to take a trip to Russia. I saw on this trip not only Russia, but prostrate Germany, which I had not seen for 30 years. It was a terrible contrast.

By 1945 all these contacts with foreign peoples and foreign problems and the combination of these problems with the race problem here was forced into one line of thought by the Second World War. This strengthened my growing conviction that the first step toward settling the world's problems was Peace on Earth.

Many men have judged me, favorably and harshly. But the verdict of two I cherish. One knew me in mid-life for 50 years and was without doubt my closest friend. John Hope wrote me in 1918:

"Until the last minute I have been hoping that I would have an opportunity to be with you next Monday when you celebrate the rounding out of 50 years in this turbulent but attractive world. But now I am absolutely certain that I cannot come, so I am writing Mr. Shillady expressing my regret and shall have to content myself with telling you in this letter how glad I am that your 50th birthday is going to be such a happy one because you can look back on so much good work done. But not the good work alone. What you may look upon with greatest comfort is good intention. The fact that every step of the way you have purposed to be a man and to serve other people rather than yourself must be a tremendous comfort to you. Sometime soon if I chance to be back in New York I am going to have you take your deferred birthday dinner with *me*. You do not realize how much that hour or two which we usually spend together when I am in New York means to me."

Joel Spingarn said:

"I should like to have given public expression by my presence and by my words, not merely to the sense of personal friendship which has bound us together for 15 years, but to the gratitude which in common with all other Americans I feel we owe you for your public service. It so happens that by an accident of fate, you have been in the forefront of the great American battle, not merely for justice to a single race, but against the universal prejudice which is in danger of clouding the whole American tradition of toleration and human equality.

"I congratulate you on your public service, and I congratulate you also on the power of language by which you have made it effective. I know that some people think that an artist is a man who has nothing to say and who writes in order to prove it. The great writers of the world have not so conceived their task, and neither have you. Though your service has been for the most part the noble one of teacher and prophet (not merely to one race or nation but to the world), I challenge the artists of America to show more beautiful passages than some of those in *Darkwater* and *The Souls of Black Folk*."

Let one incident illustrate the paradox of my life.

Robert Morse Lovett was perhaps the closest white student friend I made at Harvard; when not long before his last visit to New York about 1950 he wanted to see and talk with me, he proposed the Harvard Club of which he was a member. I was not. No Negro graduate of Harvard was ever elected to membership in a Harvard club. For a while Jews were excluded, but no longer. I swallowed my pride and met Lovett at the Club. A few months later he died. . . .

Through all our bitter tears we knew how beautiful it was to die for that which our souls called sufficient. Like all true beauty this thing of dying was so simple, so matter-of-fact. The boy clothed in his splendid youth stood before us and laughed in his own jolly way— went and was gone. Suddenly the world was full of the fragrance of sacrifice. We left our digging and burden-bearing; we turned from our scraping and twisting of things and words; we paused from our hurrying hither and thither and walking up and down, and asked in half whisper: 'Death—is this life? And is its beauty real or false?'

"Here, then, is beauty and ugliness, a wide vision of world-sacrifice, a fierce gleam of world-hate. Which is life and what is death and how shall we face so tantalizing a contradiction? Any explanation must necessarily be subtle and involved. No pert and easy word of encouragement, no merely dark despair, can lay hold of the roots of these things. And first and before all, we cannot forget that this world is beautiful. Grant all its ugliness and sin—the petty, horrible snarl of its putrid threads, which few have seen more near or more often than I—notwithstanding all this, the beauty of the world is not to be denied.

"And then—the Veil, the Veil of color. It drops as drops the night on southern seas—vast, sudden, unanswering. There is Hate behind it, and Cruelty and Tears. As one peers through its intricate, unfathomable pattern of ancient, old, old design, one sees blood and guilt and misunderstanding. And yet it hangs there, this Veil, between then and now, between Pale and Colored and Black and White—between You and Me. Surely it is but a thought-thing, tenuous, intangible; yet just as surely is it true and terrible and not in our little day may you and I lift it. We may feverishly unravel its edges and even climb slow with giant shears to where it ringed and gilded top nestles close to the throne of Eternity. But as we work and climb we shall see through streaming eyes and hear with aching ears, lynching and murder, cheating and despising, degrading and lying, so flashed and flashed through this vast hanging darkness that the Doer never sees the Deed and the Victim knows not the Victor and Each hate All in wild and bitter ignorance. Listen, O Isles, to those voices from within the Veil, for they portray the most human hurt of the Twentieth Cycle of that poor Jesus who was called the Christ!

"At last to us all comes happiness, there in the Court of Peace, where the dead lie so still and calm and good. If we were not dead we would lie and listen to the flowers grow. We would hear the birds sing and see how the rain rises and blushes and burns and pales and dies in beauty. We would see spring, summer, and the red riot of autumn, and then in winter, beneath the soft white snow, sleep and dream of dreams. But we know that being dead, our Happiness is a fine and finished thing and that ten, a hundred, and a thousand years, we shall lie at rest, unhurt in the Court of Peace."

From then until now the wraith of Death has followed me, slept with me and awakened me and accompanied my day. Only now it is more commonplace and reasonable. It is the end and without ends there can be no beginnings. Its finality we must not falsify. It is our great debt to the Soviet Union that it alone of nations dared stop that lying to children which so long disgraced our schools. We filled little minds with fairy tales of religious dogma which we ourselves never believed. We filled their thoughts with pictures of barbarous revenge called God which contradicted all their inner sense of decency. We repeated folk tales of children without fathers, of death which was life, of sacrifice which was shrewd investment and ridiculous pictures of an endless future. The Soviets have stopped this. They allow a child to grow up without religious lies and with mature mind make his own decision about the world without scaring him into Hell or rewarding him with a silly Heaven.

We know that Death is the End of Life. Even when we profess to deny this we know that this hope is mere wishful thinking, pretense broidered with abject and cowardly Fear. Our endless egotism cannot conceive a world without Us and yet we know that this will happen and the world be happier for it.

I have lived a good and full life. I have finished my course. I do not want to live this life again. I have tasted its delights and pleasures; I have known its pain, suffering and despair. I am tired, I am through.

For the souls who follow me; for that little boy born Christmas day before last, my great-grandson and his compeers, I bequeath all that waits to be done, and Holy Time what a task, forever! . . .

The highest ambition of an American boy today is to be a millionaire. The highest ambition of an American girl is to be a movie star. Of the ethical actions which lie back of these ideals, little is said or learned. What are we doing about it? Half the Christian churches of New York are trying to ruin the free public schools in order to install religious dogma in them; and the other half are too interested in Venezuelan oil to prevent the best center in Brooklyn from fighting youthful delinquency, or prevent a bishop from kicking William Howard Melish in the street and closing his church. Which of the hundreds of churches sitting half empty protests about this? They hire Billy Graham to replace the circus in Madison Square Garden.

Howard Melish is one of the few Christian clergymen for whom I have the highest respect. Honest and conscientious, believing sincerely in much of the Christian dogma, which I reject, but working honestly and without hypocrisy, for the guidance of the young, for the uplift of the poor and ignorant, and for the the betterment of his city and his country, he has been driven from his work and his career ruined by a vindictive bishop of his church, with no effective protest from most of the Christian ministry and membership or of the people of the United States. The Melish case is perhaps at once the most typical and frightening illustration of present American religion and my reaction. Here is a young man of ideal character, of impeccable morals; a hard worker, especially among the poor and unfortunate, with fine family relations. His father had helped build one of the most popular Episcopal churches in the better part of Brooklyn. He himself had married a well-educated woman, and had three sons in school. The community about it was changing from well-to-do people of English and Dutch descent, to white-collar and laboring folk of Italian, Negro and Puerto Rican extraction. Trinity church, under the Melishes, adapted itself to changing needs, and invited neighborhood membership. It was not a large church, but it was doing the best work among the young and foreign-born of any institution in Brooklyn.

The young rector took one step for which the bishop, most of his fellow clergymen and the well-to-do community, with its business interests, pilloried him. He joined and became an official of the National Council of American-Soviet Friendship. He was accused immediately of favoring communism, and to appease criticism he gave up his official position in this organization, but refused to resign his membership. Allegedly for this reason the bishop, most of the clergy and the well-to-do community proceeded to force him out of the church. The real reason behind their fight was anger because a rich, white, "respectable" church was being surrendered to workers and Negroes. It became a renewed battle between Episcopal authority and democratic rule. That his parish wanted to retain Melish as rector was unquestionable. Through the use of technicalities in the canon law and in accord with the decision of Catholic judges who believed in Episcopal power, Howard Melish lost his church, had his life work ruined, the church itself closed, and its local influence ended. There was vigorous protest against this by a few devoted colleagues, many of them Jews and liberals. But the great mass of the Episcopal church membership was silent and did nothing.

All this must not be mentioned even if you know it and see it. America must never be criticized even by honest and sincere men. America must always be praised and extravagantly praised, or you lose your job or are ostracized or land in jail. Criticism is treason, and treason or the hint of treason testified to by hired liars may be punished by shameful death. I saw Ethel Rosenberg lying beautiful in her coffin beside her mate. I tried to stammer futile words above her grave. But not over graves should we shout this failure of justice, but from the housetops of the world.

Honest men may and must criticize America. Describe how she has ruined her democracy, sold out her jury system, and led her seats of justice astray. The only question that may arise is whether this criticism is based on truth, not whether it has been openly expressed.

What is truth? What can it be when the President of the United States, guiding the nation, stands up in public and says: *"The world also thinks of us as a land which has never enslaved anyone."* Everyone who heard this knew it was not true. Yet here stands the successor of George Washington who bought, owned, and sold slaves; the successor of Abraham Lincoln who freed four million slaves after they had helped him with victory over the slaveholding South. And so far as I have seen, not a single periodical, not even a Negro weekly, has dared challenge or even criticize that falsehood.

Perhaps the most extraordinary characteristic of current America is the attempt to reduce life to buying and selling. Life is not love unless love is sex and bought and sold. Life is not knowledge save knowledge of technique, of science for destruction. Life is not beauty except beauty for sale. Life is not art unless its price is high and it is sold for profit. All life is production for profit, and for what is profit but for buying and selling again?

NOTES

1. Father Gregory S. Petrov was one of 14 priests elected to the first Duma in 1905 in Russia. He was a fiery orator, an able publicist and a liberal in politics, verging—especially for a priest in Tsarist Russia— upon radicalism. In 1906 he was sent into exile by the Tsar and efforts to free him became a celebrated case throughout the world. *See,* John S. Curtiss, *Church and State in Russia* (N.Y., Columbia Univ. Press, 1940; reprinted, 1965, Octagon Press).

2. A delegation representing the British Trades Union Congress visited the USSR for one month commencing on November 11, 1924; it consisted of ten very prominent men in trade union, government and academic life, including Alan Findlay, Harold Grenfell, A. A. Purcell and Ben Tillett.

Its "Final Report" affirmed that the USSR was a "strong and stable State" possessing the support of most of the people and one which was worthy of careful study by all. The full text makes up a volume of over 250 pages: *Russia Today: The Official Report of the British Trade Union Delegation* (N.Y., International Publishers, 1925).

16

THE FIRE NEXT TIME

James Baldwin

❏

James Baldwin (1924–1987) was born in Harlem and much of his work revolves around the issue of race prevalent in Harlem as elsewhere in the United States. From his sense of the autobiographical as an important element of the literary process, Baldwin created some of the most important material of the late twentieth century. He provided in works such as Notes of a Native Son *(Boston: Beacon Press, 1955) and* Nobody Knows My Name *(New York: Dial Press, 1961), as well as fictional works such as* Giovanni's Room *(New York: Dial Press, 1956), a glimpse into life in a racialized and homophobic United States that earned him national recognition.*

One of Baldwin's widely read books, Go Tell It on the Mountain, *which chronicles his early years, is probably his best work. It centers on his growing awareness of the white world and his relationship, as a young Black male, to this world. Baldwin outlines his relationship with his family and speaks— in soft tones—of his sexuality. One of the many powerful moments in the text revolves around his "surrender" to the Christian faith and his acceptance of a "call to preach" the Gospel.*

In the following selection from The Fire Next Time, *Baldwin is reflecting on his reasons for joining the church and beginning the preaching career portrayed in* Go Tell It on the Mountain. *He argues that to live successfully in Harlem required a "gimmick," a means of survival, and that he had few options with respect to this necessity. It was necessary, as an African American, to find a way to battle successfully the inferiority the dominant society encourages in "its" Black people. His escape, his affirmation of the ability to be and do "anything," was the church.*

It seems fairly clear that the church provided an answer to large and pressing social and cultural issues. And Baldwin embraced it to the extent it met these sociocultural needs. However, as Baldwin further notes in the following excerpt, he moved away from the church (and denounced Christianity) because it and its God did not fully respond to the existential angst he experienced as a homosexual and Black *man. Rather than alleviate his concerns, it served to promote further a sense of his* being *as inferior. The Black church provided a "rackett," lucrative but unfulfilling.*

During an interview with the Honorable Elijah Muhammad, he notes that he no longer embraced Christianity but rather found his connection to "something" larger then himself in his writing. It is the connection to human life that Baldwin embraces. In this way, Baldwin is able to maintain his commitment to the importance of the human's physicality as well as deeper self, and its connection to community. God and the church had proven unhelpful with this project. The reader will note the manner in which Baldwin's words seem to point to basic principles of humanism.

Readers interested in additional material on James Baldwin should see James Baldwin's writings, including the following not mentioned above: Another Country *(New York: Dial Press, 1962);* Tell Me How Long the Train's Been Gone *(New York: Dial Press, 1968);* Blues for Mr. Charlie *(New York: French, 1964); and* Going to Meet the Man *(New York: Dial Press, 1965). Secondary treatments include David Adams Leeming,* James Baldwin: A biography *(New York: Knopf, 1994); Keneth Kinnamon, comp.,* James Baldwin; A Collection of Critical Essays *(Englewood Cliffs, N.J.: Prentice-Hall, 1974); and Fred L. Standley and Louis H. Pratt, ed.,*

James Baldwin: Conversations with James Baldwin (*Jackson: University Press of Mississippi, 1989*). *There is also the critical collection by Harold Bloom,* James Baldwin (New York: Chelsea House, 1986). Also see Henry L. Gates, Jr., Nellie Y. McKay, et al., *The Norton Anthology of African American Literature* (New York: W. W. Norton & Company, 1997), 1650–1717.

❏

Being in the pulpit was like being in the theatre; I was behind the scenes and knew how the illusion was worked. I knew the other ministers and knew the quality of their lives. And I don't mean to suggest by this the "Elmer Gantry" sort of hypocrisy concerning sensuality; it was a deeper, deadlier, and more subtle hypocrisy than that, and a little honest sensuality, or a lot, would have been like water in an extremely bitter desert. I knew how to work on a congregation until the last dime was surrendered—it was not very hard to do—and I knew where the money for "the Lord's work" went. I knew, though I did not wish to know it, that I had no respect for the people with whom I worked. I could not have said it then, but I also knew that if I continued I would soon have no respect for myself. And the fact that I was "the young Brother Baldwin" increased my value with those same pimps and racketeers who had helped to stampede me into the church in the first place. They still saw the little boy they intended to take over. They were waiting for me to come to my senses and realize that I was in a very lucrative business. They knew that I did not yet realize this, and also that I had not yet begun to suspect where my own needs, *coming up* (they were very patient), could drive me. They themselves did know the score, and they knew that the odds were in their favor. And, really, I knew it, too. I was even lonelier and more vulnerable than I had been before. And the blood of the Lamb had not cleansed me in any way whatever. I was just as black as I had been the day that I was born. Therefore, when I faced a congregation, it began to take all the strength I had not to stammer, not to curse, not to tell them to throw away their Bibles and get off their knees and go home and organize, for example, a rent strike. When I watched all the children, their copper, brown, and beige faces staring up at me as I taught Sunday school, I felt that I was committing a crime in talking about the gentle Jesus, in telling them to reconcile themselves to their misery on earth in order to gain the crown of eternal life. Were only Negroes to gain this crown? Was Heaven, then, to be merely another ghetto? Perhaps I might have been able to reconcile myself even to this if I had been able to believe that there was any loving-kindness to be found in the haven I represented. But I had been in the pulpit too long and I had seen too many monstrous things. I don't refer merely to the glaring fact that the minister eventually acquires houses and Cadillacs while the faithful continue to scrub floors and drop their dimes and quarters and dollars into the plate. I really mean that there was no love in the church. It was a mask for hatred and self-hatred and despair. The transfiguring power of the Holy Ghost ended when the service ended, and salvation stopped at the church door. When we were told to love everybody, I had thought that that meant *everybody*. But no. It applied only to those who believed as we did, and it did not apply to white people at all. I was told by a minister, for example, that I should never, on any public conveyance, under any circumstances, rise and give my seat to a white woman. White men never rose for Negro women. Well, that was true enough, in the main—I saw his point. But what was the point, the purpose, of *my* salvation if it did not permit me to behave with love toward others, no matter how they behaved toward me? What others did was their responsibility, for which they would answer when the judgment trumpet sounded. But what *I* did was *my* responsibility, and I would have to answer, too—unless, of course, there was also in Heaven a special dispensation for the benighted black, who was not to be judged in the same way as other human beings, or angels. It probably occurred to me around this time that the vision people hold of the world to come is but a reflection, with predictable wishful distortions, of the world in which they live. And this did not apply only to Negroes, who were no more "simple" or "spontaneous" or "Christian" than anybody else—who were merely more oppressed. In the same way that we, for white people, were the descendants of Ham, and were cursed forever, white people were, for us, the descendants of Cain. And the passion with which we loved the Lord was a measure of how deeply we feared and distrusted and, in the end, hated almost all strangers, always, and avoided and despised ourselves.

But I cannot leave it at that; there is more to it than that. In spite of everything, there was in the life I fled a zest and a joy and a capacity for facing and surviving disaster that are very moving and very rare. Perhaps we were, all of us—pimps, whores, racketeers, church members, and children—bound together by the nature of our oppression, the specific and peculiar complex of risks we had to run; if so, within these limits we sometimes achieved with each other a freedom that was close to love. I remember, anyway, church suppers and outings, and, later, after I left the church, rent and waistline parties where rage and sorrow sat in the darkness and did not stir, and we ate and drank and talked and laughed and danced and forgot all about "the man." We had the liquor, the chicken, the music, and each other, and had no need to pretend to be what we were not. This is the freedom that one hears in some gospel songs, for example, and in jazz. In all jazz, and especially in the blues, there is something tart and ironic, authoritative and double-edged. White Americans seem to feel that happy songs are *happy* and sad songs are *sad,* and that, God help us, is exactly the way most white Americans sing them—sounding, in both cases, so helplessly, defenselessly fatuous that one dare not speculate on the temperature of the deep freeze from which issue their brave and sexless little voices. Only people who have been "down the line," as the song puts it, know what this music is about. I think it was Big Bill Broonzy who used to sing "I Feel So Good," a really

231

joyful song about a man who is on his way to the railroad station to meet his girl. She's coming home. It is the singer's incredibly moving exuberance that makes one realize how leaden the time must have been while she was gone. There is no guarantee that she will stay this time, either, as the singer clearly knows, and, in fact, she has not yet actually arrived. Tonight, or tomorrow, or within the next five minutes, he may very well be singing "Lonesome in My Bedroom," or insisting, "Ain't we, ain't we, going to make it all right? Well, if we don't today, we will tomorrow night." White Americans do not understand the depths out of which such an ironic tenacity comes, but they suspect that the force is sensual, and they are terrified of sensuality and do not any longer understand it. The word "sensual" is not intended to bring to mind quivering dusky maidens or priapic black studs. I am referring to something much simpler and much less fanciful. To be sensual, I think, is to respect and rejoice in the force of life, of life itself, and to be *present* in all that one does, from the effort of loving to the breaking of bread. It will be a great day for America, incidentally, when we begin to eat bread again, instead of the blasphemous and tasteless foam rubber that we have substituted for it. And I am not being frivolous now, either. Something very sinister happens to the people of a country when they begin to distrust their own reactions as deeply as they do here, and become as joyless as they have become. It is this individual uncertainty on the part of white American men and women, this inability to renew themselves at the fountain of their own lives, that makes the discussion, let alone elucidation, of any conundrum—that is, any reality—so supremely difficult. The person who distrusts himself has no touchstone for reality—for this touchstone can be only oneself. Such a person interposes between himself and reality nothing less than a labyrinth of attitudes. And these attitudes, furthermore, though the person is usually unaware of it (is unaware of so much!), are historical and public attitudes. They do not relate to the present any more than they relate to the person.

Therefore, whatever white people do not know about Negroes reveals, precisely and inexorably, what they do not know about themselves.

White Christians have also forgotten several elementary historical details. They have forgotten that the religion that is now identified with their virtue and their power—"God is on our side," says Dr. Verwoerd—came out of a rocky piece of ground in what is now known as the Middle East before color was invented, and that in order for the Christian church to be established, Christ had to be put to death, by Rome, and that the real architect of the Christian church was not the disreputable, sun-baked Hebrew who gave it his name but the mercilessly fanatical and self-righteous St. Paul. The energy that was buried with the rise of the Christian nations must come back into the world; nothing can prevent it. Many of us, I think, both long to see this happen and are terrified of it, for though this transformation contains the hope of liberation, it also imposes a necessity for great change. But in order to deal with the untapped and dormant force of the previously subjugated, in order to survive as a human, moving, moral weight in the world, America and all the Western nations will be forced to reexamine themselves and release themselves from many things that are now taken to be sacred, and to discard nearly all the assumptions that have been used to justify their lives and their anguish and their crimes so long.

"The white man's Heaven," sings a Black Muslim minister, "is the black man's Hell." One may object—possibly—that this puts the matter somewhat too simply, but the song is true, and it has been true for as long as white men have ruled the world. The Africans put it another way: When the white man came to Africa, the white man had the Bible and the African had the land, but now it is the white man who is being, reluctantly and bloodily, separated from the land, and the African who is still attempting to digest or to vomit up the Bible. The struggle, therefore, that now begins in the world is extremely complex, involving the historical role of Christianity in the realm of power—that is, politics—and in the realm of morals. In the realm of power, Christianity has operated with an unmitigated arrogance and cruelty—necessarily, since a religion ordinarily imposes on those who have discovered the true faith the spiritual duty of liberating the infidels. This particular true faith, moreover, is more deeply concerned about the soul than it is about the body, to which fact the flesh (and the corpses) of countless infidels bears witness. It goes without saying, then, that whoever questions the authority of the true faith also contests the right of the nations that hold this faith to rule over him— contests, in short, their title to his land. The spreading of the Gospel, regardless of the motives or the integrity or the heroism of some of the missionaries, was an absolutely indispensable justification for the planting of the flag. Priests and nuns and schoolteachers helped to protect and sanctify the power that was so ruthlessly being used by people who were indeed seeking a city, but not one in the heavens, and one to be made, very definitely, by captive hands. The Christian church itself—again, as distinguished from some of its ministers— sanctified and rejoiced in the conquests of the flag, and encouraged, if it did not formulate, the belief that conquest, with the resulting relative well-being of the Western populations, was proof of the favor of God. God had come a long way from the desert—but then so had Allah, though in a very different direction. God, going north, and rising on the wings of power, had become white, and Allah, out of power, and on the dark side of Heaven, had become—for all practical purposes, anyway—black. Thus, in the realm of morals the role of Christianity has been, at best, ambivalent. Even leaving out of account the remarkable arrogance that assumed that the ways and morals of others were inferior to those of Christians, and that they therefore had every right, and could use any means, to change them, the collision between cultures—and the schizophrenia in the mind of Christendom—had rendered the domain of morals as chartless as the sea once was, and as treacherous as the sea still is. It is not too much to say that whoever wishes to become a truly moral human being (and let us not ask whether or not this is possible; I think we must *believe* that it is possible) must first divorce himself from all the prohibitions, crimes, and hypocrisies of the Christian church. If the concept of God has any validity or any use, it can only be to make us larger, freer, and more loving. If God cannot do this, then it is time we got rid of Him.

17

THE LEGACY OF MALCOLM X AND THE COMING OF THE BLACK NATION

Amiri Imamu Baraka

❏

LeRoi Jones (1934–   ), later Amiri Imamu Baraka, is one of the major writers of what has been referred to as the Black arts movement and the approach known as Black aesthetics. His works, such as "The Dutchman," marked a major moment in the development of Black theater, and his writings, such as The System of Dante's Hell, *spoke to the efforts of African Americans to develop a revolutionary consciousness during the turbulent 1960s. Baraka combined his creative work with critical commentary on African American cultural production, such as* Blues People: Negro Music in White America *(New York: William Morrow, 1963). Many considered him the major African American literary voice during this period. In addition to his own plays, poetry, and prose, Baraka was also influential in the promotion of works by African Americans in New York City and New Jersey through organizations such as Black Arts Repertory Theatre/School and Spirit House.*

Both his writings and personal development spoke to a sense of the ontological

237

and epistemological location of African Americans within the United States. At times this was referred to in the language of cultural nationalism and, at other points, Baraka embraced a form of Pan-Africanism and socialism. In keeping with his changing political orientation, Baraka moved between various religious traditions—orthodox Islam, the Nation of Islam, and Yoruba religion. However, Baraka's orientation did not remain theistic. For example, at least one poem, "Lord Haw Haw (as Pygmy) #37," in the collection titled Wise, Why's, Y's (Chicago: Third World Press, 1995) speaks of God as a questionable human construct. This notion of God as a human construct, and the added responsibility this places on humans, is found in the following passage from The LeRoi Jones/Amiri Baraka Reader (New York: Thunder's Mouth Press, 1991), and it provides a sense of Baraka's development as a humanist.

The following section of the essay dealing with Malcolm X and the "Black Nation," addresses the manner in which Malcolm X's contribution to the struggles of African Americans revolves around the rich notion of nationalism, tied to internationalism, that he taught. In this way, Malcolm X proposed a sense of consciousness that incorporated African Americans into a world scene that is theoretical but also very much connected to the ownership of land. This form of progressive consciousness is connected to culture because culture outlines and, to some extent, predicts our lives or habits. He continues by saying that religion is connected to culture, but his understanding of religion is very much defined in functional terms. Religion entails humanity's "aspiration." And, God is simply the human at his/her best.

Readers interested in additional materials on Baraka should see Amiri Baraka, The Autobiography of LeRoi Jones/Amiri Baraka (New York: Freundlich Books, 1984); Amiri Baraka, Three Books by Imamu Amiri Baraka (LeRoi Jones): The System of Dante's Hell, Tales, and the Dead Lecturer (New York: Grove Press, 1967); Amiri Baraka, Selected Poetry of Amiri Baraka/LeRoi Jones (New York: Morrow, 1979). For additional information on the Black arts movement, see, for example, Larry Neal, Visions of a Liberated Future: Black Arts Movement Writings (New York: Thunder's Mouth Press, 1989).

Baraka was certainly not the only noteworthy African American literary figure during the 1950s and 1960s whose personal perspective was in line with humanist thought. One could also include in this category Lorraine Hansberry (1930–1965). The following is from an interview contained in To Be Young, Gifted and Black: Lorraine Hansberry in Her Own Words, *adapted by Robert Nemiroff (New York: New American Library, 1969.):*

INTERVIEWER: *I know that you have said that science will bring more rewards for our generation than God. Does this mean that you place your faith in a very rational, scientific approach to existence* now*—rather than in the traditional religious beliefs of, say, Mama in your play?*

L.H.: *Yes, I do. I think . . . well, you see, I don't think anything new has happened since rationalism burst forth with the Renaissance and the subsequent developments in rational thought. We only revert back to mystical ideas— which includes most contemporary orthodox religious views, in my opinion— because we simply are confronted with some things we don't yet understand. . . .*

For additional information on Lorraine Hansberry, see Lorraine Hansberry, A Raisin in the Sun *(New York: Modern Library, 1995, 1958); Lorraine Hansberry,* Les blancs: The Collected Last Plays of Lorraine Hansberry *(New York: Viking Books, 1973).*

❑

I

The reason Malik was killed (the reasons) is because he was thought dangerous by enough people to allow and sanction it. Black People and white people.

Malcolm X was killed because he was dangerous to America. He had made too great a leap, in his sudden awareness of direction and the possibilities he had for influencing people, anywhere.

Malcolm was killed because he wanted to become official, as, say, a statesman. Malcolm wanted an effective form in which to enrage a white man, a practical form. And he had begun to find it.

For one thing, he'd learned that Black Conquest will be a deal. That is, it will be achieved through deals as well as violence. (He was beginning through his African statesmanship to make deals with other nations, as statesman from a nation. An oppressed Black Nation "laying" in the Western Hemisphere.)

This is one reason he could use the "universal" Islam—to be at peace with all dealers. The idea was to broaden, formalize, and elevate the will of the Black Nation so that it would be able to move a great many people and resources in a direction necessary to spring the Black Man.

"The Arabs must send us guns or we will accuse them of having sold us into slavery!" is international, and opens Black America's ports to all comers. When the ports are open, there is an instant brotherhood of purpose formed with most of the world.

Malcolm's legacy was his life. What he rose to be and through what channels, e.g., Elijah Muhammad and the Nation of Islam, as separate experiences. Malcolm changed as a minister of Islam: under Elijah's tutelage, he was a different man—the difference being, between a man who is preaching Elijah Muhammad and a man who is preaching political engagement and finally, national sovereignty. (Elijah Muhammad is now the second man, too.)

The point is that Malcolm had begun to call for Black National Consciousness. And moved this consciousness into the broadest possible arena, operating with it as of now. We do not want a Nation, we are a Nation. We must strengthen and formalize, and play the world's game with what we have, from where we are, as a truly separate people. America can give us nothing; all bargaining must be done by mutual agreement. But finally, terms must be given by Black Men from their own shores—which is where they live, where we all are, now. The land is literally ours. And we must begin to act like it.

The landscape should belong to the people who see it all the time.

We begin by being Nationalists. But a nation is land, and wars are fought over land. The sovereignty of nations, the sovereignty of culture, the sovereignty of race, the sovereignty of ideas and ways "into" the world.

The world in the twentieth century, and for some centuries before, is, literally, backward. The world can be understood through any idea. And the purely social condition of the world in this millennium, as, say, "compared" to other millennia, might show a far greater loss than gain, if this were not balanced by concepts and natural forces. That is, we think ourselves into the balance and ideas are necessarily "advanced" of what is simply here (what's going on, so to speak). And there are rockets and super cars. But, again, the loss? What might it have been if my people were turning the switches? I mean, these have been our White Ages, and all learning has suffered.

And so Nationalist concept is the arrival of conceptual and environmental strength, or the realization of it in its totality by the Black Man in the West, i.e., that he is not of the West, but even so, like the scattered Indians after movie cavalry attacks, must regroup, and return that force on a fat, ignorant, degenerate enemy.

We are a people. We are unconscious captives unless we realize this —that we have always been separate, except in our tranced desire to be the thing that oppressed us, after some generations of having been "programmed" (a word suggested to me by Jim Campbell and Norbert Wiener) into believing that our greatest destiny was to become white people!

2

Malcolm X's greatest contribution, other than to propose a path to internationalism and hence, the entrance of the American Black Man into a world-wide allegiance against the white man (in most recent times he proposed to do it using a certain kind of white liberal as a lever), was to preach Black Consciousness to the Black Man. As a minister for the Nation of Islam, Malcolm talked about a black consciousness that took its form from religion. In his last days he talked of another black consciousness that proposed politics as its moving energy.

But one very important aspect of Malcolm's earlier counsels was his explicit call for a National Consciousness among Black People. And this aspect of Malcolm's philosophy certainly did abide throughout his days. The feeling that somehow the Black Man was different, as being, as a being, and finally, in our own time, as judge. And Malcolm propounded these differences as life anecdote and religious (political) truth and made the consideration of Nationalist ideas significant and powerful in our day.

Another very important aspect of Malcolm's earlier (or the Honorable Elijah Muhammad's) philosophy was the whole concept of land and land-control as central to any talk of "freedom" or "independence." The Muslim tack of asking for land within the continental United States in which Black People could set up their own nation, was given a special appeal by Malcolm, even though the request was seen by most people outside the movement as "just talk" or the amusing howls of a gadfly.

But the whole importance of this insistence on land is just now beginning to be understood. Malcolm said many times that when you speak about revolution you're talking about land—changing the ownership or usership of some specific land which you think is yours. But any talk of Nationalism also must take this concept of land and its

242

primary importance into consideration because, finally, any Nationalism which is not intent on restoring or securing autonomous space for
a people, i.e., a nation, is at the very least shortsighted.

Elijah Muhammad has said, "We want our people in America,
whose parents or grandparents were descendants from slaves, to be
allowed to establish a separate state or territory of their own—either
on this continent or elsewhere. We believe that our former slavemas-
ters are obligated to provide such land and that the area must be
fertile and minerally rich." And the Black Muslims seem separate from
most Black People because the Muslims have a national consciousness
based on their aspirations for land. Most of the Nationalist movements
in this country advocate that that land is in Africa, and Black People
should return there, or they propose nothing about land at all. It is
impossible to be a Nationalist without talking about land. Otherwise
your Nationalism is a misnamed kind of "difficult" opposition to what
the white man has done, rather than the advocation of another people
becoming the rulers of themselves, and sooner or later the rest of
the world.

The Muslims moved from the Back-to-Africa concept of Marcus
Garvey (the first large movement by Black People back to a National
Consciousness, which was, finally, only viable when the Black Man
focused on Africa as literally "back home") to the concept of a Black
National Consciousness existing in this land the Black captives had
begun to identify as home. (Even in Garvey's time, there was not a
very large percentage of Black People who really wanted to leave.
Certainly, the newly emerging Black bourgeoisie would have nothing
to do with "returning" to Africa. They were already created in the
image of white people, as they still are, and wanted nothing to do
with Black.)

What the Muslims wanted was a profound change. The National
Consciousness focused on actual (nonabstract) land, identifying a people, in a land where they lived. Garvey wanted to go back to Jordan.

A real one. The Nation of Islam wanted Jordan closer. Before these two thrusts, the Black Man in America, as he was Christianized, believed Jordan was in the sky, like pie, and absolutely supernatural.

Malcolm, then, wanted to give the National Consciousness its political embodiment, and send it out to influence the newly forming third world, in which this consciousness was to be included. The concept of Blackness, the concept of the National Consciousness, the proposal of a political (and diplomatic) form for this aggregate of Black spirit, these are the things given to us by Garvey, through Elijah Muhammad and finally given motion into still another area of Black response by Malcolm X.

Malcolm's legacy to Black People is what he moved toward, as the accretion of his own spiritual learning and the movement of Black People in general, through the natural hope, a rise to social understanding within the new context of the white nation and its decline under hypocrisy and natural "oppositeness" which has pushed all of us toward "new" ideas. We are all the products of national spirit and worldview. We are drawn by the vibrations of the entire nation. If there were no bourgeois Negroes, none of us would be drawn to that image. They, bourgeois Negroes, were shaped through the purposive actions of a national attitude, and finally, by the demands of a particular culture.

At which point we must consider what cultural attitudes are, what culture is, and what National Consciousness has to do with these, i.e., if we want to understand what Malcolm was pointing toward, and why the Black Man now must move in that direction since the world will not let him move any other way. The Black Man is possessed by the energies of historic necessity and the bursting into flower of a National Black Cultural Consciousness, and with that, in a living future, the shouldering to power of Black culture and, finally, Black Men . . . and then, Black ideals, which are different descriptions of a God. A righteous sanctity, out of which worlds are built.

3

What the Black Man must do now is look down at the ground upon which he stands, and claim it as his own. It is not abstract. Look down! Pick up the earth, or jab your fingernails into the concrete. It is real and it is yours, if you want it.

But to want it, as our own, is the present direction. To want what we are and where we are, but rearranged by our own consciousness. That is why it was necessary first to recrystallize national aspirations behind a Garvey. The Africans who first came here were replaced by Americans, or people responding to Western stimuli and then Americans. In order for the Americans to find out that they had come from another place, were, hence, alien, the Garvey times had to come. Elijah said we must have a place, to be, ourselves. Malcolm made it contemporarily secular.

So that now we must find the flesh of our spiritual creation. We must be conscious. And to be conscious is to be cultured, processed in specific virtues and genius. We must respond to this National Consciousness with our souls, and use the correspondence to come into our own.

The Black Man will always be frustrated until he has land (A Land!) of his own. All the thought processes and emotional orientation of "national liberation movements"—from slave uprisings onward—have always given motion to a Black National (and Cultural) Consciousness. These movements proposed that judgments were being made by Black sensibility, and that these judgments were necessarily different from those of the white sensibility—different, and after all is said and done, inimical.

Men are what their culture predicts (enforces). Culture is, simply, the way men live. How they have come to live. What they are formed by. Their total experience, and its implications and theories. Its paths.

The Black Man's paths are alien to the white man. Black Culture is alien to the white man. Art and religion are the results and ideal-ized supernumeraries of culture. Culture in this sense, as Sapir said, is "The National Genius," whether it be a way of fixing rice or kill-ing a man.

I said in *Blues People:* "Culture is simply how one lives and is connected to history by habit." God is man idealized (humanist defi-nition). Religion is the aspiration of man toward an idealized exis-tence. An existence in which the functions of God and man are harmonious, even identical. Art is the movement forward, the under-standing progress of man. It is feeling and making. A nation (social order) is made the way people *feel* it should be made. A face is too. Politics is man's aspiration toward an order. Religion is too. Art is an ordering as well. And all these categories are spiritual, but are also the result of the body, at one point, serving as a container of feeling. The soul is no less sensitive.

Nations are races. (In America, white people have become a nation, an identity, a race.) Political integration in America will not work because the Black Man is played on by special forces. His life from his organs, i.e., the life of the body, what it needs, what it wants, to become, is different—and for this reason racial is biological, finally. We are a different species. A species that is evolving to world power and philosophical domination of the world. The world will move the way Black People move!

If we take the teachings of Garvey, Elijah Muhammad and Malcolm X (as well as Frazier, Du Bois and Fanon), we know for certain that the solution of the Black Man's problems will come only through Black National Consciousness. We also know that the focus of change will be racial. (If we feel differently, we have different ideas. Race is feeling. Where the body, and the organs come in. Culture is the preservation of these feelings in superrational to rational form. Art is one method of expressing these feelings and identifying the form, as an emotional phenomenon.) In order for the Black Man in the West to absolutely know himself, it is necessary for him to see himself first as culturally separate from the white man. That is, to be conscious of this separation and use the strength it proposes.

Western Culture (the way white people live and think) is passing. If the Black Man cannot identify himself as separate, and understand what this means, he will perish along with Western Culture and the white man.

What a culture produces, is, and refers to, is an image—a picture of a process, since it is a form of a process: movement seen. The changing of images, of references, is the Black Man's way back to the racial integrity of the captured African, which is where we must take ourselves, in feeling, to be truly the warriors we propose to be. To form an absolutely rational attitude toward West man, and West thought. Which is what is needed. To see the white man as separate and as enemy. To make a fight according to the absolute realities of the world as it is.

Good–Bad, Beautiful–Ugly, are all formed as the result of image. The mores, customs, of a place are the result of experience, and a common reference for defining it—common images. The three white men in the film Gunga Din who kill off hundreds of Indians, Greek hero–style, are part of an image of white men. The various black porters, gigglers, ghostchumps and punkish Indians, etc., that inhabit the public image the white man has fashioned to characterize Black Men are references by Black Men to the identity of Black Men in the West, since that's what is run on them each day by white magic, i.e., television, movies, radio, etc.—the Mass Media (the *Daily News* does it with flicks and adjectives).

The song title "A White Man's Heaven Is a Black Man's Hell" describes how complete an image reversal is necessary in the West. Because for many Black People, the white man has succeeded in making this hell seem like heaven. But Black youth are much better off in this regard than their parents. They are the ones who need the least image reversal.

The Black artist, in this context, is desperately needed to change the images his people identify with, by asserting Black feeling, Black mind, Black judgment. The Black intellectual, in this same context, is needed to change the interpretation of facts toward the Black Man's best interests, instead of merely tagging along reciting white judgments of the world.

Art, Religion, and Politics are impressive vectors of a culture. Art describes a culture. Black artists must have an image of what the Black sensibility is in this land. Religion elevates a culture. The Black Man must aspire to Blackness. God is man idealized. The Black Man must idealize himself as Black. And idealize and aspire to that. Politics gives a social order to the culture, i.e., makes relationships within the culture definable for the functioning organism. The Black man must seek a Black politics, an ordering of the world that is beneficial to his culture, to his interiorization and judgment of the world. This is strength. And we are hordes. . . .

18

HALLEY'S COMET AND MY RELIGION

Harry Haywood

❑

Harry Haywood (1898–1985) was born in South Omaha, Nebraska, the child of former slaves. At the age of sixteen, Haywood moved to Chicago, where he spent most of the remainder of his life.

After serving in World War I, Haywood became involved in a variety of organizations that brought him in contact with the Communist Party of the U.S.A. He found its platform appealing and, within a matter of a few years, he became deeply involved in the work of the party. Haywood made an effort to bring the political philosophy of the party in line with issues of race.

In 1926, Haywood was a part of a group of African American Communists who traveled to the Soviet Union. He remained there and studied, not returning to the United States until 1930. During those four years abroad, he continued his work on race issues and the potential effect of Communism on this problem. Haywood's work gained him a major reputation and resulted in his selection to head the Communist Party's Negro Department. His work in this capacity included the "Scottsboro Boys" case. Haywood's stature in the party continued to grow through his labors with the party's League of Struggle for Negro Rights.

However, as the party's platform changed, Haywood lost ground because of his strong Black nationalist stance. Nonetheless, even as the party officially removed itself from the struggle for African American self-determination, Haywood continued to advocate African American concerns. He argued that African Americans were captives in the United States, and they must embrace Black nationalism in order to avoid the harmful effects of integration. This position ultimately resulted in his being forced out of the party. Until his death, Haywood continued to support Black nationalist organizations and strategies.

Although readers should not assume that all African American Socialists and Communists were humanists (for example, some were agnostics, atheists, and freethinkers), it is safe to say that the Communist Party and the Socialist Party provided organizational homes for those who were.[1] The following segment of Haywood's autobiography demonstrates the manner in which humanistic thought (in this case atheism) provided the religiophilosophical grounding for his praxis.

It is worth noting that Haywood was not alone in his religiophilosophical position as it connected to the issue of labor. Readers, as Norm Allen notes, should also be aware of the atheism that underpinned A. Philip Randolph's thinking and efforts on behalf of African American laborers. Randolph's position is clearly outlined in the following: Jervis Anderson, A. Philip Randolph: A Biographical Portrait *(New York: Harcourt Brace Jovanovich, 1973) and in an editorial by A. Philip Randolph, "The Failure of the Negro Church." This editorial can be found in Cary D. Wintz, ed.,* African American Political Thought, 1890–1930: Washington, Du Bois, Garvey, and Randolph *(Armonk, N.Y.: M. E. Sharpe, 1996) and in Jerome Davis, ed.,* Labor Speaks for Itself on Religion: A Symposium of Labor Leaders Throughout the World *(New York: Macmillan, 1929).*

For additional information on the Communist Party and African American humanism, see the sources listed in the Harrison summary. Also see, for example, Nell Irvin Painter, The Narrative of Hosea Hudson: His Life as a Negro Communist in the South *(Cambridge: Harvard University Press, 1979), particularly pages 128–135. Additional examples of Black nationalism can be found in the following: Wilson Jeremiah Moses, ed.,* Classical Black Nationalism: From the American Revolution to Marcus Garvey *(New York: New York University Press, 1996) and William L. Van DeBurg, ed.,* Modern Black Nationalism: From Marcus Garvey to Louis Farrakhan *(New York: New York University Press, 1997). For more information on Haywood's thought, see Harry Haywood,* Negro Liberation *(Chicago: Liberator Press, 1976). Also Philip S. Foner and James S. Allen, eds.,* American Communism and Black Americans: A Documentary History, 1919–1929 *(Philadelphia: Temple University Press, 1987). Readers may also be interested in African American Communists such as James W. Ford, who was the Communist Party's 1940 candidate for vice president. William Patterson's autobiography provides information on Ford and other prominent African American Communists* (The Man Who Cried Genocide *{New York: International Publishers, 1991}).*

Readers may also be interested in the following books by Benjamin J. Davis, Jr.: The Negro People and the Communist Party *(New York: Workers Library Publishers, 1943);* The Path of Negro Liberation *(New York: New Century Publishers, 1947); and* The Negro People in the Struggle for Peace and Freedom *(New York: New Century Publishers, 1951).*

Ewert Brown is a little-known Unitarian who worked in Harlem attempting to bring liberal religion (often resembling humanism) to African Americans. The connection between his politics and his religiophilosophical position is worth noting here. Interested readers should see, in the Schomburg Collection in New York City, the following speeches by Brown: "Naturalism" (1993); "A Debate: Does the Modern World Need a God?" (1933); and "Religious Liberalism in Harlem" (1929).

NOTE

1. For information on Christian socialists, see, for example, George Washington Woodbey, Black Socialist Preacher: The Teachings of Reverend George Washington Woodbey and His Disciple, Reverend G. W. Slater, Jr. *(San Francisco: Synthesis Publications, 1983).*

❏

On May 4, 1910, Halley's Comet appeared flaring down out of the heavens, its luminous tail switching to earth. It was an ominous sight.

A rash of religious revival swept Omaha. Prophets and messiahs appeared on street corners and in churches preaching the end of the world. Hardened sinners "got religion." Backsliders renewed their faith. The comet, with its tail moving ever closer to the earth, seemed to lend credence to forecasts of imminent cosmic disaster.

Both my Mother and Father were deeply religious. Theirs was that "old time religion," the fire-and-brimstone kind which leaned heavily on the Old Testament. It was the kind that accepted the Bible and all its legends as the literal gospel truth. We children had the "fear of the Lord" drilled into us from early age. My image of God was that of a vengeful old man who demanded unquestioned faith, strict obedience and repentant love as the price of salvation:

> I the Lord thy God am a jealous God, visiting the iniquity of the fathers upon the children unto the third and fourth gener-ation of them that hate me, and showing mercy unto thousands of them that love me and keep my commandments. Thou shalt love the Lord thy God with all thy heart, and with all thy soul, and with all thy might.

Every Sunday, rain or shine, the family would attend services at the little frame church near the railroad tracks. For me, this was a tortur-ous ordeal. I looked forward to Sundays with dread. We would spend all of eight hours in church. We would sit through the morning service, then the Sunday school, after which followed a break for dinner. We returned at five for the Young People's Christian Endeavor and finally the evening service. It was not just boredom. Fear was the dominant emotion, especially when our preacher, Reverend Jamieson, a big Black man with a beautiful voice, would launch into one of his fire-and-brimstone sermons. He would start out slowly and in a low voice, gradually raising it higher he would swing to a kind of sing-song rhythm, holding his congregation rapt with vivid word pictures. They would respond with "Hallelujah!" "Ain't it the truth!" "Preach it, brother!"

He would go on in this manner for what seemed an interminable time, and would reach his peroration on a high note, winding up with a rafter-shaking burst of oratory. He would then pause dramatically amidst moans, shouts and even screams of some of the women, one or two of whom would fall out in a dead faint. Waiting for them to subside he would then, in a lowered, scarcely audible voice, reassure his flock that it was not yet too late to repent and achieve salvation. All that was necessary was to: "Repent sinners, and love and obey the Lord. Amen." Someone would then rise and lead off with an appropriate spiritual such as:

> Oh, my sins are forgiven and my soul set free-ah,
> Oh, glory Halelua-a-a-a!
> Just let me in the kingdom when the world is all a'fi-ah,
> Oh Glory Halelu!
> I don't feel worried, no ways tiahd,
> Oh, glory Halelu!

I remember the family Bible, a huge book which lay on the center table in the front room. The first several pages were blank, set aside for recording the vital family statistics: births, deaths, marriages. The book was filled with graphic illustrations of biblical happenings. Leafing through Genesis (which we used to call "the begats"), one came to Exodus and from there on a pageant of bloodshed and violence unfolded. Portrayed in striking colors were the interminable tribal wars in which the Israelites slew the Mennonites and Pharoah's soldiers killed little children in search of Moses. There was the great God, Jehovah himself, whitebearded and eyes flashing, looking very much like our old cracker neighbor, Mr. Faught.

Just a couple of weeks before Halley's comet appeared, Mother had taken us to see the silent film, *Dante's Inferno,* through which I sat with open mouth horror. Needless to say, this experience did not lessen my apprehension.

The comet continued its descent, its tail like the flaming sword of vengeance. Collision seemed not just possible, but almost certain. What had we poor mortals done to incur such wrath of the Lord?

My deportment underwent a change. I did all my chores without complaint and helped Mama around the house. This was so unlike me that she didn't know what to make of it. I overheard her telling Pa about my good behavior and how helpful I had become lately. But I hadn't really changed. I was just scared. I was simply trying to carry out another one of God's commandments, "Honor thy father and thy mother that thy days may be prolonged, and that it may go well with thee in the land which the Lord thy God giveth thee."

Then one night, when the whole neighborhood had gathered as usual on the hill to watch the comet it appeared to have ceased its movement towards the earth. We were not sure, but the next night we were certain. It had not only ceased its descent, but was definitely withdrawing. In a couple more nights, it had disappeared. A wave of relief swept over the town.

"It's not true!" I thought to myself. "The fire and brimstone, the leering devils, the angry vengeful God. None of it is true."

It was as if a great weight had been lifted from my mind. It was the end of my religion, although I still thought that there was most likely a supreme being. But if God existed, he was nothing like the God portrayed in our family Bible. I was no longer terrified of him.

Later, at the age of fourteen or fifteen, I read some of the lectures of Robert G, Ingersoll and became an agnostic, doubting the existence of a god. From there, I later moved to positive atheism.

Two years later, the great event was the sinking of the *Titanic.* This was significant in Omaha because one of the Brandeis brothers, owners of the biggest department store in North Omaha, went down with her. In keeping with the custom of Blacks to gloat over the misfortunes of whites, especially rich ones, some Black bard composed the "Titanic Blues":

> *When old John Jacob Astor left his home,*
> *He never thought he was going to die.*
> *Titanic fare thee well,*
> *I say fare thee well.*

But disaster was more frequently reserved for the Black community. On Easter Sunday 1913, a tornado struck North Omaha. It ripped a two-block swath through the Black neighborhood, leaving death and destruction in its wake. Among the victims were a dozen or so Black youths trapped in a basement below a pool hall where they had evidently been shooting craps. Mother did not fail to point out the incident as another example of God's wrath. While I was sorry for the youths and their families (some of them were friends of Otto), the implied warning left me cold. My God-fearing days had ended with Halley's Comet.

Misfortune, however, was soon to strike our immediate family. It happened that summer, in 1913. My Father fled town after being attacked and beaten by a gang of whites on Q Street, right outside the gate of the packing plant. They told him to get out of town or they would kill him.

I remember vividly the scene that night when Father staggered through the door. Consternation gripped us at the sight. His face was swollen and bleeding, his clothes torn and in disarray. He had a frightened, hunted look in his eyes. My sister Eppa and I were alone.

Mother had gone for the summer to work for her employers, rich white folks, at Lake Okoboji, Iowa.

"What happened?" we asked.

He gasped out the story of how he had been attacked and beaten.

"They said they were going to kill me if I didn't get out of town."

We asked him who "they" were. He said that he recognized some of them as belonging to the Irish gang on Indian Hill, but there were also some grown men.

"But why, Pa? Why should they pick on you?"

"Why don't we call the police?"

"That ain't goin' to do no good. We just have to leave town."

"But Pa," I said, "how can we? We own this house. We've got friends here. If you tell them, they wouldn't let anybody harm us."

Again the frightened look crossed his face.

"No, we got to go."

"Where, where will we go?"

"We'll move up to Minneapolis, your uncles Watt and George are there. I'll get work there. I'm going to telegraph your Mother to come home now."

He washed his face and then went into the bedroom and began packing his bags. The next morning he gave Eppa some money and said, "This will tide you over till your Mother comes. She'll be here in a day or two. I'm going to telegraph her as soon as I get to the depot. I'll send for you all soon."

He kissed us goodbye and left.

Only when he closed the door behind him did we feel the full impact of the shock. It had happened so suddenly. Our whole world had collapsed. Home and security were gone. The feeling of safety in our little haven of interracial goodwill had proved elusive. Now we were just homeless "niggers" on the run.

The cruelest blow, perhaps, was the shattering of my image of Father. True enough, I had not regarded him as a hero. Still, however, I had retained a great deal of respect for him. He was undoubtedly a very complex man, very sensitive and imaginative. Probably he had never gotten over the horror of that scene in the cabin near Martin, Tennessee, where as a boy of fifteen he had seen his father kill the Klansman. He distrusted and feared poor whites, especially the native born and, in Omaha, the shanty Irish.

Mother arrived the next day. For her it was a real tragedy. Our home was gone and our family broken up. She had lived in Omaha for nearly a quarter of a century. She had raised her family there and had built up a circle of close friends. With her regular summer job at Lake Okoboji and catering parties the rest of the year, she had helped pay for our home. Now it was gone. We would be lucky if we even got a fraction of the money we had put into it, not to speak of the labor. Now she was to leave all this. Friends and neighbors would ask why Father had run away.

Why had he let some poor white trash run him out of town? He had friends there. Ours was an old respected family. He also had influential white patrons. There was Ed Cudahy of the family that owned the packing plant where he worked. The Cudahys had become one of the nation's big three in the slaughtering and meat packing industry. Father had known him from boyhood. There was Mr. Wilkins, general manager at Cudahy's, whom Father had known as an office boy, and who now gave Father all his old clothes.

A few days later, Mr. Cannon, a railroad man in charge of a buffet car on the Omaha and Minneapolis run and an old friend of the family, called with a message from Father. He said that Father was all right, that he had gotten a job for himself and Mother at the Minneapolis Women's Club. Father was to become caretaker and janitor, Mother was to cater the smaller parties at the club and to assist at the larger affairs. They were to live on the place in a basement apartment.

The salary was ridiculously small (I think about $60 per month for both of them) and the employers insisted that only one of us children would be allowed to live at the place. That, of course, would be Eppa. He said that Father had arranged for me to live with another family.

This, he said, would be a temporary arrangement. He was sure he could find another job, and rent a house where we could all be together again. As for me, Father suggested that since I was fifteen, I could find a part-time job to help out while continuing school. Mr. Cannon said that he was to take me back to Minneapolis with him, and that Mother and Eppa were to follow in a few days.

With regards to our house, Mr. Cannon said that he knew a lawyer, an honest fellow, who for a small commission would handle its sale. Mother later claimed that after deducting the lawyer's commission and paying off a small mortgage, they only got the paltry sum of $300! This was for a five-room house with electricity and running water.

The next day, Mr. Cannon took me out to his buffet car in the railroad yards. He put me in the pantry and told me to stay there, and if the conductor looked in: "Don't be afraid, he's a friend of mine." Our car was then attached to a train which backed down to the station to load passengers. I looked out the window as we left Omaha. I was not to see Omaha again until after World War I, when I was a waiter on the Burlington Railroad.

My childhood and part of my adolescence was now behind me. I felt that I was practically on my own. What did the world hold for me—a Black youth?

Arriving in Minneapolis, I went to my new school. As I entered the room, the all-white class was singing old darkie plantation songs. Upon seeing me, their voices seemed to take on a mocking, derisive tone. Loudly emphasizing the Negro dialect and staring directly at me, they sang:

> "Down in De Caun fiel—HEAH DEM darkies moan
> All De darkies AM a weeping
> MASSAHS in DE Cold Cold Ground"

They were really having a ball.

In my state of increased racial awareness, this was just too much for me. I was already in a mood of deep depression. With the breakup of our family, the separation from my childhood friends, and the interminable quarrels between my Mother and Father (in which I sided with Mother), I was in no mood to be kidded or scoffed at.

That was my last day in school. I never returned. I made up my mind to drop out and get a full-time job.

I was fifteen and in the second semester of the eighth grade.

19

"CORRUPT BLACK PREACHERS" AND "GOD IS DEAD: A QUESTION OF POWER"

James Forman

❏

James Forman (1928–) played a major role in efforts to reconstruct the United States during the civil rights movement. Born in Chicago, Forman earned a degree at Roosevelt University and began working for the Chicago Defender *newspaper. Forman also became involved with the Congress of Racial Equality's (CORE) efforts on behalf of Black farmers in the South.*

Based upon his work and his firsthand experience of racism during his travels in the South, Forman decided to become more involved in civil rights activities by joining the Student Nonviolent Coordinating Committee (SNCC). He quickly rose to a position of leadership and helped SNCC gain exposure and strength. However, differences in goals for the organization resulted in his resigning his post as executive secretary. Yet, although he no longer held an office, Forman remained involved and played a major role in the growing cooperation between the Black Panther Party and SNCC.

In 1969, Forman left SNCC and devoted his energies to the National Black Development Conference in Detroit. Many readers may remember For-man's actions as part of this group because it was as a member that Forman helped develop and then read the "Black Manifesto" at Riverside Church in

New York City. (The manifesto demanded reparations for African Americans.)
As a result of the document, the National Black Development Conference
received funding from a range of organizations, and Forman helped to establish
various projects, such as Black Star Publications, which published various
pamphlets. From that point until the present, Forman's efforts on behalf of the
oppressed have continued.

Forman's religiophilosophical position is important in that it sheds addi-
tional light on the presence of humanism as an empowering force *in civil*
rights activities. Many, when considering the civil rights movement, are hard
pressed to think beyond the Christian assumptions of figures such as Martin
Luther King, Jr. Some assume that the Christian church was the only progres-
sive force worth mentioning, other efforts being prone to what Cornel West refers
to as nihilism because they lack grounding in cosmic powers and authorities.
Forman's life and work disprove such assertions. In the following two excerpts
from his autobiography, Forman outlines his sense of humanism and its
connection to his political activities.

For additional information on SNCC, see Clayborne Carson, In Struggle:
SNCC and the Black Awakening of the 1960's *(Cambridge: Harvard*
University Press, 1981). Additional work related to Forman includes the
following: James Forman, Self Determination: An Examination of the
Question and Its Application to the African-American People *(Wash-*
ington, D.C.: Open Hand, 1984); "The Black Manifesto," 80–89, in James
H. Cone and Gayraud S. Wilmore, Black Theology: A Documentary
History, 1966–1979 *(Maryknoll, N.Y.: Orbis Books, 1979).*

❏

Corrupt Black Preachers

When I graduated from Englewood no one there even suggested that
I might apply for a scholarship to a university on the basis of my

strong high school record. No one counseled me or put me in touch with the right people to do this. It was just assumed that a black high school graduate would head for the job market or if he had money a small black college.

My dream was to go to Roosevelt University, but it cost money and I had none. Roosevelt had just opened, in 1945, on the principle of equal education for all people. While this slogan sounds like old hat today, in the city of Chicago in 1945 it was a revolutionary concept. But Roosevelt cost money. Wilson Junior College did not, so I enrolled there with the hope of being able to get a scholarship later.

At Wilson I entered the program in the humanities and took English, French, world history, and other subjects. The school was full of veterans; I always sought their company to discuss events and ideas. They were convinced I could not be serious about God. How could he exist? What type of God was he that would allow all the injustices in the world? World wars? Killing? Prejudices? Define him. Hell was here on earth, man, for black people.

By this time I began to have deep doubts about the existence of God. I had learned that matter cannot be created or destroyed. Therefore, how could God exist? I asked the ministers, the preachers. Youth wants to know the answers to these questions. The important thing about my questions was that a certain intellectual attitude had developed in me. I had to know for myself. I had to be convinced of the correctness of a position before I would accept it. I had to be committed fully to an idea and no one could explain to me the nature of God or what type of person or force he was.

This kind of debate stimulated me enormously and I had a great time during that first semester. I also worked out my long-range educational plans, which led me to a Ph.D. degree by the age of twenty-four.

During the summer of 1947, after that first semester at Wilson, I went to a youth meeting of African Methodist Episcopals from my district. It took place at a white Methodist camp in Michigan which our church rented. When I left there I had lost still more of my belief in God—and I had completely gotten over the idea of becoming a minister.

I had been assigned to a cabin where most of the ministers were staying. There were no young people in this cabin. One night I woke up and heard some ministers discussing how they planned to curb some of the power of Reverend Roberts, to whom I felt a strong attachment. Roberts was becoming too powerful, they said, and before you knew it he would be talking about running for bishop. This was politics and I did not mind politics, but I didn't think that preachers, ministers, people who were talking about a new world, should be involved in this kind of backbiting and conniving. I began to ask myself if I really wanted to be involved with this type of men. The theory of working from within lay heavy on me at that time, but I now began to think that it was nonsensical for me to dream of reforming the church, of crusading within the church. It would be too difficult, I was sure. And, then, I had some serious doubts about God. These "apostles" of God helped to confirm my doubts.

Then there was the matter of the cook.

It was my job during the meeting to ring the bells for people to go to classes, to worship, to sleep, and so forth. The bell was in front of an administrative cabin. I had to ring a bell at 10:00 for people to go to their cabins and worship, then another bell fifteen minutes later for worship to begin, and a final bell at 10:30 for lights out. One night, during the interval between those first two bells, one of the three white cooks employed by the camp came to talk to me. She was a young redhead named Ethel. I rang the second bell, went to my cabin to worship, and returned. She waited and walked me to my cabin after I rang the final lights-out bell.

The next day, one of the officials of the camp—Reverend Roberts's secretary—told me that I should just ring the two bells for worship and then remain in my cabin. It would be much easier for her to ring the last bell since it was right by her cabin, than for me to return. I thought this was a sensible idea. The next night, I rang the bell at 10:00, talked with Ethel until 10:15, and then she walked me to my cabin.

On the following morning, Reverend Roberts's secretary told me that it would be best for me to ring the bell at 10:00 and then go directly to my cabin and not be late for worship. She would ring the 10:15 bell for worship to begin. Now all this began to sound a little queer to me. Each day the bell-ringing procedure changed.

That afternoon one of the preachers who had been talking about the coup against Roberts came up to me. We were standing in some tall grass and he asked, "How are you enjoying the camp?"

"There are some good things and I have learned some things that I'm thinking about," I said.

"Well, have you seen the picture *Duel in the Sun?*"

"No, I haven't. What makes you ask that?"

"Well, in this picture Lionel Barrymore has two sons on this ranch and there is an Indian girl there played by Jennifer Jones."

He paused, looking very sheepish and then continued, "Well, in the picture Joseph Cotten falls in love with this Indian girl and Lionel Barrymore says to him 'We don't want any half-breeds on this ranch.'"

I looked at him, a preacher, a politician, and I said, "Why are you telling me this?"

"Don't you know?"

"Know what?" I exploded. It was very obvious to me what he was talking about, but I wanted him to say it. I didn't think he had the nerve.

"Well, we don't want any redheaded Negro children coming from this camp."

"Thanks for your advice," I said and walked away. How could he consider himself a preacher, a minister of the gospel, and think that way? You can't even talk to a person and be friendly without someone, a preacher at that, thinking such thoughts and then telling you. I was disgusted. Then I began to wonder if he had some other reason for having changed the ringing of the bell.

It was not until the following week, when I returned to Chicago, that I confirmed my suspicion. I had a conversation with Reverend Roberts's secretary. In the middle of other matters, I suddenly asked, "Why did you keep changing the bells at the camp?"

"Why do you ask?"

She had outfoxed me with this question. Instead of demanding an answer, I told her what that preacher of the gospel had said to me about redheaded Negro children.

"Oh, don't worry about him. You're right, there was a great deal of talk about the possibility of your association with that girl hurting our chances of getting the camp again. To deal with the gossip, I just decided to ring the bells myself. As for that character . . . I wouldn't give it a second thought.

"Listen, he called my house this morning. My husband answered the phone and said Reverend—wants to speak to you. I was very surprised to get a call from him. And do you know, he began telling me how he had fallen in love with me at the camp and he would leave his wife and four children if I would leave my husband and marry him! I was outraged," she continued. "I didn't know what to say. My husband was in the room so I had to make up something. I'm not sure what I told him, I think I said we could discuss that 'church matter' later. I had to get off the phone.

"The fool did not want to hang up. He kept telling me how much he loved me and he had to marry me. He wanted to leave everything, his family, his children, and all that he had done. He had to marry me! So it doesn't surprise me, what he said to you."

"But how could he do that? How could he, a minister, do that? How can he talk about God and ethics and do something like that?" I asked. I was convinced that reforming preachers was impossible. I suppose I was looking for some kind of consistency in ministers, a superiority to the rest of us.

Then I told her the story of the planned coup against Reverend Roberts and all my feelings about that. We talked for a long time about words and actions, consistency and honesty in your work, and how men should react to women.

God was not quite dead in me, but he was dying fast.

At the end of the summer, when I was eagerly expecting to return to Wilson Junior College for a second semester, an incident occurred which changed my big educational plans and had an undetermined effect on my life.

As in high school, I had been working off and on at my stepfather's gas station. It was a Saturday morning in mid-September and I had gone down there to work for the day, although I wanted to go to the opening football game of Englewood High School. My stepfather hadn't yet arrived and I opened up shop. The first customer was a man who wanted his battery charged. I checked the water, put some in, and then charged it while the customer went off on an errand.

He came back for his car and said it wouldn't start. My stepfather had arrived by then, and went to the car with the battery tester. He said the battery did not charge because there was no water in it.

"I put water in it," I told Pop. "There must be a leak."

Pop continued to insist that no water had been put in the battery. For what must have been the fifteenth time, he scolded, "You got to put water in the battery."

I exploded.

"I told you I put water in. If you say I didn't, you're a shittin' ass liar."

Pop froze. "What did you say?"

"Nothing," I answered. I didn't want another hassle with him, we had had enough arguments over the years.

My stepfather called to my younger brother, Bernard, who was also there that day. "What did he say?"

"He said you're a liar," Bernard answered. I was mad at him for telling on me, but glad he hadn't thrown in all the adjectives.

Then Pop said it, though not for the first time. "The house isn't big enough for both of us," he told me. "Get out."

I left and went to the football game. That night and the next I spent at the home of Mr. and Mrs. Rogers from my church. I decided to enlist in the Army. It would interrupt my education and it changed all my plans; but, I told myself, there would probably be a compulsory draft again anyway—and, in fact, it came two years later. Also, I thought the country would be at war again soon (which it was, in Korea). It might be better to get my service out of the way now, in peacetime, and have an uninterrupted education afterward.

There were other factors. I had no money to support myself while in school. The chances of my getting a decent job seemed like a hopelessly long shot. The Army was an assured means of living; I might even learn something from it. Anyway it would only be for two years. Also, I was now eighteen years old and I felt it was time to leave home. Time to get away from my stepfather.

Above all, I had little choice. In feeling that way, I was like a lot of young black brothers then, and still today—just looking for a home and holding little hope of alternatives. I accepted the idea that there might be a draft and I would be drafted. The thought of fighting the draft system did not enter my mind then. I accommodated to the seeming inevitability of the draft and also to the racism which made finding a good job impossible. For all my desire to go on in school right away and to change the society, there was a fatalistic streak in me—as in other young blacks—about our lives. I knew the Army would be segregated; still, I decided without great qualms to go into it, not to fight for so-called freedom and democracy, but to earn money, travel, and fulfill my military obligations to the United States.

That decision reflected the deadening effect that a pervasive system of racism and exploitation has on people. Growing up in a racist society, you become accustomed to a certain way of life. Although I had challenged many forms of racism, I was also inoculated against protest and resistance to a large extent. Perhaps I also had then, deep within me, a hope—a vague wish—that freedom and democracy for all would not always prove to be empty words.

Today I would never volunteer for a segregated army (or the U.S. Armed Forces in general), nor would I take a seat at the back of a bus or in the front of a train. Those battles have been won; the struggle, once so focused on segregation because it was the most blatant form of racism, passed through that stage and now stands on a higher level. And I myself changed.

But this was 1947 and I was eighteen. I had made up my mind to volunteer, and I went back to my parents' apartment just once—to tell my mother of my decision, and say good-bye. . . .

God Is Dead: A Question of Power

The next six years of my life were a time of ideas. A time when things were germinating and changing in me. A time of deciding what I would do with my life. It was also a time in which I rid myself, once and for all, of the greatest disorder that cluttered my mind—the belief in God or any type of supreme being.

When I finally entered Roosevelt University in the fall of 1954 it must have been one of the most stimulating and brotherly places of study in the country. Its birth in 1945 grew out of a decision by Dr. Edward J. Spaulding, president of the state YMCA college. The board of trustees of the YMCA college wanted Dr. Spaulding to make a head count of the black students there. He knew this meant only one thing: that they were planning to establish a quota because of all the young blacks flooding out of the Armed Forces and into the schools. Spaulding refused to do this and took the issue to the faculty. Its members agreed that, rather than submit to this kind of discrimination, they would found a new university based upon the principle of equal educational opportunities for all people and free from the unwritten quota system for the admission of black people. Spaulding became Roosevelt's first president and the university became a haven for veterans who could not get in anywhere else because of quota systems.

The staff at Roosevelt contained a high percentage of black people, blacks who occupied not just menial jobs but also important administrative positions. This I found very impressive the first day I went there; and I continued to be impressed. It was a very good thing to see that many black people handling administrative posts. It created a feeling of warmth and camaraderie all over the university and a feeling that this school, at least, was serious about its program, serious about its philosophy.

"Do you think that people who want to write are neurotic?" I had asked the doctor during a group therapy session at Brentwood Neuropsychiatric Hospital. "Well, we're all neurotic," he answered, "it's a question of how a person handles his neurosis." I suppose his answer was good enough for me, or that I stopped worrying about what my motivation might be and decided that it was the kind of work I produced that counted. One way or the other, I had left the hospital with a clear desire to be a writer—something I had never thought of before.

At Roosevelt, I wanted to switch my field from public administration to journalism, but this proved impossible. The government was paying for my education and journalism was not a career within its program for veterans; I had to stick with personnel management. But again, the program allowed me to take a wide range of courses— political science, anthropology, economics, philosophy. I made peace with myself about this arrangement by saying that it would provide a good, broad background for journalism; I could always pick up the techniques of my craft at some other point.

Later at Roosevelt I thought for a while of becoming a civil rights lawyer and even applied to the University of Chicago Law School. They rejected me and I never pursued the idea. As it turned out, the choice of a career to pursue at Roosevelt was less important than my good luck in having a number of exciting teachers and courses.

Walter Weiskopf, a professor of economics, was one of those who impressed me most. He was an Austrian Jew who had to flee Austria because of the Nazis. He had been psychoanalyzed by a student of Freud's, which gave our association additional meaning for me because I was then emerging from my experience at the Brentwood Neuropsychiatric Hospital. I did a tremendous amount of outside reading for his courses: Thorstein Veblen, Karen Horney, and particularly Erich Fromm were some of the writers whom I came to know under Weiskopf's direction.

Lionel Ruby was my professor for Philosophy 102 and important not so much for his personal qualities as for what happened to me because I took his course. Our textbook was *The Way of Philosophy,* by Cartwright [Wheelwright], which might be called an atheist's manual; during that course God finally died in my conscious mind. For the final examination, we had to write an essay discussing the most important thing we had learned from the course. This is the essence of what I wrote: The most important things I have learned from this class are a number of intellectual arguments which disprove the myth that there is a God. When I was growing up, I was taught that God was responsible for the creation of the universe and he had the power to judge men, to make them submit to his will.

Then I began to wonder, if he is all-powerful, as we are told, why do we have war and disease and poverty and natural disasters like earthquakes? Why would an all-powerful God create a world where these ills exist? It is said that God leaves these questions to be settled by man. But can he be a just God, knowing that he had the power to change conditions and yet allowing people to suffer on this earth? He cannot be a just God if he has this power and will not use it. And if he is not just, then men should not give him their allegiance, but should seek to destroy him. Which they cannot do, of course, if he is all-powerful.

As I grew older, I began to question the existence of God. If matter could neither be created nor destroyed but simply changed in form— then how was it possible that God, an entity, a being, could create the world. Out of what did he create it?

When I entered this class, I had my doubts about God; I had simply decided that he was the first cause and nothing else. He had no attributes other than being the first cause. I have learned that every cause has its effect and every effect is produced by a cause. This argument goes on ad infinitum. Cause and effect cannot be broken logically. Therefore, if God is the first cause, then what caused the cause?

St. Thomas Aquinas has said that there is a point when one can no longer prove the existence of God by logic. One has to make a leap of faith and accept that there is a God. He is correct, but most often those who believe in God are not willing to say, "I believe in God but cannot prove that he exists." No man can logically disprove the beliefs of someone who insists that his beliefs are correct despite all rational arguments.

It is that leap of faith which I now refuse to make. I reject the existence of God. He is not all-powerful, all-knowing, and everywhere. He is not just or unjust because he does not exist. God is a myth; churches are institutions designed to perpetuate this myth and thereby keep people in subjugation.

When a people who are poor, suffering with disease and sickness, accept the fact that God has ordained for them to be this way—then they will never do anything about their human condition. In other words, the belief in a supreme being or God weakens the will of a people to change conditions themselves. As a Negro who has grown up in the United States, I believe that the belief in God has hurt my people. We have put off doing something about our condition on this earth because we have believed that God was going to take care of business in heaven.

My philosophy course had finally satisfied my need for intellectual as well as emotional certainty that God did not exist. I reached the point of rejecting God out of personal experience and observations; now I had intellectual arguments to satisfy me that my private feelings were correct. It was a great load off my mind to say with conviction, "God is a myth."

The greatest, most direct, and longest-lasting influence on me at Roosevelt was that of St. Clair Drake, who also became a personal friend and collaborator in many ventures after I graduated. St. Clair was the first black teacher that I had throughout my educational experience (except for Mrs. Pearson, my gym teacher in grammar school). He and Lorenzo Turner, with whom I would have a graduate course later, were the only black teachers that I had after grammar school.

My relationship with Drake began when I went to interview him for *The Torch,* the school newspaper, in the fall of 1955. He had just come back from Africa and his excitement about the new political independence of Ghana, about the continuing liberation struggles in countries like Kenya, about the newborn struggles of countries like Algeria, was contagious. He talked in particular about the problems facing black nations with large European populations. In the courses I had with him later, anthropology and sociology, Drake stirred us by the vividness with which he lectured, the energy with which he taught and led discussions, the amount of knowledge he disseminated.

A number of us, both black and white, formed a small cadre or brotherhood, as we called it. Because of teachers like Drake and because Roosevelt had an older student population than most schools, our brotherhood included not only students but also faculty and community people. We read many of the same books, shared similar experiences, had the same basic values. We formed a sort of unity around our common interests—above all, racism U.S.A.

Roy Stell, now a teacher in the Chicago public schools, was my closest associate. He and I used to prick the conscience of many of the black students. Sometimes they didn't even want us to come over to their tables because we would always come talking race. At this time, the NAACP was coming under attack for pushing its many school cases throughout the Deep South and we used to have heated arguments with the black students who didn't want us to talk about the NAACP's struggle. We also argued with white students who felt the NAACP was "pushing too hard."

The Montgomery bus boycott, which began in late 1955, got us even more involved in such debates. There had been a court ruling in the state of Virginia which stated that bus companies could not deny Negroes any seats whatsoever on a bus. The Supreme Court refused to review this decision; this indicated that the court was in agreement with the decision. In Montgomery people continued to boycott the buses while awaiting a decision on their court case. They were testing whether or not the segregation on the Montgomery buses was legal. I was studying constitutional law at the time and believed that, given the Virginia decision and the Supreme Court's attitude, the people in Montgomery should start boarding the buses—and sitting where they wished—instead of waiting for the outcome of their legal case. If they waited, it would set a pattern of people all over the country waiting until their particular desegregation suit was decided. This was one of the weaknesses of the Supreme Court's ruling on school desegregation, that blacks had to apply to desegregate each Southern school district, one by one.

At Roosevelt, I was president of student government then and we decided to try to raise some money for some station wagons to support the Montgomery bus boycott. We made contact—I think Roy Stell spoke to Rev. Ralph Abernathy of the Southern Christian Leadership Conference—to find out what they were going to do. SCLC said that their lawyers felt that there was not enough clarity in the Virginia ruling and that the courts in Alabama would say that it did not apply. We felt that this was a very negative attitude and that King should call for a creative confrontation with the racist bus companies. The boycott had become a passive kind of protest and should be turned into a more positive, aggressive action similar to what Gandhi did at the salt mines. Of course we were sitting in Chicago, judging the situation from a great distance, which is a very dangerous thing to do. Nevertheless, we felt that we had a right to make a comment on the paramount social issue of the day.

The Montgomery bus boycott had a very significant effect on the consciousness of black people throughout the United States. In 1956 our people constantly said, "Well, black folks just can't stick together. We can never act as a unit, we can't unify to protest against this man. We're like a bunch of crabs—the minute one of us crawls through the top, the rest of us drag him back down." This idea had been instilled by the colonizing force of white society, which always played down the importance of the black man. Part of the lack of group identification also rested in the belief that there was no need for it; God was going to take care of the white man when he got him in heaven. Our songs said things like, "I'm gonna tell God how you treat me," and then justice would be done.

Some friends and I had spent hours and hours in the barber shops of Sixty-first Street, trying to talk people out of these self-destructive attitudes, these self-fulfilling prophecies of "we can't get together." When the Montgomery bus boycott came along, you could hear people in the barber shops saying, "Well, at least people in Montgomery are sticking together." The boycott had a particularly important effect on young blacks and helped to generate the student movement of 1960. I remember Ruby Doris Robinson, who became executive secretary of SNCC, saying that when she was about thirteen or four-teen and saw those old people walking down there in Montgomery, just walking, walking, walking, it had a tremendous impact. The boycott woke me to the real—not merely theoretical—possibility of building a nonviolent mass movement of Southern black people to fight segregation. I had already found this notion in Reinhold Nie-buhr's book *Moral Man and Immoral Society* and in John Steinbeck's writing. But now, in Montgomery, you could see the real thing.

My philosophy and strategy of struggle were evolving rapidly in the dynamic climate of Roosevelt. I was reading in anthropology and sociology, history and economics, many books outside the required lists, especially with Weiskopf. I had already made up my mind about passive resistance, or pacifism: It was strictly a tactic, not a way of life without limitations. Many students did not agree. Another value in dispute was integration, which had become the subject of keen debate with the 1954 Supreme Court decision ordering that all schools be desegregated. We argued over the merits of integration, which we took to mean total absorption into the mainstream of American life. Day after day, night after night, the discussions went on: "Who wants to integrate into a burning house?" some of us asked. When James Baldwin began writing these things, we had already been saying them for half a dozen years. The difference, of course, is that we just said them while Brother Baldwin put them down on paper.

As the student government president—the second black to hold that office in the school's ten-year history—I invited Autherine Lucy, who had desegregated the University of Alabama, to speak at Roose-velt. I was also working on a local issue, the desegregation of housing in Trumbull Park. Such activities brought my administration of stu-dent government under sharp attack from many whites, who felt people in my position should stick to campus affairs.

This was also the position of the National Student Association, which failed to support the Montgomery boycott. I attended the 1956 conference of NSA as head of Roosevelt's delegation and had my eyes opened to how the power structure operates and how whites use blacks to their own ends. This story begins a few weeks before the NSA conference, at the Democratic Convention. My experience there would affect my behavior at the 1964 Democratic Convention.

I went to the National Democratic Party meeting in Chicago in August, 1956, not as a representative of any group but as an individual, a person who lived in Chicago and who was interested in politics— particularly in the platform hearings which preceded nominations. I wanted to see what really went on at these sessions of the Democratic Party. And I began to learn.

One of the delegates to the Platform Committee was a short judge from Alabama, George C. Wallace. Stupid George impressed me at that meeting as an avowed segregationist with a distinctive style. He was constantly jumping up, challenging this statement and that one, arguing that the South and the state of Alabama had no problems of race relations and that people were distorting reality. He jumped up and down so much that I wanted to know what made this jumping jack tick. How could a man who claimed to be a judge jump up and down and make all that noise and know damn well he was not telling the truth? I understood why he was doing it, but I wanted to know more about the man. So one day, during a break, I decided that I would go up and say "hello" to him. I wondered if he was such a segregationist that he would refuse to shake my hand. And if he did, maybe that would embarrass him.

No. Not stupid George. George came over, shook my hand, leaned on a railing, and tried to convince me that he was right. Why, we would be surprised at the progress they were making in getting the right to vote for the nigras in Alabama before that NAACP came along and started pushing too fast. And what the NAACP did with Autherine Lucy was just awful. He went on and on, and I listened. With stupid George I just couldn't get angry. I don't know exactly what made me listen that long, maybe curiosity, but George had a style then, long before he became governor, a style that made me listen to him without getting too angry.

That was not the case with James P. Coleman, a former governor from Mississippi; now he sits on the bench of the United States Fifth Circuit Court of Appeals. To him I reacted with hostility the first time I heard him open his mouth. I wanted to punch that cracker dead in the nose, right there in the Sheraton-Blackstone Hotel. Maybe it was because he was from Mississippi and that provoked an immediate psychological response in me. I couldn't stand his so-called suave style of condescension: Why, he knew nigras that just loved him to death. Why, even before he left Mississippi, there was Old John whom he had loaned a heap of money to in the past. Old John wanted to borrow five dollars. He asked Old John what did he need it for. Just need it, boss-man. So he loaned Old John the five dollars, knowing full well he would not get it back. He never got it back; that's the way they were. He said he told this story just to show that there was a tradition of good will between the races in Mississippi. He just wished all these here Northerners would stop talking about how bad the good white folks of Mississippi treat their nigras.

During the break that day, I saw him entering the hotel and coming up the stairs to the platform hearings. I rushed up and stood by the railing, trying to block his passage, hoping, just hoping he would touch me. He saw me staring at him. He stepped back and went far to the other side of the stairs in order to enter. After he had gone to the other side, I was angry with myself for not stepping over to the other side, too. I guess I made one of those face-saving little vows that a revolutionary often makes, "You just wait."

At the caucuses of the newly formed Leadership Conference on Civil Rights, of which Roy Wilkins was chairman, the feeling was that the Platform Committee would present a very weak platform—with a minority report. The Leadership Conference wanted a floor fight on the minority resolution. If that resolution ever reached the floor of the convention, they were sure that it would be accepted by the convention. The convention just couldn't turn down a strong civil rights plank in the platform of the Democratic Party.

There was some concern that the chairman of the convention would say, "You have heard the report of the Platform Committee. All those in favor say, 'Aye.' Those not in favor, say, 'Nay.' " If this happened, according to Walter Reuther, then certainly the chairman would rule on this voice vote that ["]the ayes have it. Platform adopted. Weak."

But the convention certainly had enough labor delegates who were prepared to prevent this steamroller tactic. They would demand a roll-call vote. At that point, there would be a motion to substitute the minority report for the majority. Labor was going to make so much noise before the chairman called for the voice vote that the convention would be in pandemonium. Thus they would stop the steamroller.

I waited. I wanted to see this happen. It was crucial to the civil rights struggle, the destiny of black people. We had to win this one, I thought.

On the night that the Platform Committee was due to give its report, I sat in the balcony, tense, waiting. The drama was there, the suspense. A feeling of intrigue developed when I saw Carmine De Sapio, smoky glasses and all, walk out of the convention to caucus. What was up?

There was a minority report given and speakers for it. I remember the senator from Illinois, the white-haired Paul Douglas, who spoke in favor of the minority report.

Then came the majority report. The chairman did ask for a voice vote. Where was the noise? I didn't hear anything. I listened. They voted. The ayes had it. The majority report won. I didn't hear one foot hit the floor when the chairman of the convention called for a unanimous decision to support the civil rights plank.

But the trick was greater than I thought. Not only wasn't there a floor fight, but the white people offered up Congressman Bill Dawson, a black man, to speak about the glories of the Democratic Party. I was walking out in disgust as I heard him say he remembered when Negroes were hungry and the Democratic Party came and fed us.

I thought all night about the trick that had been played on the blacks across the country who could not see what I saw or hear what I heard. What a fake the entire platform hearings must be, I thought. They probably had the resolution already written in the National Committee meeting. They had the hearings only as a pretense of democratic procedure, to let people talk.

I learned and I remembered. I didn't know what could be done, except that I could go to the NSA conference held at the University of Chicago. There, as the chairman of the delegation from Roosevelt, I certainly could make a floor fight over civil rights. This time there would be a fight. No compromise. A fight.

The Roosevelt delegation urged that NSA accept the five points which the NAACP and the Leadership Conference on Civil Rights had put forward as a minimum plank for adoption by the Democratic Party:

1. Establishment of a Civil Rights Commission.
2. Creation of a civil rights section in the Justice Department.
3. Calling a national conference on civil rights.
4. Implementation of the 1954 Supreme Court decision.
5. Repeal of Senate Rule 22.

(The last is the rule by which the Senate deals with the filibuster; it requires a vote of two-thirds to end debate. Every time a civil rights measure had come to the Senate, it was killed by extensive filibustering on the part of Southern senators. Those senators wanting to pass civil rights legislation argued that they did not have the necessary two-thirds vote in the Senate to cut off debate. It was this rule that labor, according to Walter Reuther, wanted most to change because it affected labor legislation too.)

To strengthen our position, we lined up the support of the University of Chicago delegation and from there flanked out to get the support of students from Columbia University, the City College of New York, the University of Michigan, some California schools, and others. We were lined up solidly, along with the few black schools from the South, against the Southern whites.

We won. We got the convention to pass resolutions adopting the entire program with relative ease. We were surprised.

And then some tall delegate from a western university moved that we reconsider the vote on the repeal of Senate Rule 22. After all, this was a rule that dealt with how the U.S. Senate governed its business; NSA should not concern itself with such matters.

Our group had successfully argued the importance of civil rights from the point of view of those of us who were black. But in the long run everybody who wanted to make changes through the so-called democratic process suffered from Senate filibustering. Now there was a move to undo all our political and educational work at the convention.

People told us we were fighting an uphill battle because Allard Lowenstein opposed us. Lowenstein, who in 1968 became a congressman from New York, was indeed a powerful fellow, a graduate of the University of North Carolina, a past president of NSA, one who had addressed the convention earlier and received a tremendous response. Lowenstein, we were told, led the fight against us not from the floor but by assisting those Southerners and Westerners who wanted us to leave the business of the Senate to the senators.

It is hard to imagine today the passion and energy with which we fought to keep the NSA convention from rescinding its vote on Senate Rule 22. We were fighting for students to take a positive stand on an important issue of 1956. But the battle was larger than that. We fought to educate people and deal another blow to segregation. In many respects, the NSA convention of 1956 was similar to the halls of Congress. The Southern students lined up with the Western and Midwestern farmers and the Northern conservatives.

Finally Lowenstein pulled out his last and most effective ace. He got the student body president from the City College of New York, a Negro, to stand up and argue against us. The moment this young Uncle Tom rose to speak, I was on the floor and saw with my own eyes how Allard Lowenstein shoved him, literally pushed him, toward the microphone, saying, "Go now. Speak now."

There are some faces and expressions that one does not forget. And to this day I remember the expression on the face of Allard Lowenstein as he pushed the black cat down the aisle. This was the young white who would later build a big liberal image by organizing students to work in the South and by his trips to Africa.

It was a critical moment, for the debate had been wavering and all the blacks at the convention had lined up in favor of keeping the vote on Senate Rule 22. We had decided that this was our fight and that we blacks should speak to this issue. We had decided that if NSA meant anything, it must listen to the black delegates. We had decided that if the Southerners threatened the convention with a walkout, then we would tell the liberals gathered there to kiss them good-bye. We had argued that the question of principle should override any threats from Southern white schools that had not even desegregated themselves. Let them go.

But the black brother from New York stood up and said he was against the convention taking a stand on Senate Rule 22, although he had favored it earlier. He had thought about it and felt this was an unwise position for NSA to take. Not all Negroes were interested in the repeal of Rule 22, he said.

The brother's speech did not affect the black votes but it turned a crucial number of whites around because the argument came from a Negro. So we lost the vote on the repeal of Senate Rule 22, but we saved the rest of the program that had been passed. Afterward I talked to the brother from City College. Not only did I tell him that I felt he had been a Tom for Lowenstein and the Southern opposition, but I asked the brother about what kind of role he would play later in life, given the attitudes he had now. I later learned that this brother lost his position as chairman of his delegation when he returned to City College, primarily because of his stand.

Autherine Lucy, the expelled black student from the University of Alabama, appeared at this conference with Herb Wright, the director of youth activities of the NAACP. Sister Lucy and I had met earlier when she spoke at Roosevelt at the invitation of the student government. Wright announced that, since her case was in court, she would not speak to the body. With Autherine by his side, he proceeded to read a legal document detailing the facts of her expulsion. The white delegation from the University of Alabama and some other crackers got up and walked out, singing "Dixie." Some of us stood, singing the "Star Spangled Banner," of all things.

The last fight we made at that conference dealt with black representation on the policy-making and officer level of NSA. We severely criticized NSA for not having had a Negro as a national officer since its founding. We argued that if NSA were serious about the desegregation of Southern white schools, it should elect a Negro as educational affairs vice-president. We felt that a black would press harder for the desegregation of Southern schools than a white person.

I was then asked to run for this office, in order to make it a real issue. With great reservations I did so, fully aware that having an insurgent as a candidate would reduce us to the level of protesting, making a point. A three-way contest developed. When it was obvious that I would lose, I threw my support to another fellow who was also somewhat opposed to the administration of NSA. Their choice won, nevertheless. Some people argued that my campaigning hurt the liberal candidate. Anyway, the liberal candidate won the position of national affairs vice-president by a unanimous vote.

The 1956 NSA convention was the first and the last one I attended. I knew almost nothing about the organization before this experience. Afterward I felt NSA was irrelevant to the struggle of black people, since it was an extremely conservative organization, dominated by a body of students and former officers who saw themselves moving in governmental circles. But I underestimated the influence of NSA's International Affairs Commission. Since the 1967 disclosures about its involvement with the CIA, its relationship to African students has caused some of us great concern. (Not that we should have tried to reform the organization, but we should have developed alternatives to this government body.) I also wonder to what extent the position I took at that conference affected the way NSA would later play its cards in relation to various groups and individuals in the civil rights movement. Certainly the CIA, FBI, and others must have come to the conclusion in 1956 that I, for one, could never become "witty."

The fight over Senate Rule 22 reinforced my belief that blacks had to take the leadership in waging their struggle. If there were whites who accepted the program and were willing to work under the leadership and direction of blacks, that was another matter. Within that framework, decisions about the participation of whites should be made on the merit of each individual white and how he fitted into the total program and objectives.

The conference revealed to me the distinctions between integration and desegregation which Southerners maintained. As a member of the drafting committee of the Educational Affairs Commission, I could not understand at first some of the quarrels over the words *desegregation* and *integration.* Later I learned that the Southerners believed *integration* meant the total acceptance of the American Negro in the American way of life. *Desegregation* meant the removal of the legal barriers that prevented Negroes from having access to the American way of life.

I became convinced that Southerners deliberately fostered this distinction between integration and desegregation as a rationale for evading the 1954 Supreme Court decision. For instance, the Supreme Court decision of 1954 said that Southern schools should be desegregated. That is a legal question, a legal right which is indisputable. However, when you twist the removal of legal barriers to mean that one must accept (how gracious) us totally into the American way of

life, then the justification for hostility increases. The resistance becomes even greater when one takes the word *desegregation* to mean race
mixing, as many of the Southern white papers used to call orders to
desegregate this or that school, "The court ordered race mixing."

There were a few Southern whites at the NSA meeting who told
the truth. One of them was the son of John Patterson, then governor
of Alabama, who said "The issue is power. We control the state and
we're not going to allow any Negras to run Alabama and take our
power from us. That is why we expelled Autherine Lucy. If we allow
the Negras to crack our power in any way, that is an invitation to
further weaken it.

"Why, in the county where my friend lives, the Negras are nine to
one and his father is sheriff of that county. Do you think if the Negras
had the right to vote that they would elect his father as sheriff? We
got the power and we intend to keep it."

In the contest of power, those with the greatest force, the greatest
strength, will win. I was learning.

20

THE ONLY REASON YOU WANT TO GO TO HEAVEN IS THAT YOU HAVE BEEN DRIVEN OUT OF YOUR MIND

Alice Walker

❏

Alice Walker's (1944–   ) novels and essays have gained her an international reputation. Born in Eaton, Georgia, Walker attended Spelman College but completed her degree at Sarah Lawrence College. Walker found access to African American thought and writings wanting at Sarah Lawrence and supplemented this material with travel and involvement in social protest in the United States.

Drawing from this background, Walker's work explores various dimensions of African American experience. The themes within early works such as The Third Life of Grange Copeland *(New York: Harcourt, Brace, Jovanovich, 1970) were enhanced through her discovery of Zora Neale Hurston's writings.[1] One sees the influence of Hurston, Phillis Wheatley, and others in books such as* In Search of Our Mothers' Gardens: Womanist Prose *(San Diego: Harcourt, Brace, Jovanovich, 1983). In this text, Walker develops the notion of "womanist," which continues to serve as an organizing paradigm for Black feminist work in areas such as literary criticism and theology. Walker's exploration of the combined issues of race, gender, and class is found in all of her work, including the Pulitzer Prize–winning* The Color Purple *(New York: Harcourt, Brace, Jovanovich, 1982).*

The influence of Walker on popular literature, academic investigations, and notions of social transformation is undeniable. However, what receives less attention is her humanism. As discussed in the following article, Walker has moved beyond traditional and theistic notions, and embraces a conception of nature as the organizing principle of life. In this way, Walker grounds her thought in a healthy respect for collective life without losing sight of the importance of the human's place in this larger scheme of existence.

The reader will note the manner in which Walker's thought reflects basic humanist principles. Her connection to these principles was recognized by the American Humanist Association when it named her the "1997 Humanist of the Year." The following article is her acceptance speech.

Other interesting depictions of humanist sensibilities can be found in the work of Ernest Gaines. See, for example, John Lowe, ed., Conversations with Ernest Gaines *(Jackson: University Press of Mississippi, 1995), particularly 39–55; and Ernest Gaines,* Bloodline *(New York: Norton, 1976). Attention might also be given to the work of Cyrus Colter; see John O'Brien, ed.,* Interviews with Black Writers *(New York: Liveright, 1973), 17–33; and Cyrus Colter,* The Rivers of Eros *(Chicago: Swallow Press, 1972). In addition to the above, readers will find the humanistic tone of Robert H. deCoy's* The Nigger Bible *(Los Angeles: Halloway House, 1972) interesting. With deCoy's text, particular attention should be given to pages 17–26, 157–160, and 172–175.[2] For a more general discussion of humanism within African American literature, see Trudier Harris, "Three Black Women Writers and Humanism: A Folk Perspective," 50–74, in R. Baxter Miller, ed.,* Black American Literature and Humanism *(Lexington: University Press of Kentucky, 1981).*

Those interested in additional works by Alice Walker should see the following: Meridian *(New York: Washington Square Press, 1977);* The Temple of My Familiar *(San Diego: Harcourt, Brace, Jovanovich, 1989);* Possessing the Secret of Joy *(New York: Harcourt, Brace, Jovanovich, 1992);* You Can't Keep a Good Woman Down: Stories *(New York: Harcourt, Brace*

Jovanovich, 1981); and Living by the Word: Selected Writings, 1973–
1987 *(San Diego: Harcourt, Brace, Jovanovich 1988). For discussions of
Walker's work, see Henry L. Gates, Jr., and Anthony Appiah, ed.,* Alice
Walker: Critical Perspectives Past and Present *(New York: Amistad;
distributed by Penguin USA, 1993).*

NOTES

1. See Alice Walker, ed., I Love Myself When I Am Laughing . . . and
Then Again When I am Looking Mean and Impressive: A Zora Neale
Hurston Reader *(New York: Feminist Press, 1979).*
   2. I am grateful to Cheryl Johnson for bringing this text to my attention.

❏

Unto the woman God said: I will greatly multiply thy sorrow
and thy conception; In sorrow thou shalt bring forth children;
and thy desire shall be to thy husband, and he shall rule over
thee.
                                                    —Genesis 3:16

In my novel *The Color Purple,* Celie and Shug discuss, as all thoughtful
humans must, the meaning of God. Shug says, "I believe God is
everything that is, ever was or ever will be." Celie, raised to worship
a God that resembles "the little fat white man who works in the
bank," only bigger and bearded, learns to agree. I agree also. It was
years after writing these words for Shug that I discovered they were
also spoken, millennia ago, by Isis, ancient Goddess of Africa, who, as
an African, can be said to be a spiritual mother of us all.

There is a special grief felt by the children and grandchildren of those
who were forbidden to read, forbidden to explore, forbidden to ques-

tion or to know. Looking back on my parents' and grandparents' lives, I have felt overwhelmed, helpless, as I've examined history and society, and especially religion, with them in mind, and have seen how they were manipulated away from a belief in their own judgment and faith in themselves.

It is painful to realize they were forever trying to correct a "flaw"— that of being black, female, human—that did not exist, except as "men of God," but really men of greed, misogyny, and violence, defined it. What a burden to think one is conceived in sin rather than in pleasure; that one is born into evil rather than into joy. In my work, I speak to my parents and to my most distant ancestors about what I myself have found as an Earthling growing naturally out of the Universe. I create characters who sometimes speak in the language of immediate ancestors, characters who are not passive but active in the discovery of what is vital and real in this world. Characters who explore what it would feel like not to be imprisoned by the hatred of women, the love of violence, and the destructiveness of greed taught to human beings as the "religion" by which they must guide their lives.

What is happening in the world more and more is that people are attempting to decolonize their spirits. A crucial act of empowerment, one that might return reverence to the Earth, thereby saving it, in this fearful-of-Nature, spiritually colonized age.

In day-to-day life, I worship the Earth as God—representing everything—and Nature as its spirit. But for a long time I was confused. After all, when someone you trust shows you a picture of a blond, blue-eyed Jesus Christ and tells you he's the son of God, you get an instant image of his father: an older version of him. When you're taught God loves you, but only if you're good, obedient, trusting, and so forth, and you know you're that way only some of the

time, there's a tendency to deny your shadow side. Hence the hypocrisy I noted early on in our church.

The church I attended as a child still stands. It is small, almost
tiny, and made of very old, silver-gray lumber, painted white a couple
of decades ago, when an indoor toilet was also added. It is simple,
serene, sweet. It used to nestle amid vivid green foliage at a curve in
a sandy dirt road; inside, its rough-hewn benches smelled warmly of
pine. Its yard was shaded by a huge red oak tree, from which people
took bits of bark to brew a tonic for their chickens. I remember my
mother boiling the bark she'd cut from the tree and feeding the
reddish brown "tea" to her pullets, who, without it, were likely to
cannibalize each other. The county, years later, and without warning,
cut down the tree and straightened and paved the road. In an attempt
to create a tourist industry where none had existed before, they flooded
the surrounding countryside. The fisherpeople from far away who whiz
by in their pickup trucks today know nothing about what they see.
To us, they are so unconnected to the land they appear to hover above
it, like ghosts.

My mother, in addition to her other duties as worker, wife, and
mother of eight children, was also mother of the church. I realize now
that I was kind of a little church mother in training, as I set out for
the church with her on Saturday mornings. We would mop the bare
pine floors, run dust rags over the benches, and wash the windows.
Take out the ashes, dump them behind the outhouse, clean the outhouse, and be sure there was adequate paper. We would sweep the
carpeting around the pulpit and I would reverently dust off the Bible.
Each Saturday my mother slipped a starched and ironed snowy-white
doily underneath it.

One season she resolved to completely redo the pulpit area. With
a hammer and tacks and rich, wine-dark cloth she'd managed to
purchase from meager savings, she upholstered the chairs, including the thronelike one in which the preacher sat. She also laid new

carpeting. On Sunday morning she would bring flowers from her garden.

There has never been anyone who amazed and delighted me as consistently as my mother did when I was a child. Part of her magic was her calm, no-nonsense manner. If it could be done, she could probably do it, was her attitude. She enjoyed being strong and capable. Anything she didn't know how to do, she could learn. I was thrilled to be her apprentice.

My father and brothers cleared the cemetery of brush and cut the grass around the church while we were inside. By the time we were finished, everything sparkled. We stood back and admired our work.

Sister Walker, my mother, was thanked for making the church so beautiful, but this wise woman, who knew so many things about life and the mysteries of the heart, the spirit, and the soul, was never asked to speak to the congregation. If she and other "mothers" and "sisters" of the church had been asked to speak, if it had been taken for granted that they had vision and insight to match their labor and their love, would the church be alive today?

And what would the women have said? Would they have protested that the Eve of the Bible did not represent them? That they had never been that curious? But of course they had been just as curious. If a tree had appeared in their midst with an attractive fruit on it, and furthermore one that they were informed would make them wise, they would have nibbled it. And what could be so wrong about that? Anyway, God had told Adam about the forbidden fruit; He hadn't said a word directly to Eve. And what kind of God would be so cruel as to curse women and men forever for eating a piece of fruit, no matter how forbidden? Would they have said that Adam was a weak man who evaded personal responsibility for his actions? Would they have pointed out how quickly and obsequiously he turned in his wife to God, as if she had forced him to eat the fruit rather than simply offered him a bite? Would they have said Adam's behavior reminded them of a man who got a woman pregnant and then blamed the woman for tempting him to have intercourse, thereby placing all the blame on her? Would they have said that God was unfair? Well, He was white, His son was white, and it truly was a white man's world, as far as they could see.

Would they have spoken of the God they had found, not in the Bible but in life, as they wrestled death while delivering babies, or as they worked almost beyond, and sometimes beyond, capacity in the white man's fields? I remember my mother telling me of a time when she was hugely pregnant and had an enormous field of cotton, twenty-five or thirty acres, to chop, that is, to thin and weed. Her older children were in school, from which she refused to take them, her youngest trailed behind her and fell asleep in the furrows. My father, who was laborer, dairyman, and chauffeur, had driven the bosslady to town. As my mother looked out over the immense acreage still to be covered, she felt so ill she could barely lift the hoe. Never had she felt so alone. Coming to the end of a row, she lay down under a tree and asked to die. Instead, she fell into a deep sleep, and when she awakened, she was fully restored. In fact, she felt wonderful, as if a healing breeze had touched her soul. She picked up the hoe and continued her work.

What God rescued my mother? Was it the God who said women deserved to suffer and were evil anyway, or was it the God of non-judgmental Nature, calming and soothing her with the green coolness of the tree she slept under and the warm earth she lay upon? I try to imagine my mother and the other women calling on God as they gave birth, and I shudder at the image of Him they must have conjured. He was someone, after all, they had been taught, who said black people were cursed to be drawers of water and hewers of wood. That some people enslaved and abused others was taken for granted by Him. He ordered the killing of women and children, by the hundreds of thousands, if they were not of his chosen tribe. The women would have had to know how little they and their newborns really mattered, because they were female, poor, and black, like the accursed children of Hagar and of Ham, and they would have had to promise to be extra good, obedient, trusting, and so forth, to make up for it.

Life was so hard for my parents' generation that the subject of heaven was never distant from their thoughts. The preacher would gleefully, or so it seemed to me, run down all the trials and tribulations of an existence that ground us into dust, only to pull heaven out of the biblical hat at the last minute. I was intrigued. Where was heaven? I asked my parents. Who is going to be there? What about accommodations and food? I was told what they sincerely believed: that heaven was in the sky, in space, as we would later describe it; that only the best people on earth would go there when they died. We'd all have couches to lounge on, great food to eat. Wonderful music, because all the angels played harp. It would be grand. Would there be any white people? Probably. Oh.

There was not one white person in the county that any black person felt comfortable with. And though there was a rumor that a good white woman, or man, had been observed sometime, somewhere, no one seemed to know this for a fact.

Now that there's been so much space travel and men have been on the moon, I wonder if preachers still preach about going to heaven, and whether it's the same place.

The truth was, we already lived in paradise but were worked too hard by the land-grabbers to enjoy it. This is what my mother, and perhaps the other women, knew, and this was one reason why they were not permitted to speak. They might have demanded that the men of the church notice Earth. Which always leads to revolution. In fact, everyone has known this for a very long time. For the other, more immediate and basic, reason my mother and the other women were not permitted to speak in church was that the Bible forbade it. And it is forbidden in the Bible because, in the Bible, men alone are sanctioned to own property, in this case, Earth itself. And woman herself *is* property, along with the asses, the oxen, and the sheep.

Pagan means "of the land, country dweller, peasant," all of which my family was. It also means a person whose primary spiritual relationship is with Nature and the Earth. And this, I could see, day to day, was true not only of me but of my parents; but there was no way to ritually express the magical intimacy we felt with Creation without being accused of, and ridiculed for, indulging in "heathenism," that other word for paganism. And Christianity, we were informed, had fought long and hard to deliver us from *that*. In fact, millions of people were broken, physically and spiritually, literally destroyed, for nearly two millennia, as the orthodox Christian church "saved" them from their traditional worship of the Great Mystery they perceived in Nature.

In the sixties, many of us scared our parents profoundly when we showed up dressed in our "African" or "Native American" or "Celtic" clothes (and in my case, all three). We shocked them by wearing our hair in its ancient naturalness. They saw us turning back to something that they'd been taught to despise and that, by now, they actively feared. Many of our parents had been taught that the world was only two or three thousand years old, and that spiritually civilized life began with the birth of Jesus Christ. Their only hope of enjoying a better existence, after a lifetime of crushing toil and persistent abuse, was to be as much like the long-haired rabbi from a small Jewish sect in a far-off desert as possible; then, by the Grace of His father, who owned heaven, they might be admitted there, after death. It would be segregated, of course, who could imagine anything different? But perhaps Jesus Christ himself would be present, and would speak up on their behalf. After all, these were black people who were raised never to look a white person directly in the face.

I think now, and it hurts me to think of it, of how tormented the true believers in our church must have been, wondering if, in heaven, Jesus Christ, a white man, the only good one besides Santa Claus and Abraham Lincoln they'd ever heard of, would deign to sit near them.

But only a very small percentage of us would get into heaven. There was hell, a pit of eternally burning fire, for the vast majority.

Where was hell? I wanted to know. Under the ground, I was informed. It was assumed most of the white people would be there, and therefore it would be more or less like here. Only fiery hot, hotter than the sun in the cotton field at midday. Nobody wanted to go there.

I had a problem with this doctrine at a very early age: I could not see how my parents had sinned. Each month my mother had what I would later recognize, because I unfortunately inherited it, as bad PMS. At those times her temper was terrible; the only safe thing was to stay out of her way. My father, slower to anger, was nonetheless a victim of sexist ideology learned from his father, the society, and the church, which meant I battled with him throughout childhood, until I left home for good at seventeen. But I did not see that they were evil, that they should be cursed because they were black, because my mother was a woman. They were as innocent as trees, I felt. And, at heart, generous and sweet. I resented the minister and the book he read from that implied they could be "saved" only by confessing their sin and accepting suffering and degradation as their due, just because a very long time ago, a snake had given a white woman an apple and she had eaten it and generously given a bite to her craven-hearted husband. This was insulting to the most drowsy intelligence, I thought. Noting that my exhausted father often napped while in church. But what could I do? I was three years old.

It is ironic, to say the least, that the very woman out of whose body I came, whose pillowy arms still held me, willingly indoctrinated me away from herself and the earth, from which both of us received sustenance, and toward a frightful, jealous, cruel, murderous "God" of another race and tribe of people, and expected me to forget the very breasts that had fed me and that I still leaned against. But such is the power of centuries-old indoctrination.

In the black church, we have loved and leaned on Moses, because he brought the enslaved Israelites out of Egypt. As enslaved and oppressed people, we have identified with him so completely that we have adopted his God.

It is fatal to love a God who does not love you. A God specifically created to comfort, lead, advise, strengthen, and enlarge the tribal borders of someone else. We have been beggars at the table of a religion that sanctioned our destruction. Our own religions denied, forgotten; our own ancestral connections to All Creation something of which we are ashamed. I maintain that we are empty, lonely, without our pagan-heathen ancestors; that we must lively them up within ourselves, and begin to see them as whole and necessary and correct: their Earth-centered, female-reverencing religions, like their architecture, agriculture, and music, suited perfectly to the lives they led. And lead, those who are left, today. I further maintain that the Jesus most of us have been brought up to adore must be expanded to include the "wizard" and the dancer, and that when this is done, it becomes clear that he coexists quite easily with pagan indigenous peoples. Indeed, it was because the teachings of Jesus were already familiar to many of our ancestors, especially in the New World—they already practiced the love and sharing that he preached—that the Christian church was able to make as many genuine converts to the Christian religion as it did.

All people deserve to worship a God who also worships them. A God that made them, and likes them. That is why Nature, Mother Earth, is such a good choice. Never will Nature require that you cut off some part of your body to please it; never will Mother Earth find anything wrong with your natural way. She made it, and she made it however it is so that you will be more comfortable as part of Her Creation, rather than less. Everyone deserves a God who adores our freedom: Nature would never advise us to do anything but be ourselves. Mother Earth will do all that She can to support our choices. Whatever they are. For they are of Her, and inherent in our creation is Her trust.

We are born knowing how to worship, just as we are born knowing how to laugh.

And what is the result of decolonizing the spirit? It is as if one truly does possess a third eye, and this eye opens. One begins to see the world from one's own point of view; to interact with it out of one's own conscience and heart. One's own "pagan" Earth spirit. We begin to flow, again, with and into the Universe. And out of this flowing comes the natural activism of wanting to survive, to be happy, to enjoy one another and Life, and to laugh. We begin to distinguish between the need, singly, to throw rocks at whatever is oppressing us, and the creative joy that arises when we bring our collective stones of resistance against injustice together. We begin to see that we must be loved very much by whatever Creation is, to find ourselves on this wonderful Earth. We begin to recognize our sweet, generously appointed place in the makeup of the Cosmos. We begin to feel glad, and grateful that we are not in heaven but that we are *here*.

C

Observations

21

ON THE RELEVANCE OF THE CHURCH

May 19, 1971

Huey P. Newton

❏

The commitment to socialist thought and progressive activity outside church-centered civil rights efforts noted with respect to James Forman is also present with Huey P. Newton (1942–1989). Newton and others of a similar mind-set embraced the theme of Black Power and argued that African Americans would not thrive until the United States was purged through a socialist revolution. This philosophy took organizational form in a variety of ways, one of which was the Black Panther Party. Developed first in California as an organized effort to safeguard and mobilize African Americans, the Party understood that the basic necessities of life must be provided before African Americans could take up the revolutionary cause. In keeping with this philosophy, the Black Panthers initiated a variety of services, including a breakfast program for schoolchildren. The "authorities" objected to the attitude of the Panthers and their demand to be armed and defend themselves, in keeping with the laws of California. Leaders of the organization such as Huey P. Newton were targeted. Conflict with local authorities combined with dramatized sus-

picion by national policing agencies resulted in death for some Panthers and jail sentences for others.

Although the Black Panther Party, like other organizations, had internal problems as well as gaps between its theory and practice, what is noteworthy here is the manner in which it made use of humanist principles in carving out its agenda. At times, the Party felt it was necessary to maintain a good relationship with Black churches in order to secure a base of operation and access to large groups of African Americans. However, the religiotheological underpinning of these churches made it difficult to maintain this relationship. The following document outlines the rationale used by Newton and the Party to explain the church's existence. Newton argues that there is a period during which people make use of the God concept to explain the unknown; however, with the passage of time, science and experience replace this need for God. This move away from supernatural explanations for world events places Newton and, by extension, the Black Panther Party in line with humanism's basic principles.

Readers may also find the work of William H. Grier and Price M. Cobbs interesting because it brings into question, in similar ways, as the following article demonstrates, the function of Black churches (and by extension Christianity). They argue that religion should be mistrusted and also that it is necessary to see the survival of African Americans as not simply a result of their Christian faith. In their words: "On such a stage a million anonymous black men have stepped. They have survived an attack aimed at their lives with guns and at their secret selves with the weapon of religion" (180). See Grier and Cobbs, The Jesus Bag *(New York: McGraw-Hill Book Company, 1971), especially 166–180.*

For additional information on Huey P. Newton and the Black Panther Party, see, for example, Bobby Seale, Seize the Time: The Story of the Black Panther Party and Huey P. Newton *(New York, Random House, 1970); Huey P. Newton,* War against the Panthers: A Study of Repression in America *(New York: Harlem River Press, 1996); Charles E. Jones, ed.,* The Black Panther Party (Reconsidered) *(Baltimore: Black Classic*

Press, 1998); and Philip Sheldon Foner, The Black Panthers Speak *(Philadelphia: Lippincott 1970).*

❏

Since 1966 the Black Panther Party has gone through many changes; it has been transformed. I would like to talk to you about that and about contradictions. I would also like to talk about the Black Panther Party's relationship with the community as a whole and with the church in particular.

Some time ago when the Party started, Bobby and I were interested in strengthening the Black community—rather its comprehensive set of institutions because if there is one thing we lack it is community. We do have one institution that has been around for some time and that is the church. After a short harmonious relationship with the church, in fact a very good relationship, we were divorced from the church, and shortly after that found ourselves out of favor with the whole Black community.

We found ourselves in somewhat of a void alienated from the whole community. We had no way of being effective as far as developing the community was concerned. The only way we could aid in that process of revolution—and revolution is a process rather than conclusion or a set of principles, or any particular action—was by raising the consciousness of the community. Any conclusion or particular action that we think *is* revolution is really reaction, for revolution is a developmental process. It has a forward thrust which goes higher and higher as man becomes freer and freer. As man becomes freer he knows more about the universe, he tends to control more and he therefore gains more control over himself. That is what freedom is all about.

I want now to talk about the mistakes that were made. I hate to call them mistakes because maybe they were necessary to bring about change in the Party, the needed transformation. I am sure that we will have other kinds of contradictions in the future, some that we don't know about now. I am sure they will build up and hurl us into a new thing.

But the church also has been going through phases of development. It too has found itself somewhat isolated from the community. Today, the church is striving to get back into favor with the community. Like the church the Black Panther Party is also trying to reinstate itself with the community.

A short time ago there was an article in the Black Panther paper called "The Defection of Eldridge Cleaver from the Black Panther Party and the Defection of the Black Panther Party from the Black Community." I would like to concentrate now upon the defection of the Party. That is, the larger unit. I hate to place blame upon individuals in our Party particularly since they are always governed by a collective called the Central Committee. Even when I disagree with the Central Committee (and I did much disagreeing and arguing when I was in prison, but I was out-voted), after the vote I supported the position of the Party until the next meeting.

I think, at first, that we have to have some organized apparatus in order to bring about the necessary change. The only time we leave our political machine or our institution altogether is when we feel that we cannot bring about the necessary change through the machine, and the very posture of the organization or the institution will strip us of our individual dignity. I felt that this was true of the Party, and although it could be argued, *I personally thought that the Party should still be held together.* I knew if I left we would have to form a new Party, a new institution in order to be that spur or that guiding light in the community. Also I would have to contend with new contradictions.

We always say that contradictions are the ruling principle of the universe. I use that word time and time again because I think that it is responsible for much suffering. When things collide they hurt, but collision is also responsible for development. Without contradictions everything would be stagnant. Everything has an internal contradiction including the church.

Contradiction, or the strain of the lesser to subdue that which controls it, gives motion to matter. We see this throughout the universe in the physical as well as the biological world. We also see this in cultures. Development comes with the phenomenon we call acculturation. That is, two societies meet and when their cultures collide because they have a contradiction, both are modified. The stronger shows less change and the weaker more change. All the time the weaker is attempting to gain dominance over the stronger. But something happens, they both will never be the same again because they have reached a degree of synthesis. In other words, it is all working toward the truth of the trinity: thesis, anti-thesis, synthesis. This principle of contradiction, this striving for harmony, operates in all of our disciplines.

The Black Panther Party was formed because we wanted to oppose the evils in our community. Some of the members in the Party were not refined—we were grasping for organization. It wasn't a college campus organization; it was basically an organization of the grass roots, and any time we organize the most victimized of the victims we run into a problem. To have a Party or a church or any kind of institution, whether we like it or not, we have to have administrators. How an institution, organization, or the Party in this case, functions, as well as how effective it is depends upon how knowledgeable and advanced in thinking the administrators are. We attempt to apply the administrative skills of our grass-roots organization to the problems that are most frequently heard in the community.

History shows that most of the parties that have led people out of their difficulties have had administrators with what we sometimes call the traits of the bourgeoisie or declassed intellectuals. They are the people who have gone through the established institutions, rejected them, and then applied their skills to the community. In applying them to the community, their skills are no longer bourgeoisie skills but people's skills, which are transformed through the contradiction of applying what is usually bourgeoisie to the oppressed. That itself is a kind of transformation.

In our Party we are not so blessed. History does not repeat itself; it goes on also transforming itself through its dialectical process. We see that the administrators of our Party are victims who have not received that bourgeois training. So I will not apologize for our mistakes, our lack of a scientific approach to use and put into practice. It was a matter of not knowing, of learning, but also of starting out with a loss—a disadvantage that history has seldom seen. That is, a group attempting to influence and change the society so much while its own administrators were as much in the dark much of the time as the people that they were trying to change. In our Party we have now what we call the Ideological Institute, where we are teaching these skills, and we also invite those people who have received a bourgeois education to come and help us. However, we let them know that they will, by their contribution, make their need to exist, as they exist now, null and void. In other words, after we learn the skills their bourgeois status will evaporate once the skills have been applied.

As far as the church was concerned, the Black Panther Party and other community groups emphasized the political and criticized the spiritual. We said the church is only a ritual, it is irrelevant, and therefore we will have nothing to do with it. We said this in the context of the whole community being involved with the church on one level or another. That is one way of defecting from the community, and that is exactly what we did. Once we stepped outside of the church with that criticism, we stepped outside of the whole thing that the community was involved in and we said, "You follow our example; your reality is not true and you don't need it."

Now, without judging whether the church is operating in a total reality, I will venture to say that if we judge whether the church is relevant to the *total* community we would all agree that it is not. That is why it develops new programs—to become more relevant so the pews will be filled on Sunday.

The church is in its developmental process, and we believe it needs to exist. We believe this as a result of our new direction (which is an old direction as far as I am concerned, but we'll call it new because there has been a reversal in the dominance in the Central Committee of our Party for reasons that you probably know about). So we do go to church, are involved in the church, and not in any hypocritical way. Religion, perhaps, is a thing that man needs at this time because scientists cannot answer all of the questions. As far as I am concerned, when all of the questions are not answered, when the extraordinary is not explained, when the unknown is not known, then there is room for God because the unexplained and the unknown *is* God. We know nothing about God, really, and that is why as soon as the scientist develops or points out a new way of controlling a part of the universe, that aspect of the universe is no longer God. In other words, once when the thunder crashed it was God clapping His hands together. As soon as we found out that thunder was not God, we said that God has other attributes but not *that* one. In that way we took for ourselves what was His before. But we still haven't answered all of the questions, so He still exists. And those scientists who say they can answer all of them are dishonest.

We go into the church realizing that we cannot answer the questions at this time, that the answers will be delivered eventually, and we feel that when they are delivered they will be explained in a way that we can understand and control.

I went to church for years. My father is a minister and I spent 15 years in the church; this was my life as a child. When I was going to church I used to hear that God is within us and is, therefore, some part of us: that part of us that is mystical. And as man develops and understands more, he will approach God, and finally reach heaven and merge with the universe. I've never heard one preacher say that there is a need for the church in heaven; the church would negate itself. As man approaches his development and becomes larger and larger, the church therefore becomes smaller and smaller because it is not needed any longer. Then if we had ministers who would deal with the social realities that cause misery so that we can change them, man will become larger and larger. At that time the God within will come out, and we can merge with Him. Then we will be one with the universe.

So I think it was rather arrogant of my Party to criticize the community for trying to discover answers to spiritual questions. The only thing we will criticize in the future is when the church does not act upon the evils that cause man to get on his knees and humble himself in awe at that large force which he cannot control. But as man becomes stronger and stronger, and his understanding greater and greater, he will have "a closer walk with Thee." *Note the song says walk —not crawl.*

So along with the church we will all start again to control our lives and communities. Even with the Black church we have to create a community spirit. We say that the church is an institution, but it is not a community. The sociological definition of a community is a comprehensive *collection* of institutions that delivers our whole life, and within which we can reach most of our goals. We create it in order to carry out our desires and it serves us. In the Black community the church is an institution that we created (that we were allowed to create). The White church warred against us, but finally we won the compromise to worship as a unit, as a people, concerned with satisfying our own needs. The White church was not satisfying our needs in human terms because it felt that we were not human beings. So we formed our own. Through that negative thing a positive thing evolved. We started to organize fraternities, antilynching groups and so forth, but they still would not let our community exist. We came here in chains and I guess they thought we were meant to stay in chains. But we have begun to organize a political machine, to develop a community so that we can have an apparatus to fight back. You cannot fight back individually against an organized machine. We will work with the church to establish a community which will satisfy most of our needs so that we can live and operate as a group.

The Black Panther Party, with its survival programs, plans to develop the institutions in the community. We have a clothing factory we are just erecting on Third Street, where we will soon give away about three hundred to four hundred new articles of clothing each month. And we can do this by robbing Peter to pay Paul. What we will do is start to make golfing bags under contract to a company, and with the surplus we will buy material to make free clothes. Our members will do this. We will have no overhead because of our collective (we'll "exploit" our collective by making them work free). We will do this not just to satisfy ourselves, like the philanthropist, or to serve, or to save someone from going without shoes, even though this is a part of the cause of our problem, but to help the people make the revolution. We will give the process a forward thrust. If we suffer genocide we won't be around to change things. So in this way our survival program is very practical.

What we are concerned with is the larger problem. Therefore we will be honest and say that we will do like the churches—we will negate our necessity for existing. After we accomplish our goals the Black Panther Party will not need to exist because we will have already created our heaven right here on earth. What we are going to do is administer to the community the things they need in order to get their attention, in order to organize them into a political machine. The community will then look to the Party and look to those people who are serving their needs in order to give them guidance and direction, whether it is political, whether it is judicial, or whether it is economic.

Our real thing is to organize across the country. We have thirty-eight chapters and branches and I would like to inform you that the so-called split is only a myth, that it does not exist. We lost two chapters in that so-called split and I will tell you that the burden is off my shoulders. I was glad to lose them because it was a yoke for me; I was frozen. Even though I couldn't make a move I wouldn't get out of the whole thing then because certain people had such an influence over the Party. For me to have taken that stand would have been individualism. Now we're about three years behind in our five-year plan, but we will *now* move to organize the community around the *survival* programs.

We have a shoe factory that we're opening up on 14th and Jefferson. The machines and everything else were donated. We'll use it to get inmates out of prison because most of us learned how to make shoes in prison. So it will serve two purposes: we can make positions in the shoe factory available and thereby get somebody out on parole; and since the parolees must agree to give a certain amount of shoes away each week, we will have a "right to wear shoes" program. We'll point out that everyone in the society should have shoes and we should not have a situation like the one in Beaufort County, South Carolina, where 70 percent of the children suffer brain damage because of malnutrition. They have malnutrition because of the combination of not enough food and parasites in the stomach. The worms eat up half the food that the children take in. Why? Because the ground is infested with the eggs of the worms and the children don't have shoes to wear. So as soon as we send a doctor there to cure them, they get the parasites again. We think that a shoe program is a very relevant thing, first to help them stay alive, then to create conditions in which they can grow up and work out a plan to change things. If they have brain damage, they will never be revolutionists because they will have already been killed. That is genocide in itself.

We will inform this government, this social order, that it must administer to its people because it is supposed to be a representative government which serves the needs of the people. Then serve them. If it does not do this then it should be criticized. What we will not do in the future is jump too far ahead and say that the system absolutely cannot give us anything. That is not true; the system can correct itself to a certain extent. What we are interested in is its correcting itself as much as it can. After that, if it doesn't do everything that the people think necessary, then we'll think about reorganizing things.

To be very honest I think there is great doubt whether the present system can do this. But until the people feel the same way I feel then I would be rather arrogant to say dump the whole thing, just as we were arrogant to say dump the church. Let's give it a chance, let's work with it in order to squeeze as many contributions and compromises out of all the institutions as possible, and then criticize them after the fact. We'll know when that time comes, when the people tell us so.

We have a program attempting to get the people to do all they will do. It is too much to ask the people to do all they can do even though they can do everything. But that is not the point. The point is how do we get them to do all they *will* do until they eventually get to the place where they will have to be doing all they can.

We organized the Party when we saw that growing out of the Movement was what was called a cultural cult group. We defined a cultural cult group as an organization that disguised itself as a political organization, but was really more interested in the cultural rituals of Africa in the 1100's before contact with the Europeans. Instead of administering to the community and organizing it, they would rather wear bubas, get African names and demand that the community do the same, and do nothing about the survival of the community. Sometimes they say, "Well, if we get our culture back then all things will be solved." This is like saying to be regenerated and born again is to solve everything. We know that this is not true.

Then the Party became just as closed as the cultural cultist group. You know many churches that are very reactionary which you describe as a religious cult. They go through many rituals but they're divorced from reality. Even though we have many things in common with them, we say they isolate themselves from reality because they're so miserable and reality is so hard to take. We know that operating within reality does not mean that we accept it; we're operating within it so that the reality can be changed. For what we did as revolutionists was abstract, and the people are always real. But we know that reality is changing all the time, and what we want to do is harness those forces that are causing the change to direct them to a desirable goal. In other words developments will continue, but we have no guarantee that they will be developments that allow man to live. We have no guarantee that the bomb won't be dropped, but we know that there are certain ways that we can plan for the new reality. In order to do this we have to take some control over the present. So the people who withdraw, like the religious cultist group, do the same thing as the cultural cultist group.

These are words that we have coined. The Panthers are always coining words because we have to keep defining the new reality, the new phenomena. The old words confuse us sometimes because things have changed so much. So we try to stay abreast by developing or stipulating definitions. The old lexical definitions become so outdated after the qualitative leap (the transformation) that it does not match at all what we are talking about now.

One new word related to what we have been talking about describes something I was guilty of. I was guilty of this when I offered the Black troops to Vietnam. I won't talk about whether it was morally right or wrong, but I will say that anything said or done by a revolutionist that does not spur or give the forward thrust to the process (of revolution) is wrong. Remember that the people are the makers of history, the people make everything in their society. They are the architects of the society and if you don't spur them on, then I don't care what phrases you use or whether they are political or religious, you cannot be classified as being relevant to that process. If you know you're wrong and do certain things anyway, then you're reactionary because you are very very guilty. You deserve many stripes. Some of us didn't know. I keep searching myself to see whether I knew we were going wrong. I couldn't influence the Central Committee and maybe I should have risked being charged with an individual violation and said that they didn't know. I think most of them didn't know, so they're not as guilty as I am. I'm probably more guilty than anyone. But anyway, the new word that describes what we went into for a short length of time—a couple of years—is revolutionary cultism.

The revolutionary cultist uses the words of social change; he uses words about being interested in the development of society. He uses that terminology, you see; but his actions are so far divorced from the process of revolution and organizing the community that he is living in a fantasy world. So we talk to each other on the campuses, or we talk to each other in the secrecy of the night, concentrating upon weapons, thinking these things will produce change without the people themselves. Of course people do courageous things and call themselves the vanguard, but the people who do things like that are either heroes or criminals. They are not the vanguard because the vanguard means spearhead, and the spearhead has to spearhead something. If nothing is behind it, then it is divorced from the masses and is not the vanguard.

I am going to be heavily criticized now by the revolutionary cultists and probably criticized even more in the future because I view the process as going in stages. I feel that we can't jump from A to Z, we have to go through all of the development. So even though I see a thing is not the answer, I don't think it's dishonest to involve myself in it for the simple reason that the people tend to take not one step higher; they take a half step higher. Then they hang on to what they view as the reality because they can't see that reality is constantly changing. When they finally see the changes (qualitatively) they don't know why or how it happened. Part of the reason reality changes around them is because they are there; they participate whether they like it or not.

What we will do now is involve ourselves in any thing or any stage of development in the community, support that development, and try to introduce some insight into it. Then we will work very hard with the people in the community and with this institution so that it can negate itself. We will be honest about this and we hope they are honest too and realize that everything is negated eventually; this is how we go on to higher levels.

I was warned when I got up here that it would be appropriate to have a question and answer period, so I guess we should start now because I'm subject to go on and on.

QUESTION: I would like to know in your re-evaluation of your former stance in relationship to the community, in what ways do you expect to merge or bring together the community of the Catholic Church into the Black Panther Party?

NEWTON: First, we can't change the realities, direct them, or harness their forces until we know them. We have to gather information. We can gather information about the church by experiencing the church. As a matter of fact this is how we gain facts: through empirical evidence, observation, and experience. In order to do this we have to go to the church. You see, the only laboratory in society we have is the community itself, and we view ourselves not only as scientists but also as activists.

Now we say we try to merge theory with practice, so we're going to churches now. I went to church last week for the first time in ten years, I guess. We took our children with us. We have a youth institute, the Samuel Napier Youth Institute. We have about thirty children now and we took them to church and involved ourselves. We plan to involve ourselves in many community activities, going through the behavior the church goes through in order to contribute to the community. We also hope to influence the church, as I'm sure the church will influence us. Remember that we said that even when whole societies and cultures meet they are both modified by each other. And I am saying that the very fact that we're there is the new ingredient in the church, and we know that we will be affected and hope that they will be affected. But I warn you that we hope to have more effect than they.

Just briefly I mentioned our Youth Institute. We have children from three to fourteen years old; most of them have already been kicked out of schools and we have a shortage of facilities because the hard core Black community is just an aggregate now. People who happen to be Black.

We are teaching them first what I mentioned earlier, bourgeois skills. It is necessary for us to learn these skills in order to understand the phenomena around us, the society. On the other hand, we don't like the way the skills have been used, so we're going to use them a different way. Thirdly, our children are not going to withdraw. I don't like parochial schools; I don't like separate schools, but I think that sometimes you have to use that strategy. For example, the Black Panther Party is a Black organization. We know that we live in a world of many cultures and ethnic groups and we all interconnect in one way or another. We say that we are the contradiction to the reactionary Western values, but we cannot separate because we're here. Technology is too far advanced for us to isolate ourselves in any geographical location—the jet can get there too fast and so can the early-bird TV set—so what we have to do is share the control of these devices.

So far as our children are concerned, the only reason they are at this separate school is because the public schools were not giving them the correct education. They can hardly learn to read and write. I don't want them to end up as I did: I only learned how to read after I was seventeen and that must not happen to them. I've only been reading for about 10 years or so and that is not very good—I still don't read very well. Our plan is not to have our children graduate from our school and live in a fantasy. Our effort is to keep them in there just as long as it will take for them to organize the school and make it relevant. In other words we are going to send them back into the wilderness, but we're going to send them with their purse and their scribes with them this time.

QUESTION: When David Hilliard spoke to the National Committee of Black Churchmen that met in Berkeley, he called the preachers who were gathered there a bunch of bootlicking pimps and motherfuckers, a comment that never should have been made public anyway. And he threatened that if the preachers did not come around that the Panthers would "off" some of the preachers. If you're not able to influence the Black church as much as you think, will the Panther Party return to this particular stance?

NEWTON: The Black Panther Party will not take the separate individual stand. We'll only take the stand of the community because we're interested in what the community will do to liberate themselves. We will not be arrogant and we would not have the most rudimentary knowledge if we did not know that we alone cannot bring about change. It was very wrong and almost criminal for some people in the Party to make the mistake to think that the Black Panther Party could overthrow even the police force. It ended up with the war between the police and the Panthers, and if there is a war it needs to be between the community and the reactionary establishment, or else we are isolating ourselves.

As for what David Hilliard said, what he did was alienate you. That kind of alienation put us in a void where blood was spilled from one end of this country to the other, our blood, while the community watched. Our help watched on, you see? But it was more our fault than theirs because we were out there saying that we were going to lead them into a change. But we cannot lead them into a change if they will not go. As a matter of fact, we cannot exist individually if we don't band together to resist the genocide against all of us. So just as I criticized David Hilliard, I criticize myself, because I knew that stuff was going on and I argued against it, but I didn't leave the Party. Finally the change came about.

And so what I am saying is that I understand, and the reason that I didn't leave was that it wasn't an outrage to my humanity even though I cringed every time. Because I understood that he did it not out of hatred, but love. He did it because he was outraged by the church's inactivity, as you are outraged (not you personally, but you in the plural) at this situation, and he was outraged, of course, because of your isolation. So we are all in the same boat; and when we end up in the same boat that means we are unified.

22

AN AFRICAN-AMERICAN
HUMANIST DECLARATION

African Americans for Humanism

❏

As this book has demonstrated, African American humanists are alive and well, and have been so for a very long time. However, in most cases African American humanists have worked within organizations that had humanistic philosophies or sympathies. Only in a few instances have African American humanists developed unique organizations with the term humanism *in the title. One of the best examples of such an organization is African Americans for Humanism (AAH), an international organization connected to the Council for Secular Humanism, headed by Paul Kurtz.*

The AAH developed as a result of Norm Allen, Jr.'s 1989 inquiry to Paul Kurtz concerning the involvement of African Americans in his organization. Kurtz's response entailed an invitation for Allen to relocate to Buffalo, New York, and begin work on the needs and interests of African American humanists. With time, Allen's efforts resulted in an organization with a strong base and potential for tremendous growth. The AAH publishes a newsletter and various members of the board regularly lecture on issues related to humanism. The members of the AAH, during its first year of existence, recognized the need for a basic statement concerning the organization's goals and philosophical underpinnings. What resulted is the African-American Humanist Declaration reprinted below.

Those interested in additional information on the AAH should see the following works: Norm Allen, Jr., African American Humanism: An Anthology *(Buffalo: Prometheus Books, 1991); Norm Allen, Jr., "Humanism in the Black Community,"* Sunrays *1, no. 1 (October–December 1991) : 11–13; and back issues of* AAH Newsletter. *Also see Anthony Pinn,* Varieties of African American Religious Experience *(Minneapolis: Fortress Books, 1998), chap. 4.*

Readers may also find the connection between African American involvement in humanism and the Unitarian Universalist Association (UUA) interesting. The UUA has long been, although this may change, a "safe haven" for humanists, and roughly 1 percent of its membership is African American. Related to this, see Mark D. Morrison-Reed, Black Pioneers in a White Denomination, *3d ed. (Boston: Skinner House Books, 1994); the Unitarian Universalist Commission on Appraisal to the General Assembly,* Empowerment: One Denomination's Quest for Racial Justice, 1967–1982 *(Boston: UUA, 1984), and the UUA's publication* Black Caucus Controversy II *(Boston: UUA, 1968).*

❏

Slavery and racism have taken their toll on the African-American community. It seems as though every possible solution to the problems that have resulted from these twin evils has been advocated or implemented on some level. But the problems have remained, and in some cases have worsened.

Many thinkers maintain that the history of African-Americans is unique. Unlike any other group, African-Americans were kidnapped from their homeland, enslaved, and brutally victimized in every way imaginable by a strict system of segregation. Only during the past three decades has it become popular for mainstream Americans to oppose racism. Segregation was "officially" practiced in the South on a large scale until the 1960s. Thus slavery and segregation have characterized most of the history of African-Americans. (It must also be noted that the enslavement and segregation of a minority by a majority differs greatly from the oppression of a majority by a minority.) Many other factors have been attributed to the unique condition of African-Americans.

Some have boldly stated that unless these factors are properly recognized and understood, the quest for freedom, justice, and equality will be in vain. As Lyndon B. Johnson said in 1965, "Freedom is not enough. You do not wipe away the scars of centuries by saying: Now you are free to go where you want, do as you desire."

But not everyone agrees with this analysis. Some maintain that opportunities for African-Americans have increased dramatically. They believe that the legacy of slavery and rigidly enforced segregation have been grossly exaggerated. They claim that many of the problems attributed to slavery did not arise until a hundred years after it was abolished, and that therefore slavery is irrelevant to today's problems. They believe that racism is a relic of the past or an insignificant factor in the problems plaguing the African-American community. They claim that liberal programs have been great failures, and further maintain that African-Americans could solve their problems if they would only modify their behavior and emulate the good habits of other ethnic groups.

Moderates, liberals, radicals, socialists, conservatives, anarchists, and others who cannot be categorized, have presented many conflicting ideas regarding the past, present, future, and even the identity of African-Americans. Never in the history of the United States has a people been plagued with so many problems and so much confusion.

Many strategies to end the confusion and solve the problems have been tried, with few positive results. But if more critical thought had gone into the planning of these strategies, they either would have been successful, or would never have been tried at all.

There are still many questions that seem almost to defy answers. How much does racism affect American society today? How limited or plentiful are the opportunities for African-Americans? What effects have the distortion, destruction, and suppression of African history had on African-Americans and on the way they are viewed and treated by the rest of society? How committed is white America to equality and the elimination of racism? If racism still exists and cannot be eradicated, is there anything African-Americans can do to solve their problems? Do African-Americans have an identity crisis, and must they pursue an identity other than "American"?

These questions are uncomfortable, and even frightening to some. But they must be answered. And they are by no means the only questions that must be answered. There are arguments from all points of view and from people of all backgrounds. But the best way to determine the proper course of action of society is through the free flow of humane ideas. If an argument or proposed solution is in error, the best way to detect the error is through the use of reason. But humanism will not live up to its full potential if most of its adherents will not open their minds and honestly pursue the truth. Everyone must be willing to reexamine their beliefs and reassess the arguments they have rejected.

And no matter how bleak the present or future looks, one must never despair of the human species. When one struggles for the betterment of humanity, there is glory even in the face of defeat.

Today the world needs a critical, rational, and humane approach to living. This is what humanism is all about.

African-Americans in general might not be familiar with the true humanist outlook—an outlook that is essential to the modern world.

Because many scholars have viewed society and history from a biased Eurocentric viewpoint, the significance of African-Americans to the humanist tradition has not been widely known. Racism and racial insensitivity have affected the entire nation, humanists included. But a new initiative has been taken to broaden the humanistic world view by making humanism more attractive to African-Americans.

Humanism incorporates a number of important ethical principles, including:

- A commitment to the application of reason and science to the understanding of the universe and to the solving of human problems.
- A concern with securing justice and fairness in society, and with eliminating discrimination and intolerance.
- A belief in enjoying life here and now and in developing humanity's creative talents to their fullest.
- A belief in the cultivation of moral excellence.
- Skepticism toward untested claims to knowledge.
- Openness toward new ideas.
- A belief in optimism rather than pessimism, hope rather than despair, learning in the place of dogma, truth instead of ignorance, joy rather than guilt or sin, tolerance in the place of fear, love instead of hatred, compassion over selfishness, beauty instead of ugliness, and reason rather than blind faith or irrationality.

Historically, the churches have been the most influential institutions in the African-American community, and African-Americans have been ardent believers. Church leaders have professed to have the solutions to the social, political, and economic ills with which African-Americans must contend. But despite their claims—or perhaps because of them—problems continue to plague the African-American community. Great strides have been made during the past forty years, but many problems have worsened, and new ones have arisen. More attention must be given to the importance of critical thinking in the quest for freedom, justice, and equality for African-Americans.

The African-American community is confronted by moral dilemmas that free thought, reason, good conduct, and proper action can best help solve. Examples include:

1. Unwanted pregnancy. Many religious leaders stress abstinence and marital fidelity as panaceas for the social problems resulting from human sexuality. But most humanists believe that all rational and humane solutions must be discussed, including the use of contraceptives and abortion. Attention must also be given to education, family counseling, and self-esteem building.

2. Alcohol and substance abuse. Alcoholism and drug abuse are major problems in the African-American community. These problems are of pressing concern, and solutions may require urgent, thorough, and rational measures. African-Americans as a group have been unfairly maligned by the media and targeted by police and the government in the War on Drugs. Yet many white drug dealers continue to grow rich and go virtually unmolested.

Many controversial solutions have been proposed, including the decriminalization of certain drugs. Humanism can be influential in the search for solutions to these problems and others that may arise from them. Humanism stresses abstinence from dangerous drugs, and moderation in the consumption of alcohol. It promotes self-love, and realizes that abusive and self-destructive behaviors interfere with the pursuit of happiness. It acknowledges the need for Secular Organizations for Sobriety (SOS).

3. Economic development. Although many African-American religious institutions have made laudable efforts toward economic development, millions of African-Americans have been attracted to Bible passages that teach that the accumulation of wealth is immoral and a complete waste of time. By thinking freely and challenging long-held beliefs and traditions, African-Americans can avoid economic stumbling blocks. Because African-Americans have always been at an economic disadvantage, many seek comfort in a possible reward in the afterlife. But fatalism is always dangerous, and "wait for the rapture" is questionable advice.

4. Organ transplants. The United States has an acute shortage of vital organs. Forty percent of the people awaiting organ transplants are African-Americans. But ironically and sadly, largely because of deep spiritual beliefs, African-Americans are the least likely to donate their organs. Openly discussing and challenging religious beliefs may convince more African-Americans to become voluntary organ donors, thereby helping potential organ recipients from all backgrounds.

Further research could also be stimulated to help find out why so many African-Americans are in need of organs. More attention must also be given to diseases—such as sickle-cell anemia—to which African-Americans are prone. Ways to improve health care and insurance should also be addressed.

5. Self-reliance. Too much emphasis has been placed on faith in charismatic African-American leaders, and not enough on individual responsibility, self-confidence, and freedom of thought. Through humanism, African-Americans can learn to have at least as much faith in themselves as they have in their leadership, because ultimately, individual choices become crucial factors in the shaping and modeling of one's life.

6. Unity. Humanism can teach African-Americans to unite around goals that are common to humanity. To unite mainly on religious grounds excludes some of the community's greatest minds and impedes progress.

The organizational aims of African-Americans for Humanism are to:

- Fight against racism in every form.
- Incorporate an Afrocentric outlook into a broader world perspective.
- Add depth and breadth to the study of history by acknowledging the great contributions made by people of African descent to the world, with the purpose of building self-esteem among African-Americans and helping to demonstrate the importance of all peoples to the development of world civilization.
- Develop eupraxophy, or "wisdom and good conduct through living" in the African-American community by using the scientific and rational methods of inquiry.
- Solve many of the problems that confront African-Americans through education and self-reliance, thereby affirming that autonomy and freedom of choice are basic human rights.
- Develop self-help groups and engage in any humane and rational activity designed to develop the African-American community.
- Emphasize the central importance of education at all levels, including humanistic moral education, developing a humanistic outlook, and providing the tools for the development of critical reason, self-improvement, and career training.

Never has a large, significant international humanist organization attracted great numbers of people of color. But this objective can be attained if we make a concerted effort to demonstrate how humanism is, has been, and can be relevant to the entire world community.

ACKNOWLEDGMENTS

The editor would like to thank the following organizations for permission to reprint documents contained in this volume.

William R. Jones, "Religious Humanism: Its Problems and Prospects in Black Religion and Culture." Reprinted by permission of *The Journal of Religious Thought.*

Herbert Aptheker, "An Unpublished Frederick Douglass Letter." Reprinted by permission of The Association for the Study of African American Life and History, Inc.

William L. Van Deburg, "Frederick Douglass: Maryland Slave to Religious Liberal." Reprinted by permission of the Maryland Historical Society.

Sterling Brown, "Negro Folk Expression: Spirituals, Seculars, Ballads, and Work Songs." Reprinted by permission of *Phylon.*

"Ideas of God Involving Frustration, Doubt, God's Impotence, and His Non-Existence." Reprinted with the permission of Scribner, a division of Simon & Schuster, Inc., from *The Negro's God as Reflected in His Literature,* by Benjamin E. Mays (New York: Russell & Russell, 1968).

Zora Neale Hurston, "Religion," from *Dust Tracks on a Road.* Copyright renewed 1970 by John C. Hurston. Reprinted by permission of HarperCollins Publishers, Inc.

Richard Wright, *Black Boy: A Record of Childhood and Youth,* 113–115, 122–128. Copyright 1937, 1942, 1944, 1945 by Richard Wright.

Copyright renewed by Ellen Wright. Reprinted by permission of HarperCollins Publishers, Inc.

Excerpt from *On Being Negro in America,* by J. Saunders Redding. Copyright © 1951 by J. Saunders Redding. Reprinted with the permission of Simon & Schuster.

Lyle Saxon, ed., "Experiences of a Chimney Sweeper," 489–495. In *Gumbo Ya-Ya.* © 1945. Reprinted by permission the State Library of Louisiana.

William Edward Burghardt Du Bois, *The Autobiography of W. E. B. Du Bois: A Soliloquy on Viewing My Life from the Last Decade to Its First Century,* 41–43, 285–288, 411–413, 416–418. Reprinted by permission of the International Publishers Company.

James Baldwin, The Fire Next Time, 55–67. Excerpted from "Down at the Cross: Letter from a Region in My Mind." Copyright 1962 by James Baldwin. Copyright renewed. Originally published in the *New Yorker.* Collected in *The Fire Next Time,* published by Vintage Books. Reprinted by arrangement with the James Baldwin Estate.

Amiri Imamu Baraka, "The Legacy of Malcolm X, and the Coming of the Black Nation," 161–167, in *The LeRoi Jones/Amiri Baraka Reader,* 1st ed. Reprinted by permission of Thunder's Mouth Press.

Harry Haywood, "Halley's Comet and My Religion," 29–35, in Harry Haywood, *Black Bolshevik: Autobiography of an Afro-American Communist.* Copyright 1978 by Harry Haywood. All rights reserved. Reprinted by permission of Lake View Press (Chicago).

James Forman, "Corrupt Black Preachers," 55–59, and "God Is Dead: A Question of Power," 80–92, in James Forman, *The Making of Black Revolutionaries* (Washington, D.C.: Open Hand Publishing, 1985). Reprinted by permission of the University of Washington Press.

Alice Walker, "The Only Reason You Want to Go to Heaven Is That You Have Been Driven Out of Your Mind," in *Anything We Love Can Be Saved* by Alice Walker. Copyright 1997 by Alice Walker. Reprinted by permission of Random House, Inc.

Huey P. Newton, "On the Relevance of the Church: May 19, 1971," in Toni Morrison, editor, *To Die for the People: The Writings of Huey P. Newton.* Reprinted by permission of the Writers and Readers Publishing, Inc.

"An African-American Humanist Declaration." Reprinted by permission from *Free Inquiry,* published by the Council for Secular Humanism, Amherst, N.Y.

The following documents have been reprinted in keeping with fair use policies.

William Loren Katz, editor, *Five Slave Narratives: A Compendium* (New York: Arno Press and The New York Times, 1968), "The Story of James Hay," 49–50.

Daniel Payne, "Daniel Payne's Protestation of Slavery," *Lutheran Herald and Journal of the Franckean Synod* (Fort Plain, N.Y.: Committee of Publication of the Franckean Synod, 1839): 113–115.

Hubert H. Harrison, "On a Certain Conservatism in Negroes," 41–47. In *The Negro and the Nation* (New York: Cosmo-Advocate Publishing Co., 1917).

INDEX

Abachi, Sani, 156, 157
Abernathy, Ralph, 275
Abolitionists, 19, 75, 88; epistemology of, 90
Adams, E. C. L., 121
African-Americans for Humanism (AAH): aims of, 325–26; described, 319–20; views on social issues, 324–25. *See also* Humanism
African Methodist Episcopal Church, 28, 123
African Pioneer Nationalist Movement (APNM), 155. *See also* Black Nationalism
Africans: arrival in the Americas, 17; and humanism, 155; traditional beliefs of, 49
Agassiz, Louis, 132
Algeria, 273
Allen, Norm R., Jr., 147–48, 319; *Anthology of African American Humanism*, 12
American Anti-Slave Society, 79, 91
American Civil Liberties Union (ACLU), 8
American Humanist Association, 288
Andrews, William, *To Tell a Free Story*, 57
Anthony, Aaron, 85
Aptheker, Herbert, 75–76
Armed Forces: and Army as segregated, 268; racism within, 132

Assing, Ottilia, 78, 79
Auld, Hugh, 84
Auld, Sophia, 84
Auld, Thomas, 85
"Aunt Jemima," 65, 66

Baldwin, James, 227–29, 276
Baraka, Amiri Imamu, 237–39; *Blues People*, 246; on the origin of the blues, 35
Beecher, Henry Ward, 89
Bennett, Lerone, 17
Bible: justifying slavery, 166; and violent images, 253–54; and the white man in Africa, 233; women's role in, 294. *See also* Christian Church; Christianity; Religion
Black arts movement, 237
Black Arts Repertory Theatre/School, 237
Black Nationalism, 132, 133; Black Nation, 238, 240; Black National Consciousness, 240–46; Black nationalists, 154, 155, Black Power, 133, 155, 301; importance of land ownership, 242, 243, 245; separatism, 246–47. *See also* Black Panther Party; Garvey, Marcus; Farrakhan, Louis; Malcolm X; Muhammad, Elijah; Nation of Islam (NOI)
Black nationalists. *See* Black Nationalism

Black Panther Party, 133, 261, 301; and the church, 303–17; and community activities, 303, 304, 309–11; education programs of, 315; humanistic principles of, 302. *See also* Black Nationalism

Black Power. *See* Black Nationalism

Blues: as born of the city, 120; as descendant of the seculars, 31; ironic nature of, 231; as post-Civil War in consciousness, 35; as "secular spirituals," 35; and work songs, 115. *See also* Jazz; Seculars; Songs

Blyden, Edward W., 32

Bolingbroke, Henry Saint John, 89

Bradford, Roark, 121

Braxton, Jo Anne, 58

Brent, Linda. *See* Jacobs, Harriet

British Trades Union: Congress, 224n. 2; report on Soviet Union, 215

Broonzy, Big Bill, 119, 231

Brotherhood of Sleeping Car Porters, 149

Brown, Ewert, 251

Brown, Hallie Q., 59

Brown, Sterling, 29, 103

Bunche, Ralph, 153

Campbell, Bishop, 80, 81

Campbell, Jim, 241

Carby, Hazel, *Reconstructing Womanhood: The Emergence of the Afro-American Women Novelist*, 59

Central Intelligence Agency (CIA), 284

Chesnutt, Charles, on Frederick Douglass, 96n. 3

Christian Church: as divorced from reality, 311–12; hypocrisy of, 229, 230; as mask for hatred and self-hatred, 230; role in oppression, 216; role of women in, 292–93; as source of release, 231. *See also* Bible; Christianity; Religion

Christianity: calendar of, 48; communism of, 217; and eschatology, 49–50; failings of, 165, 231, 234; influence in Russia, 214–15; as opposed to reality, 185, 197, 234, 244; principles of, 1; in relation to paganism, 179, 295; role in oppression, 71, 28, 85, 168, 167, 183, 234, 296, 308; role in the politics, 233–34; teachings of, 75, 204, 213; Whitianity, 47, 49. *See also* Bible; Christian Church; Religion; Theology

Christians. *See* Christianity

Civil rights movement: "Big Four" leaders, 153; and Christian association, 133; and nonreligious origins in Thoreau's writings and actions, 148–49; role of humanism in, 262

Civil War, 19, 91, 93

Clay, Henry, 87, 88

Cleage, Albert, 151

Clinton, Bill, 159

Coleman, James P., 278

Colored Socialist Club, 163

Committee of Racial Equality. *See* Congress of Racial Equality (CORE)

Communist Party: attraction of, 132; and Harry Haywood, 249; Negro Department, 249; as organizational home of humanists, 250; and Richard Wright, 183. *See also* Socialism; Socialist Party

Comte, Auguste, 38, 41, 43

ABOUT THE EDITOR

Anthony Pinn is Director of the African American Studies program and Associate Professor of Religious Studies at Macalester College.